Presidentialism, Parliamentarism, and Democracy

Are newly established presidential democracies doomed to fail? In support of their positive answer to this question, advocates of parliamentarism point out that these regimes tend to last longer than presidential ones. This book takes a contrary view. It argues that most of the reasons offered for the poor survival record of presidential democracies – that they are prone to deadlocks, offer no incentives for coalition formation, make political parties weak, and fragment decision making – have neither sound theoretical foundations nor any empirical support. In fact, what has made presidential democracies more fragile is that they typically emerged in countries where the military was already strong, which placed democracy of any kind at risk. Therefore, the prospects of new democracies that have established a directly elected president as their head of government may be better than usually considered. Instead of attempting to change the form of government, institutional reformers should thus concentrate on designing a better presidential democracy.

José Antonio Cheibub is Associate Professor and Harold Boeschenstein Scholar in Political Economy and Public Policy at the University of Illinois at Urbana-Champaign. He earned his Ph.D. from the University of Chicago and has previously taught at the University of Pennsylvania and Yale University. He is a co-author of *Democracy and Development: Political Institutions and Well-Being in the World, 1950–1990* (Cambridge, 2000), which won the 2001 Woodrow Wilson Foundation Award given by the American Political Science Association. He is also co-editor of the *Democracy Sourcebook* (2003). Professor Cheibub has published articles in numerous edited volumes and journals, including *Annual Review of Political Science, British Journal of Political Science, Comparative Political Studies, Journal of Democracy*, and *World Politics*.

Cambridge Studies in Comparative Politics

General Editor

Margaret Levi   *University of Washington, Seattle*

Assistant General Editor

Stephen Hanson   *University of Washington, Seattle*

Associate Editors

Robert H. Bates   *Harvard University*
Helen Milner   *Princeton University*
Frances Rosenbluth   *Yale University*
Susan Stokes   *Yale University*
Sidney Tarrow   *Cornell University*
Kathleen Thelen   *Northwestern University*
Erik Wibbels   *University of Washington, Seattle*

Other Books in the Series

Continued after the Index

Presidentialism, Parliamentarism, and Democracy

JOSÉ ANTONIO CHEIBUB

University of Illinois

CAMBRIDGE
UNIVERSITY PRESS

CAMBRIDGE UNIVERSITY PRESS
Cambridge, New York, Melbourne, Madrid, Cape Town, Singapore, São Paulo

Cambridge University Press
32 Avenue of the Americas, New York, NY 10013-2473, USA

www.cambridge.org
Information on this title: www.cambridge.org/9780521834674

First published 2007

Printed in the United States of America

A catalog record for this publication is available from the British Library.

Library of Congress Cataloging in Publication data
Cheibub, José Antonio
Presidentialism, parliamentarism, and democracy / José Antonio Cheibub.
p.   cm. – (Cambridge studies in comparative politics)
Includes bibliographical references and index.
ISBN-13: 978-0-521-83467-4 (hardback)
ISBN-10: 0-521-83467-8 (hardback)
ISBN-13: 978-0-521-54244-9 (pbk.)
ISBN-10: 0-521-54244-8 (pbk.)
1. Presidents.   2. Cabinet system.   3. Democracy.   4. Coalition governments.
I. Title.   II. Series.

JF255.C45   2007
321.8 – dc22   2006019362

ISBN-13   978-0-521-83467-4   hardback
ISBN-10   0-521-83467-8   hardback

ISBN-13   978-0-521-54244-9   paperback
ISBN-10   0-521-54244-8   paperback

Presidentialism, Parliamentarism, and Democracy

JOSÉ ANTONIO CHEIBUB

University of Illinois

CAMBRIDGE
UNIVERSITY PRESS

CAMBRIDGE UNIVERSITY PRESS
Cambridge, New York, Melbourne, Madrid, Cape Town, Singapore, São Paulo

Cambridge University Press
32 Avenue of the Americas, New York, NY 10013-2473, USA

www.cambridge.org
Information on this title: www.cambridge.org/9780521834674

First published 2007

Printed in the United States of America

A catalog record for this publication is available from the British Library.

Library of Congress Cataloging in Publication data
Cheibub, José Antonio
Presidentialism, parliamentarism, and democracy / José Antonio Cheibub.
p.   cm. – (Cambridge studies in comparative politics)
Includes bibliographical references and index.
ISBN-13: 978-0-521-83467-4 (hardback)
ISBN-10: 0-521-83467-8 (hardback)
ISBN-13: 978-0-521-54244-9 (pbk.)
ISBN-10: 0-521-54244-8 (pbk.)
1. Presidents.   2. Cabinet system.   3. Democracy.   4. Coalition governments.
I. Title.   II. Series.

JF255.C45   2007
321.8 – dc22   2006019362

ISBN-13   978-0-521-83467-4 hardback
ISBN-10   0-521-83467-8 hardback

ISBN-13   978-0-521-54244-9 paperback
ISBN-10   0-521-54244-8 paperback

To Gabriel and Isabel,
two of the loves of my life

Contents

Figures and Tables

Figures

Tables

Acknowledgments

Many people contributed to making this book possible. I first want to thank five individuals who have been central to its development from the very beginning. First, my sister Argelina Figueiredo, with whom I spent countless hours talking about every single aspect of the book. Not only have I benefited from her written work, but, most importantly, I profited from her insight, her patience, and her willingness to talk with me about anything related to this project and to read countless drafts and early papers. Second, Adam Przeworski – mentor, co-author, and friend – whose direct and indirect roles in developing the ideas presented here have been crucial. Finally, my friends and co-authors Jennifer Gandhi, Fernando Limongi, and Sebastian Saiegh, with whom I wrote papers that have, in part, been incorporated here.

My colleagues at Yale provided me with an intellectual environment that I believe will be difficult ever to reproduce. In particular I would like to thank Geoffrey Garrett, Greg Huber, Tasos Kalandrakis, Pierre Landry, Ellen Lust-Okar, Nicholas Sambanis, Ken Scheve, Andrew Schrank, and Jim Vreeland (especially Jim!) for reading parts of the manuscript and listening to me in their offices, over coffee, or at lunch. I would like especially to mention the late Michael Wallerstein, whose presence at Yale was short but significant, as it marked the lives of all of us who were lucky enough to have him as a colleague. Susan Stokes and Libby Wood also read the manuscript and offered written comments, for which I thank them.

For the help I received along the way, I am also grateful to Amel Ahmed, Octavio Amorim Neto, John Bowman, David S. Brown, Eric Budd, Sercan Celebi, Zairo Borges Cheibub, Marcus Figueiredo, Steffen Ganghoff, Nate Jensen, Herbert Kitschelt, Richard Locke, Frank London, Beatriz Magaloni, Scott Mainwaring, Carol Mershon, Kurt von Mettenheim, Dan Miodwnik, Sophia Moestrup, Shaheen Mozaffar, Gerry Munck, Aki Peretz, Jonathan Rodden, Nasos Rousias,

Mehmet Adil Tezgul, David Zaragoza, and Arthur Zimmerman. They helped in many ways: some read early drafts or parts of the final manuscript; others listened to me talking about it in a formal or informal setting; others helped me with data, either by collecting them for and with me or by making their data sets available; some did all of that. Their suggestions, comments, and criticisms made this book better than it would have otherwise been.

I thank Lew Bateman, political science editor at Cambridge, for his interest in this project from its early phases; Margaret Levi, series editor, who pushed me to make my ideas more clear and demonstrated extreme generosity with her time; as well as the anonymous readers of the manuscript for their suggestions.

Finally, I thank my wife, Janet Morford, for the patience, continuous support, and love that she has demonstrated as I agonized over this (and other) projects. It is hard to put in words what this all meant and means ... but I hope she knows how much it did and does.

Part of this book reproduces or relies on work that has been previously published. Chapter 3 draws heavily on "Government Coalitions and Legislative Success under Parliamentarism and Presidentialism," co-authored with Adam Przeworski and Sebastian Saiegh and published in the *British Journal of Political Science* (2004); parts of Chapter 4 appeared in "Minority Governments, Deadlock Situations, and the Survival of Presidential Democracies," published in *Comparative Political Studies* (2002); Chapter 5 is partly based on "Democratic Institutions and Regime Survival: Parliamentarism and Presidentialism Reconsidered," co-authored with Fernando Limongi and published in the *Annual Review of Political Science* (2002); and the argument in Chapter 6 first appeared in "The Military–Presidential Nexus," co-authored with Adam Przeworski and presented at the 2003 Annual Meeting of the American Political Science Association. I am grateful to the *Annual Reviews,* Cambridge University Press, and Sage Publications for allowing me to reprint parts of those papers. But I am especially grateful to my co-authors, not only for letting me use something that we did together but also for their willingness to work with me in the first place. In particular, I am grateful to Adam Przeworski and Sebastian Saiegh for letting me use the formal analysis that appears in Chapter 3; I played a secondary role in its development, but without it this book would not have come together.

1

Introduction

What difference does the form of government make for the chances that a democratic regime will survive? There are two basic forms of democratic governments. In one the government depends on the confidence of the legislature in order to exist. In the other the government, or more precisely its head, serves for a fixed term; thus the executive and the legislature are independent from one another. In systems of the former type, which are parliamentary, a legislative majority may remove the government from office – either by passing a vote of no confidence in the government or by rejecting a vote of confidence initiated by the government. When this happens, one of two things takes place: either a new government is formed on the basis of the existing distribution of legislative seats or, if this proves impossible, new elections are held in the hope that the new seat distribution will be such that a government will become viable (i.e., will not be immediately subject to a vote of no confidence from the legislative majority). In systems of the latter type, which are presidential, no such mechanism exists for removing the government. The head of the government may or may not be chosen by the legislative body, but once chosen he or she serves a fixed term in office: in presidential systems, the head of the government cannot be removed from office even if he or she favors policies opposed by the legislative majority. This book is thus about the impact of parliamentary or presidential institutions on the survival of democracy.

Presidential democracies are considerably more brittle than parliamentary ones. A cursory look around the world will show that there is only one long-lived democracy that is also presidential: the United States. At the same time, Latin America – the region of the world where presidential institutions have dominated since the nineteenth century – is also the region with the highest level of regime instability, understood here as shifts between dictatorship and democracy. The 18 countries that comprise the core of Latin America are home to only 9% of the world's population, yet they experienced 37% of the 157 regime transitions that took place between 1946 and 2002. Finally, whereas the expected life of a parliamentary democracy that existed during the 1946–2002 period was 58 years, that of presidential democracies was only 24 years.[1]

One of the questions that have driven a great deal of research in recent years is whether the difference in longevity between parliamentary and presidential democracies is due to the intrinsic features of the respective systems or rather to the conditions under which these systems emerged and function. Linz (1978, 1990a,b, 1994) has been the foremost proponent of the first thesis, whereas several scholars have attempted to find exogenous conditions that would account for this difference (see e.g. Shugart and Carey 1992; Power and Gasiorowski 1997; Shugart and Mainwaring 1997; Bernhard, Nordstrom, and Reenock 2001; Foweraker and Landman 2002).

In explanations based on the intrinsic features of parliamentarism and presidentialism, survival is endogenous to the form of government. Such theories spell out causal chains beginning with the separation of powers that defines presidentialism, derive the claim that this system is prone to irresolvable conflicts, and conclude that such conflicts undermine democratic institutions. Yet, as I will show in this book, attempts to validate endogenous theories have not been successful: at least some of the hypothesized links that need to exist in order for these theories to be true are just not there. However, efforts to find exogenous conditions under which the difference in longevity would disappear have fared no better. Whatever one controls for, a difference in the survival rates of parliamentary and presidential democracies is still there. Hence, the puzzle remains open: either we have not correctly identified the mechanism by which the intrinsic features of democratic institutions affect their longevity, or we have not found the exogenous conditions that account for the observed difference in the survival rate of presidential and parliamentary democracies.

In this book I argue that intrinsic features of presidentialism are not the reason why presidential democracies are more prone to break down. On the basis of an original data set covering all democratic regimes that existed between 1946 and 2002, I show that the alleged consequences of presidential institutions are either not observed or not sufficient to account for the difference in the survival prospects of presidential and parliamentary democracies. In line with those who have advanced "exogenous" explanations, I claim that what causes presidential democracies' brittleness is the fact that presidential institutions have been

---

[1] The probability that a parliamentary democracy would die at any time during the 1946–2002 period was 0.0171, against 0.0416 for a presidential democracy.

adopted in countries where any form of democracy is likely to perish. Existing work has singled out the level of economic development in addition to the size of the country and its geographic location as explanatory factors for the higher instability of presidential democracies.[2] I shall demonstrate that none of these factors, important as some of them may be, is sufficient to account for the variation in the survival rates of parliamentary and presidential democracies.

The reason for the instability of presidential democracies, I argue, lies in the fact that presidential institutions tend to exist in countries that are also more likely to suffer from dictatorships led by the military. I show that there is a nexus between military dictatorships and presidentialism that fully accounts for the differences in democratic survival. Democracies that are preceded by military dictatorships are more unstable than those that are preceded by civilian dictatorships; in turn, presidential democracies are more likely to follow military dictatorships. It is therefore the nexus between militarism and presidentialism, not the inherent institutional features of presidentialism, that explains the higher level of instability of presidential democracies.

In other words, the problem of presidential democracies is not that they are "institutionally flawed." Rather, the problem is that they tend to exist in societies where democracies of any type are likely to be unstable. Fears stemming from the fact that many new democracies have "chosen" presidential institutions are therefore unfounded. From a strictly institutional point of view, presidentialism can be as stable as parliamentarism. Given that constitutional frameworks, once adopted, are hard to change, it follows that striving to replace them may be wasteful from a political point of view. It would be a misguided use of resources to attempt to change an institutional structure on the grounds of democratic stability when the source of instability has nothing to do with that structure.

Explaining Presidential Instability

The comparative study of political institutions has made large strides in the past two decades as scholars began paying attention not so much to whether democracy would emerge as to the ways in which existing democracies operate. Prompted by the permanence of democracy in many heretofore unstable

---

[2] Democracies are unstable in poor countries, and presidential democracies are poorer than parliamentary ones; large countries are hard to govern, and countries with presidential democracies are larger than countries with parliamentary democracies; Latin America is inherently unstable, and the instability of presidentialism is due to the fact that most presidential systems exist in this region of the world.

countries, by a stronger theoretical integration of political science (with theories developed to study institutional structures in the United States and in European democracies finding their way into studies of democracy in developing countries), by the dissemination of institutionalist and rational choice perspectives in the profession, and by technological advances that have allowed the collection and analysis of large databases, many scholars have shifted their attention to "lower-level" institutions: subconstitutional features of a country's institutional framework that might account for observed political, economic, and social outcomes. In the face of these developments, a focus on the impact of broad constitutional frameworks may seem a bit anachronistic, particularly if one considers that few people today explicitly subscribe to the Linzian view of presidentialism. Is the endogenous theory of presidential instability, the implications of which will be tested in the chapters to come, a straw man?

My answer, of course, is that it is not. There are several reasons why a thorough examination of the leading explanation for the instability of presidential democracies is necessary from both a practical and a theoretical point of view. For one, the empirical puzzle is there – presidential democracies do have shorter lives than parliamentary ones – and, as I will show, the Linzian explanation is unable to account for it. Second, the form of government is probably the most important aspect of how a democracy is to be organized, and debates about it remain a feature of the political landscape in many countries.[3] Finally, although an increasing number of scholars claim not to agree with the Linzian framework, the notion continues to loom large that presidential systems are inherently ungovernable, structurally problematic, likely to generate crises, chronically incapable of dealing with crises once they erupt, and hence bad for the consolidation of democracy. Thus Valenzuela (2004), for example, believes that the presence of presidential institutions is at the root of Latin America's recent "failed" presidencies. Lijphart (2000), in turn, is optimistic about the prospects of democracy in the twenty-first century as long as the lessons drawn from the twentieth century – including that about "the danger of presidential governments" (p. 21) – are accepted. For O'Donnell (1994), presidential institutions are at the heart of the descent of many Latin American regimes into "delegative" democracy. Van de Walle (2003) lists presidentialism as one of the causes of the weak political parties found in Africa's recently established competitive systems. Fish (2001) identifies "superpresidentialism" as one of the main causes of "the degradation

---

[3] It re-emerged in Brazil in 2005 in the wake of the corruption charges waged against the Worker's Party and the Lula government. The possibility of changing the system away from presidentialism is also being discussed in Argentina, Colombia, Indonesia, Mexico, and the Philippines.

of Russian politics," a view that is extended by himself and others to many post-Soviet regimes. For Samuels and Eaton (2002:22), minority government under presidentialism "tends to further increase the probability of presidential collapse." For Shugart and Haggard (2001:82), divided government, which is possible under presidentialism but not under parliamentarism, increases "the potential for stalemate."

The examples can go on. Shugart and Carey (1992), who must be credited with calling our attention to the fact that presidential regimes are not all alike, remain within the Linzian framework insofar as their work presupposes an inherently conflictual relationship between the executive and the legislature in presidential regimes. It is this view that leads them to believe that regimes whose constitutions endow presidents with considerable legislative powers have a greater probability of breaking down. Strong presidents, they argue, have the institutional means to impose their will on congress and, for this reason, will have fewer incentives to negotiate with the legislature. Paralysis and crisis become more likely. Weak presidents, in turn, know that they have no alternative but to negotiate with congress. Thus, interbranch conflict dominates cooperation and the possibility is not considered that presidents with strong legislative powers may operate, much like prime ministers in parliamentary systems, as organizers (and not antagonists) of the majority.

We find traces of the traditional view of presidential and parliamentary systems even in Tsebelis's work on veto players, work that was motivated by a desire to overcome the pairwise structure of institutional analyses and to provide a "consistent framework for comparisons across regimes, legislature and party systems" (1995:292; see also Tsebelis 2002). Thus, the consequences of policy stability, which is determined by the number of veto players in a system, is a function of the broad constitutional framework. In parliamentary systems, policy stability is associated with government instability because governments that have become immobile may be changed through constitutional means (a vote of no confidence); in regimes where "government change is impossible (except for fixed intervals like in presidential systems), policy immobilism may lead to the replacement of the leadership through extra-constitutional means (regime instability)" (p. 321).

It is clear from these examples that the notion of presidential regimes undermining democracy is alive and well in the comparative literature. Although not explicitly elaborated, the reasons are invariably related to presidentialism's defining feature – the separation of executive and legislative powers – and the difficulties that are supposed to follow from it. The sense that there is something inherently problematic about presidential institutions, something that needs to be neutralized in order for the system to operate properly and generate positive outcomes, is as present in the comparative analysis of institutions today as it was twenty years ago.

The goal of this book is to make a strong statement that this view is not defensible. One of the book's main messages is that there is nothing wrong with presidential institutions per se. Or, to be more precise, presidential institutions do not cause the instability of presidential democracies. This conclusion will follow from a detailed examination of the implications of the so-called Linzian view. As will become clear, this view generates specific empirical predictions about the operation of presidential systems. If this view is correct, then: incentives for coalition formation in presidential democracies will be minimal or nonexistent; we will rarely observe coalition governments in presidential democracies or, if we do, they will be flimsy and ephemeral; presidents who do not form coalitions to govern and/or whose governments do not reach majority status should be unable to see their legislative agenda approved in congress; and, most importantly, presidential systems that produce such presidents will be much more likely to die – to become dictatorships – than presidential systems that are governed by presidents who belong to majority parties. As I will show in the chapters to follow, these implications find no support in the evidence and thus call into question the validity of the theory that underlies them: although presidential democracies are more unstable than parliamentary ones, this is not because presidential institutions provide the wrong type of incentives for democratic consolidation.

Part of the value of this book, therefore, lies in its systematic refutation of the leading explanation for the higher level of instability of presidential democracies; in this sense it establishes a "negative finding." Yet there are several positive things about how presidential democracies work that we learn in the process of subjecting the Linzian view to empirical testing. Thus, we learn about the conditions under which presidents will make coalition offers and the conditions under which parties will accept them, and we learn that the rate of coalition formation is lower in presidential democracies than in parliamentary ones but that it is higher than what we would have expected under the prevailing theory. We also learn that presidential democracies are able to survive as such under all sorts of governmental configurations and that minority presidential governments do as well legislatively as majority coalition ones; we see how the legislative powers of the president vary across presidential constitutions and how there is a wide range of configuration of constitutional presidential powers under which presidential democracies survive; and we learn that party discipline in presidential democracies can be enforced by mechanisms other than the parliamentary democracy's vote of no confidence. In sum, as we test and reject a theory based on the deleterious effect of presidential institutions on the survival of democracy, we are able to learn quite a bit about how presidential democracies actually operate.

But that is not all. In this book I also propose an alternative to the Linzian explanation of presidential instability. I suggest that the instability of presidential democracies is due to the fact that we observe presidential institutions in countries where democracy of any type would be unstable. Thus, I argue, it is not the institution itself but rather the conditions under which it exists that leads to the instability of presidential democracies. I provide some evidence in support of this explanation, but my main concern is more with clearly and precisely formulating the theory than with testing all its implications. This choice does not come from the belief that such testing is not necessary, as I do hope the theory of presidential instability proposed in this book will be the object of an examination no less meticulous than the one I perform of the Linzian view. However, before we proceed with building new theories we must be sure that the path is clear of old ones, and it is toward that end that I have devoted a significant part of the resources available to me.

The Pitfalls of Presidentialism: The Linzian View

Most (if not all) of the arguments claiming the existence of a causal relationship between presidentialism and the instability of democracy are based on the work of Juan Linz. The point of departure of Linz and his many followers is that the separation of powers that defines presidentialism implies a relationship of "mutual independence" between the executive and the legislature, which contrasts with the relationship of "mutual dependence" that is presumed to characterize executive–legislative relations under parliamentarism (Stepan and Skach 1993). Thus, it all starts with the separation of powers that defines presidentialism and, through a series of implications that are summarized in Figure 1.1, ends with the breakdown of democratic regimes.

Incentives for Coalition Formation

Presidential constitutions, contrary to parliamentary ones, are supposed to provide few or no incentives for coalition formation. According to Mainwaring and Scully (1995:33), they "lack the institutionalized mechanisms of coalition building that exist in parliamentary democracy." For Linz and Stepan (1996:181), "parliamentarism over time develops many incentives to produce coalitional majorities" whereas "presidentialism has far fewer coalition-inducing incentives."

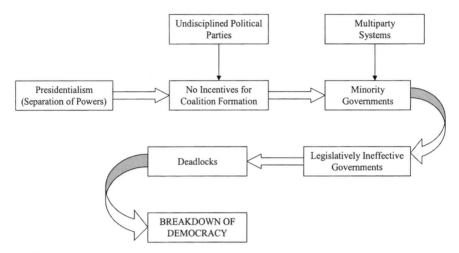

Figure 1.1 From Presidentialism to the Breakdown of Democracy.

For Valenzuela (2004:16), "parliamentary regimes are based on a political logic that urges cooperation and consensus within the context of coherent policies" yet "the underlying logic of presidentialism is far more conflict-prone."

There are three reasons why presidential democracies would lack incentives for coalition formation. The first follows directly from the principle of separation of powers: because the president's survival in office does not depend on any kind of legislative support, a president need not seek the cooperation of political parties other than his or her own; moreover, parties are not committed to supporting a government even if they join it. As Mainwaring and Scully (1995:33) put it:

> in [parliamentary systems] party coalitions generally take place after the election and are binding; in [presidential systems] they are often arranged before the election and are less binding after it. Executive power is not formed through post-election agreements among parties and is not divided among several parties that are responsible for governing, even though members of several parties often participate in cabinets. Parties or individual legislators can join the opposition without bringing down the government, so a president can finish her/his term with little congressional support.

Second, the nature of presidential elections also gives presidents incentives to avoid seeking cooperation. Cooperation requires compromises and possibly the modification of one's position in order to accommodate eventual partners, a situation that presidents may well resist. Presidents, after all, run in national districts – unlike legislators, who often have a more parochial base of representation.

Presidents are thus in a position to claim that they are the rightful interpreters of the national interest, superseding legislators' partial and parochial perspectives. Because presidents believe they have independent authority and a popular mandate,[4] they may view the opposition as irksome and demoralizing and hence may be less inclined to seek its cooperation when needed (Linz 1994). Thus, when it comes to survival in office, presidents' independence of the legislature – combined with the nationwide character of the presidential election – inflates their sense of power and makes them overestimate their ability to govern alone.

Finally, presidential politics is a zero-sum, winner-take-all affair, which is hardly conducive to cooperation or coalition formation. In presidential regimes the presidency is the highest prize in the political process. Because the presidency is occupied by a single person, it is not divisible for the purposes of coalition formation. As Lijphart (2004:7) puts it: "Parliamentary systems have collective or collegial executives whereas presidential systems have one-person, non-collegial executives." As a consequence, "the winning candidate wins all of the executive power that is concentrated in the presidency and it is 'loser loses all' for the defeated candidate, who usually ends up with no political office at all and often disappears from the political scene altogether" (p. 8). Politics, therefore, revolves around capturing the presidency to the exclusion of other political parties. Parliamentary politics is cabinet politics and, as a consequence, the government can be partitioned to accommodate a plurality of political parties. In contrast to presidentialism, politics under parliamentarism is best characterized as a mixed-motive, positive-sum game among political parties.

For these reasons, coalitions are difficult to form and do form "only exceptionally" (Linz 1994:19) under presidentialism (Mainwaring 1990; Stepan and Skach 1993:20; Linz and Stepan 1996:181). As Niño (1996:169) puts it, presidentialism "operates against the formation of coalitions"; for this reason, according to Huang (1997:138), "the very notion of majority government is problematic in presidential systems without a majority party."

Party Discipline

Even if coalitions were to form under presidentialism, they would be fragile and composed of undisciplined parties incapable of offering reliable legislative support to the government. According to Huang (1997:139), the absence of

---

[4] As Hartlyn (1994:222) wrote: "Presidents, even minority ones, as both holders of executive power and symbolic heads of state, are more likely to perceive their election as a mandate, even as popular expectations by their supporters may also be greater due to their plebiscitarian relationship."

disciplined parties is "an unavoidable result of a presidential system." Likewise, for Linz (1994:35), "the idea of a more disciplined and 'responsible' party system is structurally in conflict, if not incompatible, with pure presidentialism." For him, "the weakness of parties in many Latin American democracies ... is not unrelated to the presidential system but, rather, [is] a consequence of the system" (p. 35). He concludes this aspect of his analysis by stating that, "while the incentive structure in parliamentary systems encourages party discipline and therefore consolidation of party organizations, presidential systems have no such incentives for party loyalty (except where there are well-structured ideological parties)" (pp. 41–2).

The key to this argument is the notion that the threat of government dissolution and early elections – absent, by design, in presidentialism – is necessary and sufficient to induce party discipline. Under parliamentarism, undisciplined parties may mean a failure to obtain majority support in parliament, the defeat of government bills, and consequently the fall of the government. In order to remain in government, political parties enforce discipline so that their members in parliament can be counted on to support the bills proposed by the government. Individual legislators, in turn, have an incentive to support the government in order to prevent the occurrence of early elections in which they might lose their positions. Under presidentialism, since the government and the legislature are independently constituted, office-seeking political parties have no reason to impose discipline on their members; their survival in office does not depend on the result of any particular vote in the legislature. Individual members of congress also lack any incentive to accept the discipline of political parties (if they were to try imposing it) since there is no provision for early elections that could remove the wayward representatives from office.

Thus, given office-seeking politicians, the fusion of power that characterizes parliamentary regimes generates incentives for individual legislators and political parties to cooperate with the government, resulting in a high level of party discipline. The separation of powers that characterizes presidentialism, on the contrary, implies low levels of party discipline. Even a president lucky enough to belong to a party that controlled a majority of congressional seats could not necessarily count on the support of that majority when governing.

Minority Governments

In the Linzian framework, we have seen that parliamentary regimes are supposed to foster cooperation whereas presidential regimes encourage independence. Under parliamentarism, political parties have an incentive to cooperate with one another. Parties in government will support the executive, and parties out of government will refrain from escalating any conflict because they may, at any time, become part of the government; individual members of parliament, in turn, will align themselves with their parties. The consequence is that parliamentary governments are supported by a majority composed of highly disciplined parties that are prone to cooperate with one another. Presidentialism, on the other hand, is characterized by the absence of such incentives and hence is likely to generate either minority governments or governments that are only nominally majority governments.

Parliamentarism can thus be characterized by a majoritarian imperative that is absent in presidentialism. This imperative follows, again, from the very principle that defines parliamentary democracies. Parliamentarism is a regime in which the government, in order to assume and retain power, must enjoy the confidence of the legislature. Since these are systems in which decisions are made according to majority rule, it follows that no government that does not enjoy the support of a majority will exist under parliamentarism. Minority governments could occasionally emerge, but these would be relatively infrequent and necessarily ephemeral occurrences reflecting the temporary inability of the current majority to crystallize. This inability, however, would be necessarily temporary because the system contains automatic correctives for such situations: either a new government supported by a majority would be formed or, if this is not possible, new elections would be held so that such a majority can emerge.

Presidential regimes, in contrast, lack the majority imperative. But majorities also matter under presidentialism. In these systems voters have two agents who, by design, do not necessarily represent the same majority (Shugart and Carey 1992). These agents have fixed terms in office and do not depend on each other to exist. As a consequence, there is nothing in the system that guarantees the executive will enjoy the support of the majority in the legislature. If the majority that elected the president is different from the majority that elected the legislature – so that the president will be supported by only a minority in the legislature – then there is no automatic corrective that can be applied. Hence minority governments, although "automatically corrected" in parliamentary democracies when they emerge, would linger until the next elections in presidential systems.

Multiparty systems would only compound the problem by making the emergence of minority governments chronic. Whereas parliamentary regimes are equipped to deal with such situations – since cooperation is inherent to the regime – the problems with presidentialism are only compounded when legislatures are fragmented. As Valenzuela (2004:13) puts it, "the more fragmented the opposition and the smaller the president's own party, the greater becomes the challenge of cobbling together a majority ruling coalition." There are, according to Mainwaring (1993), three reasons why this is so. First, the likelihood that the president's party will be able to secure a majority of seats in the legislature obviously declines with the number of political parties. This is a point emphasized by Jones (1995:78), who reasons: "in presidential systems, high levels of multipartism reduce the size of the president's legislative contingent and hence increase the likelihood that the president will lack a legislative majority or near-majority. Where the president lacks this level of legislative support, effective governance will be more difficult, creating a greater opportunity for the emergence of ungovernability, the negative impact of which is felt throughout the nation." Second, ideological polarization is likely to be higher in multiparty systems (Mainwaring 1993). Finally, coalitions, which could remedy the previous factors, are supposed to be more difficult to form and more unstable in presidential than in parliamentary systems. As Jones (1995:6) puts it, whereas coalition formation when no party controls a majority of legislative seats is an "institutionalized mechanism" in parliamentary democracy, it simply does not exist in presidential ones.

Deadlocks and Legislative Ineffectiveness

The lack of incentives for coalition formation and the resulting high incidence of minority governments under multiparty presidentialism imply conflict between the executive and the legislature as well as governments that are legislatively ineffective. As Jones (1995:38) states, "when an executive lacks a majority in the parliamentary systems the norm tends to be what Lijphart terms 'consensual government' (i.e., government by coalition). In presidential systems, when the executive lacks a majority (or close to it) in the legislature, the norm is conflictual government." The higher likelihood of executive–legislative conflict and deadlock in presidential democracies is thus the product of the system's defining feature. It "stems primarily from the separate election of the two branches of government and is exacerbated by the fixed term of office" (Mainwaring 1993:209).

This suggests that the institutional strength of presidents is only superficial. As Valenzuela (2004:12) puts it with respect to Latin American democratic presidents, they " 'reign' rather than 'rule'." He continues:

The weakness of state institutions is usually less at fault than the sheer difficulty of building and maintaining support in a political environment of fragmented parties with little or no internal discipline. Compounding this problem is a lack of institutional incentives to prevent unchecked party splits, floor crossings, and the like. In the absence of congressional majorities, presidents struggle to generate legislative support only to find that legislators – often including members of the president's own party – have no interest in either collaborating with a weak chief executive or aiding the success of a strong one. Rather than generating a logic of cooperation, presidential regimes seem to give rise to a logic of confrontation precisely because the president's foes see a successful chief executive as bad for their own interests and a failed president as someone to avoid.

Presidents who do not have legislative support will try to bypass congress in order to implement their programs. They will, for instance, make increasing use of their decree powers and, in the process, undermine democratic legitimacy. As Valenzuela (2004:14) states, "by resorting to decree powers presidents may become stronger, but the presidential system becomes weaker and more brittle, encouraging confrontation rather than accommodation." Hence they undermine democratic institutions as they try "to shore up their weaknesses as presidents." Under these circumstances, democracy is delegative rather than liberal (O'Donnell 1994); that is, it relies on the plebiscitary link between voters and the president at the expense of "horizontal" links of accountability.

Breakdown of Democracy

In sum, because there are no incentives for interbranch cooperation, presidentialism will be characterized by frequent minority governments as well as conflict and deadlocks between the government and the legislature. Because these regimes lack a constitutional principle that can be invoked to resolve conflicts between the executive and the legislature, such as the vote of no confidence of parliamentary regimes, minority presidents and deadlock would provide incentives for actors to search for extra-constitutional means of resolving their differences. As a consequence, presidential democracies become more prone to instability and eventual death.

As Linz (1994:7) puts it:

since both [the president and the congress] derive their power from the vote of the people in a free competition among well-defined alternatives, a conflict is always latent and sometimes likely to erupt dramatically; there is no democratic principle to resolve it, and the mechanisms that might exist in the constitution are generally complex, highly technical, legalistic, and, therefore, of doubtful democratic legitimacy for the electorate. It is therefore no accident that in some of those situations the military intervenes as "poder moderador".

This view is echoed by many scholars: by Mainwaring and Scully (1995:33) when they assert that, "because of the fixed terms of office, if a president is unable to implement her/his program, there is no alternative but deadlock";

by González and Gillespie (1994:172), for whom "policy disagreement between president and opposition very easily become institutional conflicts between the legislature and the president"; by Riggs (1988), who claims that "when serious tensions between president and congress arise in countries following the U.S. model, constitutionalism typically loses out"; by Ackerman (2000:645), who describes the predicament of Latin American democracies by affirming that, "in an effort to destroy its competitor, one or another power assaults the constitutional system and installs itself as the single lawmaker, with or without the redeeming grace of a supportive plebiscite"; by Stepan and Skach (1993:17), for whom "incentives and decision rules for encouraging the emergence of minority governments, discouraging the formation of durable coalitions, maximizing legislative impasses, motivating executives to flout the constitution, and stimulating political society to call periodically for military coups predictably flows" from what they see as the defining (and confining) condition of presidentialism – namely, that it is a system of mutual independence; and by Valenzuela (2004:16) when he contrasts the "suppleness" of parliamentarism, where "automatic safety-valves" usually prevent crises of government from becoming crises of regime, with the "rigidity" of presidentialism, "under which a defect in leadership or failure of policy can quickly tailspin into institutional and even mass confrontations with a frightening potential for violent instability and all the human and political costs it portends."

Presidential institutions are thus thought to be simply not conducive to governments' capability of handling the explosive issues that populate the political agenda in many countries. These issues make governing difficult under any circumstances. Governing becomes almost impossible when the institutional setup is likely to generate governments with weak legislative support as well as parties and politicians whose dominant strategy is to act independently. Given the lack of constitutional solutions to the crises that are likely to erupt, political actors have no choice beyond appealing to those with guns to intervene and put an end to their misery.

What Kills Presidential Democracies? – A Summary

The general argument in this book is developed in two steps. The first step is to examine each of the mechanisms that, in the Linzian view, lead from presidential institutions to the breakdown of democracy. Through a combination of theoretical and empirical analysis I show that the consequences of this view do not follow from its premises and either are not observed empirically or, when they are observed, are not sufficient to account for the observed difference in the survival rates of presidential and parliamentary democracies. In addition to what it teaches us about the functioning of presidential democracies, this analysis clearly shows that presidentialism cannot be causally related to the breakdown of democratic regimes. The second step of the argument is to provide an alternative account for the higher regime instability of presidential democracies. I do so by focusing on the "authoritarian legacy" of these democratic regimes, thus suggesting that there is nothing inherently destabilizing in presidential institutions.

Since the goal of this book is to examine empirically what causes the instability of presidential democracies, the first order of business is to identify the set of democracies that are at risk of breakdown. This requires that we identify the set of countries and the time periods in which a democratic regime is observed and then identify the democratic regimes that have a system in which the government and the assembly are independent from one another. I do this in Chapter 2, which I begin by presenting the rules for classifying political regimes into democracies and dictatorships. These are the same rules developed by Alvarez et al. (1996) and Przeworski et al. (2000), which are based on a definition of democracy as those regimes in which government offices (specifically the executive and the legislature) are filled through contested elections.

Once democracies are distinguished from dictatorships, I proceed to review the criteria underlying existing classifications of democratic forms of government. Since existing classifications use redundant and/or insufficient criteria and are thus unable to unambiguously classify all democratic systems, I offer an alternative that focuses exclusively on the relationship between the government and the legislative assembly. The main issue is whether the government can be removed by the assembly in the course of its constitutional term in office. Systems in which governments cannot be removed by the assembly are *presidential*. Systems in which they can be so removed are either *parliamentary* (when only the assembly is allowed to remove the government) or *mixed* (when either the assembly or the directly elected president can remove the government). Answers to the following three questions unambiguously identify each form of democratic government.

1. Is there an independently elected president?
2. Is the government responsible to the assembly?
3. Is the government responsible to the president?

After providing operational criteria for answering these questions – most importantly, for deciding about government responsibility to the assembly and to the president – I classify the constitutional framework of all democratic systems that have existed between 1946 and 2002. This amounts to 135 countries observed over a total of 3,382 years and constitutes the basic data to be used for empirical analyses throughout the book.

Recall that at the root of the view that presidentialism causes democratic instability is the idea that presidential institutions – owing to the independence of the executive and the legislative branches – provide no incentive for coalition formation. This, as we have seen, could have disastrous consequences: minority presidents unable to obtain support from a majority of legislators; deadlock as legislative activity is brought to halt; and, given the impossibility of constitutionally removing the government from office, an incentive for political actors to invoke extra-constitutional solutions.

There is no doubt that presidential and parliamentary institutions prescribe different relations between the executive and the legislature, but the question is whether this difference is sufficient to generate opposite incentives for coalition formation. I address this issue in Chapter 3, where I consider (from a theoretical point of view) what these incentives are and their consequences in each kind of regime.

Parliamentary and presidential systems are indeed different when it comes to the institutional features relevant for coalition formation. To begin with, in presidential democracies the president is always the government *formateur*; in parliamentary democracies, any party is a potential *formateur*. The number of possible government coalitions is therefore smaller in presidential than in parliamentary systems and, as small as it is, the party of the president will always be in the government. Moreover, failure to form a coalition government – the reversal point of the bargaining game in which political parties engage as they attempt to form a government – leads to different outcomes in each system. In parliamentary democracies (with the exception of Norway), it is the occurrence of new elections: voters are given the chance to return a new distribution of seats that will, it is hoped, lead to the formation of a viable government. In presidential systems, failure to form a coalition implies that the party of the president is the only one to hold government portfolios (cabinet positions), and policies may or may not remain at the status quo. Finally, the legislative powers of the president, and hence the extent to which the president controls the legislative process, vary in a way that the powers of the government in a parliamentary system do not. There is a range from institutionally weak presidents who do not hold any active legislative powers to institutionally strong ones who essentially dominate the legislative process. With parliamentary systems, in contrast, governments generally exert a high degree of control over legislation within a considerably smaller range.

Are these differences between presidential and parliamentary systems sufficient to make coalition governments rare under presidentialism? I address this question by first developing a formal model in which I postulate the existence of an identical distribution of power (as expressed by seats in the legislature) and identical preferences among the parties and then vary the form of government in order to study the conditions under which a government coalition will be formed. In this framework, parties derive utility from both office and policies, and the emergence of a coalition or a minority government will depend on the distance between the party of the president and the next party in the policy space. If presidents do not dominate the legislative process and if parties have widely disparate policy preferences, then presidents will offer – and nonpresidential parties will accept – portfolios in the government in exchange for policy cooperation; then a coalition government will be formed. If parties have policy positions that are close to each other, then presidents will keep all portfolios for their party and will allow policy to be set by a nonpresidential party; then a minority single-party government will emerge.

Of great relevance here is that, given a lack of presidential dominance over the legislative process, the conditions under which a coalition government will emerge are identical in presidential and parliamentary systems. This is not so when presidents dominate the legislative process, in which case the outcome will depend on the location of the status quo. If the status quo is situated between the ideal policies of two nonpresidential parties then, as before, the outcome (coalition or minority governments) will depend on how close the parties' policy positions are to one another. If the status quo is situated between the ideal policy of the president and that of a nonpresidential party, then the Linzian scenario may emerge: there will be no combination of policy and portfolio that can entice a nonpresidential party into participating in the government; yet, since the president dominates the legislative process, the nonpresidential parties cannot ally in the legislature and set policies that they prefer over those proposed by the president. Thus, while confirming that under presidentialism – but not under parliamentarism – a minority portfolio government may face a hostile legislative majority, the results of this analysis show that coalition governments are far from abnormal in presidential democracies.

There are several implications of this analysis that speak directly to the Linzian view of presidentialism. To begin with, it shows that under some circumstances coalition and minority governments will emerge for exactly the same reasons in both presidential and parliamentary systems. Moreover, it follows from this analysis that the absence of coalition governments does not automatically imply a lack of cooperation among political parties. The crucial distinction here is that between *government* (or portfolio) and *legislative* coalitions, which do not always coincide: there will be governments composed of a single party that are nonetheless supported by a legislative coalition. Thus, given that no party holds more than 50% of legislative seats, some minority governments occur under presidentialism for the same reason that they emerge under parliamentarism: no legislative majority wants to replace them because enough parties get policies they like. In this sense they are *supported* minority governments that should be no less effective legislatively than coalition governments.

The overall message of the analysis developed in Chapter 3 is that the structure of presidentialism is not sufficient to make coalition governments atypical. These governments may be more frequent under parliamentarism than under presidentialism, but they form in the latter in response to the same incentives that lead parties to coalesce in the former: a desire to balance their simultaneous objectives of being in office and securing enactment of preferred policies. Those who see presidential institutions as providing no incentives for coalition formation have placed excessive emphasis on the first goal (offices) to the detriment of the second (policies). It is only by seeing politicians as actors who care about both these goals that we can understand why presidents, in spite of the fact that they need not share office in order to survive, may want to do so in order to govern.

The analysis in Chapter 3 can be seen as both a formalization and a refutation of the Linzian view of presidential democracies. It formalizes this view in the sense that it shows the conditions under which the Linzian scenario will be realized – that is, the conditions under which, given the constitutional framework and a distribution of preferences and power, legislative ineffectiveness or deadlock will emerge in presidential systems. Linz and the literature that followed him assumed that these conditions were pervasive under presidentialism, but the analysis in Chapter 3 shows that they are not. It also shows that there are conditions under which minority presidents will have an incentive to form coalition governments and that, when they do not, a crisis of governability necessarily follows. In this sense our analysis refutes the Linzian view.

Analyzing the incentives for coalition formation in parliamentary and presidential systems yields four predictions that address the mechanisms underlying the Linzian view of presidentialism. First, the analysis suggests that, although government coalitions should be more frequent in parliamentary than in presidential democracies, they are by no means rare in the latter. Second, it implies that parliamentary governments should be more successful legislatively than presidential ones, although minority governments in both systems should be at least as effective as majority coalitions. Third, it suggests that coalition governments should be less frequent in presidential systems that are characterized by constitutionally strong presidents. Finally, it follows that the failure to form a coalition government does not spell disaster for presidential democracies;

specifically, we see that the coalition and the majority status of the government are not correlated with legislative paralysis and with the death of democracies.

These claims are investigated in Chapter 4 on the basis of a data set that combines the classification of democratic forms of government with information on the government's partisan composition and legislative support. The findings are straightforward. Coalition governments are more frequent in parliamentary democracies but are common in presidential ones: between 1946 and 2002, they occurred in about three fifths of the "country-years" when no party commanded a majority of legislative seats. In almost three fourths of these cases the coalition reached majority status and lasted at least as long as the coalitions formed in parliamentary or mixed systems. Thus, coalition governments are not rare in presidential systems. Contrary to the view espoused by Mainwaring (1993) and Jones (1995), among others, the legislative fragmentation we observe in multi-party systems actually makes coalition governments more likely. This effect is stronger in presidential than in parliamentary democracies. The notion that coalitions are rare events in presidential democracies – and that the difficulties of coalition formation will become even more apparent when there are more than two political parties – finds no support in a data set consisting of all democracies that have existed in the past sixty years.

With respect to legislative effectiveness, the expectation derived from the analysis developed in Chapter 3 is strongly supported by the data: minority governments in presidential systems, just as in parliamentary systems, are not any less effective than majority coalition governments. Controlling for per capita income, the age of the democratic regime, and the effective number of political parties, we find that the status of the government has no effect on the proportion of bills introduced by the executive that are approved in a year. Moreover, the status of the government – whether it is single- or multi-party, whether or not it holds more than 50% of the seats – has no effect on the probability that a democracy will survive. Thus, the chain of events to be set in motion by the separation of powers that defines presidentialism (i.e., minority governments with no legislative support, deadlock, and democratic breakdown) does not materialize in the presidential systems that have actually existed since 1946.

Chapter 4 generates a number of additional findings. For one, we discover that democratic survival is not threatened by legislative fragmentation. The probability of a parliamentary democracy breaking down increases only slightly with the number of political parties; on the other hand, in presidential democracies this probability first increases and then decreases, suggesting that these systems are at their highest level of risk when party pluralism is "moderate." Thus, it is not that presidential institutions are unable to handle situations in which there are many parties in the legislature; on the contrary, it is precisely in these cases that the incentive for coalition formation will be the strongest and that governments will eventually work out a way to find support for their program.

In addition, presidential systems in which the president dominates the legislative process are neither legislatively ineffective nor any more prone to die than those in which the president does not dominate the legislative process. Presidential dominance over the legislative process here is observed in two ways: presidential control over the budget process and an effective presidential veto. Neither of these aspects of presidential strength is detrimental to the legislative effectiveness of the government or to the survival of the democratic regime. True, the types of government that emerge will differ depending on the strength of the president, with coalition governments being more frequent in contexts where the president is institutionally weaker. But the overall outcome, as far as capacity to govern and maintenance of democracy are concerned, is not affected by these institutional traits of presidential systems.

Thus, the picture that emerges from analysis of the historical record is damaging to the arguments of those who would deduce, from the separation of powers, a process that leads to crises of governability and increased likelihood of democratic breakdown. If we look back at Figure 1.1, we see that every link in the chain of reasoning it represents is somewhat impaired, if not altogether rejected, by the findings generated when we compare the way presidential and parliamentary democracies function under a variety of conditions. The one link that remains to be examined in that figure is the one between separation of powers and party (in)discipline. Such an examination requires a move from considering interparty competition to considering intraparty cooperation under different forms of government. This is the aim of Chapter 5.

Recall that the argument about party discipline in the Linzian framework sees the vote of no confidence as the crucial mechanism for inducing party discipline in parliamentary systems. No such mechanism exists in presidential systems and so intraparty cooperation is thereby weakened. Since by design there is no connection between legislative activities and the survival of the government in office, parties and legislators have few incentives to cooperate with one another to assure the government's continued existence.

Note that my goal is not to argue that party discipline is higher, or at least as high, in presidential as in parliamentary democracies. I grant from the start that, were we able to compare this feature across the two systems (which is inherently difficult, if not impossible), we would probably find that average levels of party discipline are indeed higher under parliamentary democracies than under presidential democracies. Yet I argue that this is not really what matters. Party discipline is important primarily because it is considered to be one of the main mechanisms through which governments are able to obtain consistent and predictable legislative support for their policies. In other words, party discipline matters because it enables governments to govern. However, that parties in presidential democracies cannot be disciplined via the confidence mechanism, and hence may have lower overall levels of party discipline, does not mean that presidential governments will necessarily have a hard time obtaining such legislative support. It is this particular step in the discussion of party discipline across democratic systems – that is, the step that goes from recognizing that party discipline may be on average higher in parliamentary democracies to concluding that, for this reason, presidential governments have a hard time eliciting the consistent support of a legislative majority – that is problematic, both logically and empirically.

In contrast to the analysis of coalition propensity and its consequences, the discussion of party discipline in parliamentary and presidential systems presented in Chapter 5 does not contain any new data analysis. Rather, it surveys existing studies of party discipline in order to argue that party discipline, and the predictable and steady legislative support it affords the government, is not endogenous to the form of government. For one thing, informal models of party discipline are inconsistent and hence of little help in providing insights on the matter. Formal models, in turn, demonstrate that parliamentary systems will have higher levels of discipline than presidential ones but do not rule out the possibility that the latter will achieve sufficient levels of discipline by other means. As a matter of fact, existing models actually demonstrate that what really matters for party cohesion is the government's control of the legislative agenda, which is achieved in parliamentary systems by the vote of no confidence but can be achieved in other ways in systems that have no such provision. Thus, to the extent that there exist institutional mechanisms (other than the confidence vote) that allow the government to control the legislative agenda, the absence of the confidence vote in presidential democracies can be "compensated" for and so a predictable basis of legislative support to the government may emerge. Since these mechanisms are not themselves associated with the form of government, it follows that sufficient levels of party discipline may be obtained through mechanisms that are available to presidential governments, such as the president's legislative power and the organization of the legislative body. The presence of these instruments may increase discipline in a presidential democracy, just as their absence may decrease discipline in a parliamentary democracy. Thus, the absence of the confidence vote in presidential democracies may be less of a handicap than it is often assumed to be.

Having shown that the mechanisms that supposedly connect presidential institutions to democratic breakdown do not find support in theory or data, I proceed to account for the fact with which this book started: that presidential democracies are more likely to become dictatorships than parliamentary ones. In Chapter 6, I show first of all that this fragility is not due to the fact that parliamentary democracies exist in richer countries. Although the level of development (as indicated by real per capita income) matters for the survival of democracy, differences in income do not entirely account for the differences in survival rates across types of democracy. I also show that democratic fragility arises not because parliamentary democracies tend to exist in smaller countries, where governments supposedly face relatively few challenges, while presidential democracies tend to exist in larger countries, where the tasks of government may be daunting. The size of the country, as measured by the size of the population, has no impact on the survival chances of democratic regimes. Hence the factors (apart from presidentialism itself) that are most commonly invoked to account for parliamentary democracies outliving presidential ones are not sufficient to remove the observed differences across the two systems.

There is, however, a military–presidential nexus, and it is this nexus that makes presidential democracies more fragile. Dictatorships bestow different legacies on the democratic systems that replace them. Democracies that follow military dictatorships have considerably shorter lives than democracies that follow civilian dictatorships: the expected life of the former is twenty years, whereas the expected life of the latter is almost ninety years. The reason for this is probably related to the fact that the military, once activated into politics, is hard to control: several countries in the world (e.g., Argentina, Ghana, Guatemala, Sudan, Thailand, Uruguay) have experienced more than one democratic collapse in the twentieth century; in all of these cases democracy broke down when the military – not civilian elites backed by military power – directly took over the government. Presidential democracies, in turn, follow military dictatorships more frequently than parliamentary democracies (66% versus 28% of the time). It is the combination of these two facts – that democracies that follow military dictatorships are more likely to become dictatorships and that presidential democracies are more likely to follow military dictatorships – that accounts for the higher overall regime instability of presidential democracies. Once the current democracy's authoritarian legacy is held constant, we find that presidential and parliamentary democracies have relatively equal chances of surviving: about 19 years for pure parliamentary and presidential democracies, 24 years if we add parliamentary and mixed systems.

There is no question about the military–presidential nexus, as its existence is strongly supported by the data. The question remains of how such a nexus comes into being. I argue in Chapter 6 that it is unlikely this nexus is the product of a preference by the military for presidential over parliamentary forms of government. According to this view, the military – when faced with the possibility of democratization – condition their acceptance of the new regime on the adoption of presidential institutions. Although this theory is plausible, in truth there is simply no evidence from real democratization processes that this preference exists or, if it does, that it has ever been a factor in bringing democracy about.

My own view, which is developed in Chapter 6, is that the military–presidential nexus is the product of a historical accident: it exists because the countries where militarism remained strong at the middle of the twentieth century were also countries that had adopted presidential institutions. In order for us to understand how this coincidence came about, we must consider the following factors. First, countries vary in their propensity for military intervention. Militarism may be a function of social structure or it may be a recurrent phenomenon in contexts where the military, for exogenous and conjunctural reasons, was first mobilized into politics. For instance, the first two decades of the twentieth century witnessed a sharp increase in the number of military dictatorships throughout the world, due perhaps to the combination of profound social changes brought about by industrialization and the emergence of professional armies. Second, countries *adopt* initial institutions for reasons that are unrelated to the ones that lead to the occurrence of military dictatorships. There may be common factors accounting for the adoption of these institutions, but a role is played also by factors that are specific to each "wave" of independence the world has witnessed since the beginning of the nineteenth century. Third, countries *retain* the institutions under which they consolidated their existence as a nation-state. Institutions in general are sticky, and major institutions such as the form of government are even more so than less encompassing ones.

Military intervention took place in many countries, but it persisted (at least until the 1980s) in countries that had adopted presidential institutions. This persistence, in turn, had little to do with the fact that these countries were presidential and a lot to do with the onset of the Cold War and the role of the military in "fighting" it. The instability of presidential democracies is thus due to their existence in countries where the military has endured. If they had also endured in countries with parliamentary institutions, then the rate of breakdown of parliamentary democracies would have been much higher and the difference compared to the breakdown of presidential democracies much smaller – and this book would probably not have been written. It is therefore clear that the intrinsic features of presidentialism are not the reason why presidential democracies tend to break down more frequently than parliamentary ones. The problem of presidential democracies is not that they are "institutionally flawed." Rather, the problem is that they tend to exist in societies where democracies of any type are likely to be unstable. In other words, the problem of the survival of presidential democracies is a problem of the survival of democracies in general, regardless of their form of government.

Much of the literature about democratic forms of government has focused on the relationship between the government and the legislature and on the alleged implications of the ways in which this relationship is organized: conflict under presidentialism and cooperation under parliamentarism. This book should make it apparent that these consequences have been at least exaggerated and that differences in interbranch relationships across the two systems are more of degree than of quality. In light of this, we should re-examine our thinking about the role of some institutions in presidential systems. The general tone in the literature has been to emphasize the role of specific institutional arrangements in helping to circumvent the presidential system's propensity for conflict and paralysis. Thus, strong presidential powers are viewed as undesirable because they may lead to conflicts with the legislature and eventual governability crises; moreover, concurrent and/or two-round presidential elections are considered a positive feature of presidential systems given that they tend to reduce the number of political parties and thereby (allegedly) increase the survival chances of presidential democracies. In contrast, legislative elections organized on the basis of proportional representation might lead to a relatively high number of political parties and so could be bad for the survival of democracy. Finally, presidential term limits are deemed necessary to curb presidential powers, which, if left unchecked, might have a detrimental effect on democracy.

In the concluding chapter of this book I discuss these institutions from a different perspective. Given that presidential institutions per se do not kill democracy and given that countries that are now presidential are likely to remain so in the future, institutions such as presidential powers, electoral systems, and presidential term limits can be seen as ways of advancing goals other than governability, such as representation and accountability. This, I believe, will help us refocus the academic agenda for the study of institutions under presidentialism and, it is hoped, lead to a reconsideration of the aims and strategies for institutional reforms in existing presidential systems.

In addition to providing a better understanding of patterns of democratic instability in the world, the findings presented throughout this book have important

implications for institutional analysis and design. First, they suggest that existing presidential democracies are not doomed. There are conditions, both social and institutional, that make them as likely to survive as parliamentary democracies. Second, the findings presented here draw attention to the fact that institutions, particularly such fundamental ones as the form of government, are sticky and that their "stickyness" has consequences. Countries that democratize are not presented with a clean slate on which to carve the most efficient institutional form. The language of institutional "choice" must be used carefully, since this choice is usually constrained by historical circumstances. Furthermore, because presidentialism is – from an institutional point of view – a viable form of government, countries that are locked into a presidential form of government do not necessarily face a high probability of authoritarianism. Hence it may be more prudent and effective from a political point of view to take the form of government as given and concentrate instead on improving the system that is in place and that key actors take for granted. Institutional choices at a level below the broad constitutional framework are wider and less constrained, since they represent institutional details that do not fundamentally modify expectations induced by the form of government. Such choices include electoral systems, specific powers of the chief executive, legislative organization, and so forth – choices that interact with the form of government to make democracy more or less viable. They also include mechanisms for dealing with a country's authoritarian legacy and controlling the military. Finally, the analysis in this book suggests that institutions alone are not sufficient to provide a complete understanding of broad political outcomes. Their interaction with the conditions under which they exist also needs to be taken into consideration in order for us to account for such outcomes.

The question that dominated the research agenda fifteen or twenty years ago – whether institutions matter – is beyond discussion; few people today would make a case that they do not. Yet institutions are not the whole story, and specifying how they are supposed to work is not sufficient for providing a full account of how they actually work. For otherwise we would, in an ironical twist, be regressing to a view that pre-dates the behavioral revolution in political science. The problem with the literature that identified presidentialism as a cause of democratic instability is that it placed too much emphasis on the principles defining the different forms of government and then simply derived from those principles the behavior that would, or perhaps that should, follow. In this book I provide a corrective to this view by offering a more realistic analysis of how different democratic systems operate and of the factors that allow them to survive.

2

Presidential, Parliamentary, and Mixed Democracies

The concern with presidential democracies stems from the constitutional separation between the executive and the legislative assembly: the government, headed by the president, does not require any legislative support in order to exist. From this fact are supposed to follow, as I demonstrated in the previous chapter, a number of consequences that may eventually lead to the death of the democratic regime.

The first step in evaluating the empirical validity of this view is to identify the set of democracies that should be at risk. This requires that we first identify the set of countries that are democratic and then the democratic regimes that have a system in which the government and the assembly are independent from one another. Therefore, in this chapter I start by presenting the rules for classifying political regimes into democracies and dictatorships. I then review the criteria underlying existing classifications of democratic forms of government and provide an alternative that focuses exclusively on the relationship between the government and the legislative assembly. Following the existing literature, I distinguish three types of regimes: pure presidential democracies, pure parliamentary democracies, and mixed systems.

Democracies and Dictatorships

Since the concern of this book is with the survival of democracies, the first order of business is to separate democracies from dictatorships. Here I use the classification of political regimes first proposed in Alvarez et al. (1996) and updated in Przeworski et al. (2000). There are, as anyone who has done empirical work on democracy knows, several alternative ways to observe political regimes. However, the dichotomous regime classification employed here is superior on several

grounds – most importantly that it provides a nonarbitrary and entirely reproducible way of distinguishing democracies from dictatorships.[1]

Given that there have been no changes in the rules for classifying political
regimes presented in Przeworski et al. (2000), here I simply summarize those
rules and discuss one modification I make in the way they are applied. I also
discuss why extending the period of coverage to 2002 (the original classification
ended in 1990) leads to changes in the coding of specific cases. As will become
clear in what follows, these changes were entirely due to the fact that new information about specific cases became available and not to the application of new
rules.

Democracies are regimes in which governmental offices are filled as a consequence of contested elections (Przeworski 1991). This definition has two main
parts: "offices" and "contestation." For a regime to be democratic, both the chief
executive office and the legislative body must be filled by elections.[2]

Contestation occurs when there exists an opposition that has some chance of
winning office as a consequence of elections. This entails three features:

1. *ex ante uncertainty* – the outcome of the election must be unknown before
   it takes place;
2. *ex post irreversibility* – the winner of the electoral contest must be the one
   who actually takes office;
3. *repeatability* – elections that meet the first two criteria must occur at regular and known intervals.

The challenge is to provide an operational definition for these features. We
need rules to assess whether the relevant offices are filled through elections as
well as rules to assess whether elections are competitive. A regime is classified as
a democracy if it meets the requirements stipulated in *all* of the following rules.

1. The chief executive must be elected.
2. The legislature must be elected.

---

[1] An extensive comparison between the dichotomous classification of political regimes adopted
here and existing alternatives (such as the Freedom House and Polity measures) can be found in
Cheibub and Gandhi (2006).

[2] That not all offices need to be filled by elections is uncontroversial. Collier and Adcock (1999:549),
in fact, believe that having only one of those offices filled by elections should be sufficient for a
regime to qualify as "at least partially democratic." Yet I have serious reservations about classifying as a democracy any regime in which the president is elected in contested elections but the
laws are made by a legislative body consisting of presidential appointees.

3. There must be more than one party competing in the elections. This condition is violated (and so the regime is nondemocratic) if (a) there are no political parties; (b) there is only one political party; (c) the current term in office ended in the establishment of no-party or one-party rule; or (d) the incumbents unconstitutionally closed the legislature and rewrote the rules in their favor.

4. Given that the first three conditions have been met, an alternation in power under rules identical to the ones that brought the incumbents to power must have taken place.

Implementing the first two rules presents no problem because it is simple to observe whether the relevant offices are filled as a result of elections. Implementing the third and fourth rules is more complex, and their implementation requires some discussion.

The "Party" Rule

The party rule can be conceived of as having two components. The first, represented by conditions 3(a) and 3(b) in the previous listing, is straightforward. This component says that, in order for a contested election to take place, voters must have at least two alternatives to choose from, and any year in which these alternatives do not exist cannot be considered democratic. Hence, elections in which voters are presented with a single list do not qualify as contested, and the years during which these elections occur – as well as the subsequent years up to the next election – cannot be considered as democratic.[3]

The second component of the party rule can be thought of as the "consolidation rule." Consolidation of no-party or one-party rule occurs whenever incumbents either ban all parties (or all opposition parties) or force all parties to merge with the ruling one. If the incumbents instituted a one-party or no-party rule during their current tenure in office then, according to 3(c), the regime is considered to have been authoritarian from the moment the present incumbents

---

[3] Note that what matters is not the number of parties represented in the legislature but rather the number of choices that voters have. Even though three parties and several Catholic groups were represented in the Polish legislature under communist rule, voters were offered only one list at elections. Similarly, the Vanguard of the Malagasy Revolution (AREMA) did not control all the seats in the parliament in Madagascar from 1976 to 1990, yet during this period the High Constitutional Court had decreed (in allowing multipartism) that all political associations had to operate within the National Front of the Malagasy Revolution, which was the only list offered to voters (Freedom House 1992:318).

assumed office. Consolidation of incumbent rule also applies, according to 3(d), whenever there was more than one party but at some time the incumbents unconstitutionally closed the legislature and rewrote electoral rules to their own advantage.

Such actions constitute prima facie evidence that incumbents were not prepared to yield office as a result of elections (thus violating the ex post certainty and repeatability provisos of the definition of contested elections), so the entire period preceding the legislature's closing is then considered authoritarian. To see how this works, consider the following examples.

- In South Korea, President Chung-Hee Park held elections in 1963 and 1967, when he obtained (respectively) 43% and 52% of the vote. His party was able to secure legislative majorities of 63% and 74%, respectively. After a constitutional amendment was approved in 1969 allowing him to seek re-election for a third term in office, elections were held in 1971, when Park obtained 51% of the vote and his party secured "only" 55% of the legislative seats. Not satisfied with these results, he proclaimed martial law in October 1972, dissolved congress, and called legislative elections under new rules. Between elected and appointed representatives, the government party was able to secure 67% of the seats. Under the party rule, the years prior to the closing of congress in 1972 are considered authoritarian, even though there were elections for the presidency and congress in which more than two parties competed.
- Alberto Fujimori was elected president of Peru in competitive elections in 1990. In April 1992 he dissolved congress and announced the formation of an Emergency Government of National Reconstruction. Under the party rule, transition to dictatorship in Peru occurred in 1990, when Fujimori first came to power.
- In the Philippines, Ferdinand Marcos first came to power when he won 52% of the vote in presidential elections in 1965. Re-elected in 1969 with 62% of the vote, he proclaimed martial law in 1972 when his ability to remain in power became uncertain. Under the party rule, the breakdown of democracy occurred in 1965, when Marcos first came to power.
- Finally, there had been three legislative elections in Malaysia since independence in 1957. The incumbents won an absolute majority of votes in the first two elections but not in the third. They then declared a state of emergency, closed the congress, and changed the rules in a way that secured their permanence in power. According to Ahmad (1988:357), "the better showing by the opposition caused a temporary loss of confidence and even the conclusion by some in the ruling party that it had lost its mandate." The parliament was

dissolved in 1969, a state of emergency was proclaimed, and a tough internal security law was adopted. The constitution was rewritten to assure that no more electoral defeats would occur. Under the party rule, Malaysia has never had any democratic experience because the elections that occurred between 1957 and 1968 led to the consolidation (perhaps the perpetuation) of the incumbent party in office.

The Alternation Rule: Extension to the Post-1990 Period

Implementing the last operational rule – the alternation rule – requires that we make one assumption and one decision about what kind of error we are willing to accept. It does not, however, require any subjective judgment on the part of the analyst and hence does not compromise the classification's reproducibility – probably the one attribute that any measure of political regimes should strive to guarantee and one that distinguishes the classification of democracy used here from existing alternatives.[4]

An alternation in power takes place when the individual or party occupying the chief executive office is replaced through elections that were organized under the same rules as the ones that brought the executive to office. For obvious reasons, alternation becomes relevant only in cases where the first three rules apply. However, implementing this rule is complicated by the fact that, given the occurrence of elections in which two or more parties compete, it is difficult to distinguish regimes where incumbents never lose power because they are popular from regimes in which incumbents hold elections only because they know they will not lose them. Since there is nothing in any conception of democracy that precludes the emergence of a highly popular incumbent who is repeatedly returned to office by very pleased voters, the first case should be considered a democracy; and since incumbents who are ready to call off elections at the moment they anticipate a defeat violate the ex ante uncertainty and repeatability conditions for contested elections, the second case should be considered a dictatorship. But these two cases are observationally equivalent, so it is impossible to distinguish them empirically.

Part of the problem can be addressed if we assume that current actions reveal what incumbents would have done at different moments in time. Thus, Japan's Liberal Democratic Party was in office continually until the 1993 election, when

---

[4] As discussed in Cheibub and Gandhi (2006), one advantage of this regime classification over existing alternatives is that it is exclusively based on explicit criteria and observable events. For this reason it is *reproducible* in a way that the alternatives are not.

it finally lost its legislative majority. A coalition government (not including the LDP) was formed, thus characterizing an alternation in power – the first since the end of World War II. Japan is therefore classified as a democracy under the assumption that the LDP would have yielded power had it lost elections prior to 1993.

Yet even if such assumptions are made, there are cases in which it is impossible to tell what type of incumbent is in office. The best example is Botswana, where seven multiparty elections were held since independence in 1966 under conditions that most analysts consider to be free and fair (no constraints on the opposition, little visible repression, no apparent fraud)[5] and where the incumbent won each by an atypically (for democratic elections) high margin of victory.[6] Had the Botswana Democratic Party lost one of these elections and allowed a different party to form a government – or, in the face of defeat, had it closed parliament and changed the electoral rules – then we would be able to identify the regime either as a democracy or a dictatorship. As it is, however, we simply do not know; until one of these events happens, we need to accept that we are simply not capable of classifying Botswana with the rules we now have.[7] We can exclude all cases such as Botswana from the data set, we can call them democracies, or we can call them dictatorships. The decision is a function of the kind of systematic error one is willing to risk in classifying political regimes – that is, whether one prefers to risk calling a real democracy a dictatorship (Type I error), or calling a real dictatorship a democracy (Type II error). Whatever our preferences, the fact remains that we cannot say for sure what kind of regime exists in Botswana. The choice here is to avoid committing Type II errors; hence regimes that meet the first three rules but have not experienced an alternation in power are classified as dictatorships.[8]

---

[5] According to the U.S. Department of State's country profile, "each of the elections since independence has been freely and fairly contested and has been held on schedule"; (http://www.state.gov/r/pa/ei/bgn/1830.htm). The Freedom House, in turn, states that "international observers declared polling free and fair" (2005:95).

[6] Przeworski et al. (2000) estimate that the conditional probability that the share of seats obtained by the largest party is larger than two thirds, given that a regime is democratic, is 0.126. By Bayes' rule, the probability that a country is democratic – given that the share of seats for the largest party is larger than two thirds – is 0.0877.

[7] It is important to emphasize that this is not an argument for the necessity of creating some sort of intermediate regime category. The fact that we cannot tell which regime it actually is does not make Botswana any less of a democracy or dictatorship.

[8] In practical terms this decision makes little difference. The data set contains a variable, TYPEII, which identifies the cases that are coded as a dictatorship because of this decision. Consequently, it is easy to reclassify political regimes so that Type I errors are avoided, or simply to exclude these cases from specific analyses.

One consequence of formulating the rule for regime classification in this way is that the uncertainty inherent in cases such as Botswana may be resolved as history unfolds. Indeed, the regime classification is inherently "dated" in the sense that decisions will be made on the basis of the information available *at the time the classification is being implemented.* Uncomfortable as this may be, in 1990 Japan would thus have been classified as a Type II dictatorship.

In the original classification (Przeworski et al. 2000), 92% of the regimes of all the countries that existed between 1950 and 1990 were unambiguously classified by the application of the four rules; 8% of the cases were classified as a dictatorship because multiparty elections occurred but with no alternation. As we extend the classification to 2002, these proportions remain exactly the same: 8% of country-years between 1946 and 2002 are classified as dictatorships on the grounds that they fail the alternation rule. The particular cases, however, are not the same – either because new countries have emerged since 1990 and events were not sufficient to allow us to determine their regime type (e.g., in Georgia, Kyrgyzstan, and Tajikistan) or because history provided the needed information to resolve the uncertainty about the type of political regime, thus requiring that the original coding be revised (e.g., for Mexico and Senegal).

The issue that arises with countries such as Mexico under Vicente Fox and Senegal under Abdoulaye Wade, where the opposition won after a long period of incumbent victory in multiparty elections, is to determine when exactly the transition occurred. That the new government should be classified as a democracy according to our rules is not problematic. But should the government that allowed the alternation to take place be also classified as a democracy? If we answer Yes, then what about the government prior to that one, the previous one, and so on? Specifically, does the fact that Fox took office in Mexico in 2000 require that we recode the regime as a democracy all the way back to the 1920s, when the PRI first came to office?

This issue is addressed by focusing on the rules under which the incumbent came to power. If the opposition wins under rules that are identical to the ones that led to the victory of the incumbent, then the incumbent is considered democratic: the years under that person's rule meet all four rules for classifying a regime as a democracy. This is done with all previous governments up to the point where the rules under which the incumbent came to power were changed.

The rules that matter are the broad electoral rules: who votes, how votes are counted, and who counts the votes. Thus, in the case of Mexico, we date the transition to democracy to 2000, when Fox – the candidate of one of the opposition parties – was sworn into the presidency. The electoral rules were changed under the Zedillo presidency (1994–2000) when, in 1996, an accord between the ruling PRI and the two opposition parties (PAN and PRD) ended the PRI's control of the Federal Electoral Institute. Similarly, transition to democracy in Senegal occurred in 2000 when the incumbent Abdou Diouf, of the Socialist Party, lost to Abdoulayé Wade, of the Democratic Party. Diouf's last victory had been in the 1993 election, prior to the creation of the independent National Observatory of Elections in 1997.

Applying these rules leads to the identification of 3,273 years of democracy in 129 countries between 1946 and 2002. Appendix 2.1 lists these cases, which represent 41.5% of the 7,880 possible years experienced by the 199 countries that existed at some point since 1946. These are the cases for which we must now identify the form of government.

Presidential, Parliamentary, and Mixed Democracies

There is, of course, more than one way to distinguish democracies. Given the necessity of organizing competitive elections and alternation in power, rules – that is, institutions – are paramount in democracies. A moment's consideration of what these rules entail is sufficient to convey the complexity and the variety of what needs to be specified for *competitive elections* to take place.[9] There are hundreds of ways to combine these rules and thus, in principle, hundreds of ways to differentiate democratic regimes. The focus here is on the form of government, that is, on the rules defining who the government is, how it comes to power, and how it remains in power. As seen in Chapter 1, there is a vast literature that suggests the form of government is causally related to the survival chances of democratic regimes.

Classifications of forms of democratic government abound in the literature. There seems to be a general consensus that there are two "pure" types of systems, parliamentary and presidential, as well as one system that combines features of both – variously called a mixed, semipresidential, or parliamentary–presidential system.[10] The classification to be presented in this chapter likewise

---

[9] This includes, *at the least,* rules about how to run the elections; about what is to be the object of competition, which includes the organization of the legislature and the definition of the government; about who is entitled to vote and to run in the election, which includes whether parties (universally the main vehicle for electoral competition) are to be organized and financially supported; and about who counts the votes and who proclaims the winner.

[10] Shugart and Carey (1992) seem to depart from this consensus in distinguishing two "nonpure" regime types: premier-presidential and president-parliamentary. Their distinction, however, is subsumed by the classification here in that all such cases fall within our category of mixed regimes.

groups democracies into these three categories. Existing classifications, however, use redundant and/or insufficient criteria and thus are unable to unambiguously place all cases into one of the three categories. What is distinctive about the classification offered here is that it provides a clear set of operational criteria by which democratic regimes are distinguished according to their form of government.

Conceptually, the form of government in a democracy depends on the relationship between the government, the assembly, and (where they exist) elected presidents. The main issue is whether the government can be removed by the assembly in the course of its constitutional term in office. Systems in which governments cannot be removed by the assembly are *presidential*. Systems in which they can be so removed are either *parliamentary* (when only the assembly is allowed to remove the government) or *mixed* (when either the assembly or the directly elected president can remove the government). The mechanism of removal by the legislature is the vote of no confidence initiated by the legislature – or by a failed vote of confidence that was initiated by the government itself (Huber 1996). The mechanism of removal by the elected president may be direct, such as when the president can partially or completely replace the government unilaterally, or indirect, such as when the president dissolves the assembly, calls early elections, and thus causes the government to fall.

There are several other important aspects related to the nature and operation of the government in democracies, some of which have been made into defining features of democratic forms of government. These include the nature of executive power, thought to be collective or collegial in parliamentarism and individual in presidentialism (Verney 1992; Lijphart 1999:118); the separation of heads of state and government under parliamentarism and their fusion under presidentialism (Verney 1992); the indirect election of government in parliamentarism and popular election in presidentialism (Lijphart 1999:117); the existence of a president with "constitutionally granted lawmaking authority" in presidential regimes or with "considerable powers" in "mixed" regimes (Shugart and Carey 1992:19, 24).

These features of democracies, however, are not sufficient to distinguish forms of government. Uruguay is a presidential democracy that had a collective executive between 1952 and 1967; in contrast, decisions within the British government, dominated as they are by the prime minister, can hardly be characterized as collegial.[11] Between 1996 and 2001, Israel popularly elected its prime minister while retaining the basic features of a parliamentary system: the

---

[11] There is a relatively large literature that emphasizes the different ways in which executive power is organized in parliamentary democracies. See Sartori (1994), Elgie (1997), and Figueiredo (2005).

Presidential, Parliamentary, and Mixed Democracies

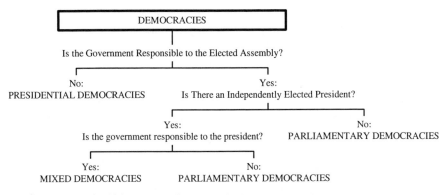

Figure 2.1 Classifying Forms of Democratic Government.

government could be removed in its entirety if the parliament passed a vote of no confidence in it. In Bolivia the president is, under some circumstances, elected by the assembly and yet the regime is not parliamentary; Venezuela prior to its 1999 constitution had a president with no constitutionally mandated legislative powers, but it was universally considered to be a presidential democracy.

Some might suggest that these constitute anomalous or intermediate cases, hybrid regimes that fall into neither the parliamentary nor the presidential category (see Mainwaring 1993; Lijphart 1999). Yet, unless we are able to provide a positive criterion for identifying these regimes, this does not seem to be a satisfactory solution because it simply creates a residual category that lumps together some very heterogeneous cases.[12] We therefore need to produce a set of criteria that unambiguously classify democratic regimes according to their form of government.

Thus: systems in which governments must enjoy the support of a legislative majority in order to exist are classified as parliamentary; systems in which governments do not need the support of a legislative majority in order to exist are classified as presidential; and systems in which governments depend both on a majority in the legislative assembly *and* on elected presidents in order to exist are classified as mixed. Operationally, the following three questions provide a sequence of steps – summarized in Figure 2.1 – that unambiguously identify presidential, parliamentary, and mixed democracies.

---

[12] Incidentally, as will become clear shortly, the "mixed" democracy in my classification is not a residual category. Although it combines features of both pure parliamentarism and pure presidentialism, the mixed system is a well-defined type of democracy. In this sense, it is not an intermediate or somewhat blurred category lying between the two pure forms.

Is the Government Responsible to the Assembly?   Assembly responsibility means that a legislative majority has the constitutional power to remove the government from office. Since assembly responsibility is a necessary condition for the existence of a parliamentary or a mixed system, cases where there is no assembly responsibility cannot be either; hence they are presidential. In turn, cases in which assembly responsibility exists can be either parliamentary or mixed.

Formally, assemblies may affect both the formation and the survival of governments, and whether it does one or the other (or both) has been made one of the dimensions along which democratic regimes are classified (Shugart and Carey 1992; Mainwaring 1993). However, the crucial aspect for assembly responsibility is not formation of but rather survival of the government. Theoretically the latter subsumes the former: an assembly deprived of the right to elect the government yet able to pass a vote of no confidence can do so immediately following the government's formation, thereby preventing it from coming into existence. Conversely, an assembly that is allowed to elect the government may, as in Switzerland and Bolivia (when popular elections do not produce a majority winner), be barred from removing it from office, thus characterizing effective independence of the executive with respect to the legislature. As Strøm (2000:265) points out, "in the real world ... parliamentarism rarely means that the legislature actually elects the executive."[13] What matters, he continues, "is that the cabinet must be tolerated by the parliamentary majority, not that the latter actually plays any direct role in the selection of the former." Note also that the nature of the executive – collective or not – is immaterial for the classification of forms of democratic regimes. Thus Switzerland, where the assembly elects a collective government that cannot be removed before the end of its term, is classified as a presidential regime: the assembly does not affect the survival of the government.

Identification of cases in which the government is responsible to the assembly is fairly unproblematic. The language in the vast majority of constitutions is unambiguous when it allows the assembly to initiate a vote of no confidence in the existing government, or when it stipulates that governments may request such a vote in connection with specific pieces of legislation. There are, however, two points that need to be clarified. First, it does not matter whether the assembly's ability to pass a no-confidence vote is restricted. For example, article 87 of the 1996 Ukrainian constitution allows the assembly to consider a vote of

---

[13] As a matter of fact, such an election is not that rare. According to Laver and Schofield (1998:64), it is required in nine out of twenty European parliamentary democracies. Nonetheless, a formal vote of investiture is not required at all in a significant number of parliamentary democracies.

no confidence in the government only once in each of the two annual legislative sessions. Article 117 of the 1993 Russian constitution – probably the most restrictive in the set of democratic constitutions – requires that the Duma approve a motion of no confidence in the government twice within three months before the president is forced to choose between the resignation of the government and the dissolution of the assembly. But even in these restrictive cases the government is subject to the confidence of the assembly in a way that it is not under presidential constitutions, where the government cannot under any circumstances be removed by a vote of the legislative assembly.

Second, government removal by the assembly means that the entire government must resign when the assembly approves a no-confidence vote. This implies that cases in which the assembly can remove individual ministers but not the government as a whole – as in Chile during its "parliamentary" republic (Stanton 1997) – are not instances of assembly responsibility. Similarly, cases in which there is a council of ministers that can be removed by the assembly but in which the head of the government serves a fixed term, as in most Peruvian constitutions, do not qualify as cases of assembly responsibility either.[14]

Is There an Independently (either Directly or Indirectly) Elected President? By itself the existence of a directly elected president is neither a necessary nor a sufficient condition for identifying a democratic system: direct presidential elections take place in both presidential and mixed systems; and indirect presidential elections may be a feature of both presidential systems (as in the United States or in Argentina until 1994) and parliamentary systems (e.g., Germany, Italy, Greece). However, in conjunction with information about assembly confidence, the lack of a directly elected head of government identifies most cases of parliamentary democracies. Hence, this question allows us to identify countries that, owing to the absence of a directly elected head of government (in combination with assembly confidence), can neither be presidential nor mixed. These countries must therefore be parliamentary, even if their heads of government are – as in South Africa, Kiribati, and the Marshall Islands – called "presidents."

---

[14] The 1993 Peruvian constitution stipulates that the president is the head of the government (article 118) who chooses the president of the council of ministers (i.e., the prime minister) and the other ministers independently (article 122). The president of the council of ministers as well as the ministers themselves are individually and collectively subject to assembly confidence, but the president is not. This has been a feature of Peruvian constitutions since the one promulgated in 1856 (Paz-Soldan 1943). The 1978 constitution in Sri Lanka has similar provisions: article 30 names the president as the head of the government, and article 43 creates a cabinet of ministers of which the president is a member and the head. The cabinet is subject to assembly confidence, but if dissolved the president remains in office.

Is the Government Responsible to the President?   Given assembly responsibility, the issue is to determine whether the government is responsible to the president. Government responsibility to the president can be direct, as when the president can unilaterally dismiss the government in its entirety or one minister at a time. It can also be indirect, as when the president dismisses the government by dissolving the assembly. In both cases the government depends on the support of a legislative majority *and* an independently elected president in order to stay in office. Thus, given assembly responsibility and an independently elected president, either type (direct or indirect) of government responsibility to the president is sufficient to characterize the regime as "mixed."[15] Cases in which the president cannot dismiss the government and/or dissolve the assembly are classified as parliamentary democracies.

Operationally, answering these questions and identifying the form of government is largely unproblematic. Both popular election of the president and government responsibility to the legislative assembly are easily identified in the existing constitutions. Government responsibility to the president is slightly more difficult to determine.

A government is responsible to the popularly elected president when at least one of the following three facts is true: (1) the president is the head of the government; (2) the president can dissolve the assembly to which the government is responsible (this will cause the government to fall); or (3) the president has some discretionary power, as indicated by the language in the constitution, to appoint and dismiss the government or individual members of the government.

It turns out that, with two exceptions, all cases in which the president is popularly elected meet at least one of these conditions. The two exceptions – the cases in which there is a popularly elected president to whom the government is *not* responsible – are Finland, where the 2000 constitution instituted a parliamentary form of government by removing the president's power to dissolve the assembly and appoint/remove the government, and Ireland under its 1937 constitution. The language in these constitutions is subtle but clear. Regarding dissolution, the president in Finland can act only in response to a proposal by the prime minister. Section 26 of its 2000 constitution states: "The President of the Republic, in response to a reasoned proposal by the Prime Minister, and after having heard the parliamentary groups, and while the Parliament is in session, may order that extraordinary parliamentary elections shall be held.

---

[15] This distinction is the basis for Shugart and Carey's (1992) definition of "premier-presidential" and "president-parliamentary" democracies, although it is unclear in their detailed discussion of these systems (pp. 55–75) whether the distinction really matters.

Thereafter, the Parliament shall decide the time when it concludes its work before the elections." In Ireland, the constitution allows the president to refuse dissolution suggested by the prime minister,[16] but it does not grant the president the power to initiate dissolution. As for appointment of the government, in both Finland and Ireland it is simply ratification by the president of an election in parliament; removal of the government is required when the assembly approves a vote of no confidence in the government.[17] Thus, with the exception of these two cases, all systems with a popularly elected president and government responsibility to the legislative assembly are mixed.

Observe that the classification of democracies here is entirely based on the rules prescribed in the country's constitution. This decision is justified, in part, because we are dealing with a set of countries that have been classified as democratic on other grounds. Given this fact, it makes sense to take the constitution as the document that effectively stipulates the way in which governments are formed and survive in power. In the vast majority of cases this leads to clear and uncontroversial decisions, since the rules of government formation are well-defined and political practice conforms to the constitutional provisions. In some cases, however, there will be ambiguity – mostly because some of the scenarios prescribed by the constitution have never materialized, but also because of misconceptions induced by the language adopted in the constitution (or by the translations upon which I relied when assessing the constitutions of some countries).

The best example of the latter issue comes from South Africa, where the head of state and government are one and the same person who is called the president. However, according to the 1996 constitution (as well as the interim 1994 constitution), this "president" is subject to a vote of no confidence by a majority of the

---

[16] Article 13, 2.2° of the 1937 constitution states that "the President may in his absolute discretion refuse to dissolve Dáil Éireann on the advice of a Taoiseach who has ceased to retain the support of a majority in Dáil Éireann."

[17] Section 61 of the 2000 Finnish constitution reads: "The Parliament elects the Prime Minister, who is thereafter appointed to the office by the President of the Republic. The President appoints the other Ministers in accordance with a proposal made by the Prime Minister." In turn, section 64 reads: "The President of the Republic grants, upon request, the resignation of the Government or a Minister. The President may also grant the resignation of a Minister on the proposal of the Prime Minister. The President shall in any event dismiss the Government or a Minister, if either no longer enjoys the confidence of Parliament, even if no request is made." The text of the Irish constitution is as follows: "Article 13.1.1°: The President shall, on the nomination of Dáil Éireann, appoint the Taoiseach, that is, the head of the Government or Prime Minister; 2° The President shall, on the nomination of the Taoiseach with the previous approval of Dáil Éireann, appoint the other members of the Government; 3° The President shall, on the advice of the Taoiseach, accept the resignation or terminate the appointment of any member of the Government."

National Assembly; if approved, the president must resign and a new government must be formed.[18] The fact that votes of no confidence have been unlikely in South Africa has nothing to do with what its constitution says, I believe, and everything to do with the dominance in parliament of a party holding about two thirds of the seats since competitive elections were held in 1994. Had such a large majority not existed, the relationship between the government and the parliament in South Africa would have been considerably different, with issues of government survival vis-à-vis legislative action probably occupying the forefront of political life.

Regarding the former issue – constitutional scenarios that do not materialize – the major uncertainty emerges with respect to mixed democracies, where the room for ambiguity is the largest and where the feeling is strongest that a mixed system is in fact a pure parliamentary or pure presidential democracy in disguise. In Iceland, for example, the directly elected president is commonly perceived as "a figurehead and symbol of unity rather than a political leader" (Kristinsson 1999:87). Hence, as Kristinsson puts it, "it is customary in Iceland to regard the form of government as a parliamentary one, essentially similar to the Danish one, despite the different ways heads of states come into office" (p. 86). Yet the Icelandic constitution is ambiguous with regard to the powers of the president. The president may dissolve parliament (article 24) and appoint and discharge ministers, including the prime minister (article 15). At the same time, the constitution also states that ministers execute the power of the president (article 13), thus providing the grounds for the "passive presidency" view of Icelandic politics. At the opposite extreme, although many African countries have adopted "French style" (i.e., mixed) constitutions, there is a strong sense that real power lies with the president (Bratton and van de Walle 1997; Carlson 1998).

Note, however, that it should matter whether the rules in a country *allow* for behavior that is proscribed elsewhere. In almost every instance of formal rules that do not seem to match political practices, we do find examples of behavior that conform to the constitutional prerogatives of the president and/or the assembly. Thus, in Iceland, the president's constitutional prerogative of choosing the *formateur* was crucial for bringing to power the coalition between the Social Democratic Party and the Independence Party, a coalition that governed between 1959 and 1971. Similarly, the head of state's decision to form a nonpartisan government – after two legislative elections and successive failed attempts at government formation by different parties – played an important role in the formation of subsequent governments in Iceland (Kristinsson 1999:93–4).

---

[18] This is also true in the constitutions of the Marshall Islands and Kiribati.

With respect to the mixed democracies that may look more like presidential ones, examples of government change due to confidence votes, or threats of confidence votes, abound. On 11 April 1995 the prime minister of the Central African Republic, Jean-Luc Mandaba, resigned upon the filing of a no-confidence motion signed by a majority of National Assembly members; on 19 May 1993, the prime minister of the Comoro Islands resigned after losing a vote of no confidence in the legislature; on 18 June 1995, the Comoran president dissolved the assembly to forestall a vote of no confidence in the government; the Congolese government of Stéphane Maurice Bongho-Nouarra fell on 14 November 1992 as a result of a vote of no confidence approved by the assembly; the government of prime minister Rosny Smarth in Haiti survived a vote of no confidence on 27 March 1997; in Madagascar, the government of prime minister Emmanuel Rakotovahiny fell on 17 May 1996 after a motion of no confidence was approved by a vote of 109 to 15; in Niger, the government of Souley Abdoulaye resigned on 16 October 1994 after losing a no-confidence vote in the assembly. Faced with the choice of appointing a prime minister supported by opposition parties or dissolving the National Assembly, Niger's president Mahamane Ousmane chose to dissolve the assembly and call elections for January 1995; the government of Abdirizak Hadji Husseing in Somalia lost a vote of no confidence on 13 July 1964, after which it resigned. In other countries, such as Albania, Armenia, Brazil (in 1962), Senegal, Sri Lanka, and Taiwan, there is evidence that political practice was clearly guided by the possibility that the legislature could pass a vote of no confidence in the government.

Thus, the presence of a constitutional provision allowing or forbidding the president, the assembly, or both to affect a government's survival matters for the way the system works, and it is these provisions that are used here to classify democratic regimes. Of course, politics may unfold differently under similar constitutional provisions. Consider, for example, the constitutions of Germany (1919), Iceland (1944), and France (1958), whose stipulations regarding the president's power to dissolve the assembly and to appoint or remove the government are reproduced in Appendix 2.2. The German (Weimar Republic) and French constitutions read very much like the Icelandic constitution.[19] Nonetheless, we have seen that Iceland's political system functions like a parliamentary democracy; Weimar is considered to be the epitome of presidential–parliamentary

---

[19] The Icelandic constitution seems to give more power to the president than either the Weimar constitution or de Gaulle's constitution: in the former, the president is limited in his ability to dissolve parliament because he can only do it once for the same reason; in France, the president is supposed to consult the prime minister and the presidents of both legislative assemblies before dissolution. No such limitations exist in Iceland.

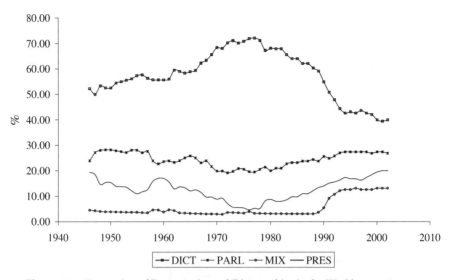

Figure 2.2 Proportion of Democracies and Dictatorships in the World, 1946–2002.

systems, which are characterized not only by the government's assembly responsibility but also by the primacy of the president (Shugart and Carey 1992:24); and France is considered to be the prototypical mixed or semipresidential system (Duverger 1980; Shugart and Carey 1992; Sartori 1994). Clearly the system's actual operation cannot itself be taken as the basis of regime classification, because politics actually unfolds in ways that necessarily depend on factors that are extra-constitutional. That mixed constitutions accommodate polities that operate sometimes like a presidential regime, sometimes like a parliamentary one, and sometimes like a "true" mixed system is intriguing and should be the object of investigation. Perhaps there is something about mixed constitutions that, in combination with some other factors, tilts the system in one way or another. Nonetheless, the constitutions in all these systems are similar in the sense that they make the government responsible to both the president and the assembly.

A Note about Mixed Systems

It is a well-known fact that the number of democracies in the world has increased considerably, in both absolute and relative terms, since the 1980s. Whereas 110 of the 162 countries (68%) that existed in 1982 had nondemocratic regimes, in 2002 only 76 out of 190 countries (40%) were not living under some form of democratic system. This evolution is displayed in Figure 2.2. The 114 democracies

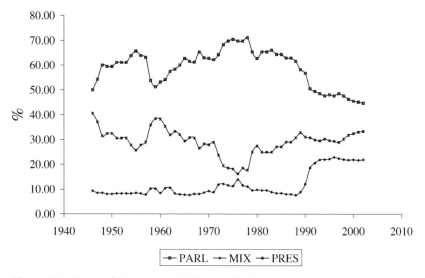

Figure 2.3 Forms of Government in Democratic Systems.

that existed in 2002, as can be seen in Figure 2.3, were distributed in terms of their form of government as follows: 45% of them were parliamentary, 33% presidential, and 22% mixed. This is in contrast with the distribution in 1946, when only three countries – Austria, Finland, and Iceland – out of 32 (about 9%) with a democratic form of government had a mixed constitution. In relative terms, the expansion of mixed systems took place at the expense of both parliamentary and presidential democracies: the increase in the number of mixed democracies by thirteen percentage points was accompanied by a reduction of five and eight percentage points in the number of parliamentary and presidential democracies, respectively.

It took some time for mixed systems to be more widely adopted. The first addition to the three systems in existence in 1946 came when France adopted de Gaulle's constitution in 1958. There were short-lived experiences in Brazil (1961–1963) and Pakistan (1972–1977); Portugal, which democratized in 1976, adopted a mixed system that remains in place to this date. The steady increase in the absolute and relative number of countries with mixed constitutions started with the 1989 transition to democracy in Poland. Between 1990 and 1992, mixed constitutions were adopted in Bulgaria, Cape Verde, the Central African Republic, the Comoros Islands, the Congo, Lithuania, Macedonia, Madagascar, Mali, Mongolia, Niger, Romania, Russia, São Tomé e Príncipe, Slovenia, and the Ukraine. Some of these regimes (e.g., the Congo, the Comoros Islands, and

Niger) have collapsed since they were first adopted, but the proportion of mixed democracies among the set of democracies was about the same in 2002 as it was in 1992.

The amount of scholarly attention paid to mixed democracies has followed a similar pattern, with a flurry of recent studies that seek to understand whether the government's responsibility to both the president and the assembly is a curse or a blessing and with – to no one's surprise – positions varying considerably from one scholar to another.[20] Well-deserved as this attention may be, the current study shall not be joining the fray.

The main reason for this is theoretical. Without denying the importance of systematically considering the consequences (if any) of a mixed constitution, I argue that, for the purposes of the arguments of interest in this book, these systems are equivalent to parliamentary democracies. My aim here is to study the effect of the separation of power systems on the survival of democracy. In terms of the propositions evaluated in this book – namely, claims about the deleterious consequences of the constitutional separation of executive and legislative powers – mixed and parliamentary systems are equivalent. In both cases, the government lacks a fixed mandate and hence the rigidity that is characteristic of presidential systems is not present. Therefore, in most of the book I compare presidential with nonpresidential democracies, that is, both parliamentary and mixed systems. The results reported in the following chapters are not dependent on whether the set of countries to which presidential democracies are compared includes mixed systems or not, since nothing of substance is changed by treating parliamentary and mixed systems together.

Appendix 2.1: Classification of Democratic Forms of Government

Parliamentary Democracies   Albania (1992–2002), Andorra (1993–2002), Antigua (1981–2002), Australia (1946–2002), Bahamas (1973–2002), Bangladesh (1991–2002), Barbados (1966–2002), Belgium (1946–2002), Belize (1981–2002), Canada (1946–2002), Czechoslovakia (1990–1992), Czech Republic (1993–2002), Denmark (1946–2002), Dominica (1978–2002), Estonia (1991–2002), Finland (2000–2002), France (1946–1957), Germany (1949–2002), Ghana (1969–1971), Greece (1946–1966), Greece (1974–2002), Grenada (1974–1978), Grenada (1984–2002), Hungary (1990–2002), India (1947–2002), Ireland (1946–2002), Israel

---

[20] See Roper (2002), Schleiter (2003), Moestrup (2004), Elgie (2004, 2005), and Schleiter and Morgan-Jones (2005).

(1948–2002), Italy (1946–2002), Jamaica (1962–2002), Japan (1947–2002), Kiribati (1979–2002), Laos (1954–1958), Latvia (1991–2002), Lebanon (1946–1974), Lesotho (1993–2002), Liechtenstein (1990–2002), Luxembourg (1946–2002), Malta (1964–2002), Marshall Islands (1991–2002), Mauritius (1968–2002), Myanmar (1948–1957), Myanmar (1960–1961), Nauru (1968–2002), Nepal (1991–2001), Netherlands (1946–2002), New Zealand (1946–2002), Nigeria (1960–1965), Norway (1946–2002), Pakistan (1947–1955), Pakistan (1988–1998), Papua New Guinea (1975–2002), St. Kitts & Nevis (1983–2002), St. Lucia (1979–2002), St. Vincent (1979–2002), Sierra Leone (1961–1966), Slovak Republic (1993–2002), Solomon Islands (1978–2002), Somalia (1960–1968), South Africa (1994–2002), South Korea (1960), Spain (1977–2002), Sri Lanka (1948–1976), Sudan (1956–1957), Sudan (1965–1968), Sudan (1986–1988), Suriname (1975–1979), Sweden (1946–2002), Thailand (1975), Thailand (1983–1990), Thailand (1992–2002), Trinidad & Tobago (1962–2002), Turkey (1961–1979), Turkey (1983–2002), United Kingdom (1946–2002), and Vanuatu (1980–2002).

Mixed Democracies   Armenia (1995–2002), Austria (1946–2002), Brazil (1961–1962), Bulgaria (1990–2002), Cape Verde (1991–2002), Central African Republic (1993–2002), Comoros (1990–1994), Republic of Congo (1992–1996), Croatia (1991–2002), Finland (1946–1999), France (1958–2002), Haiti (1994–2002), Iceland (1946–2002), Lithuania (1991–2002), Macedonia (1991–2002), Madagascar (1993–2002), Mali (1992–2002), Moldova (1996–2002), Mongolia (1992–2002), Niger (1993–1995), Niger (2000–2002), Pakistan (1972–1976), Poland (1989–2002), Portugal (1976–2002), Romania (1990–2002), Russia (1991–2002), São Tomé e Príncipe (1991–2002), Senegal (2000–2002), Slovenia (1991–2002), Taiwan (1996–2002), Ukraine (1991–2002).

Presidential Democracies   Argentina (1946–1954), Argentina (1958–1961), Argentina (1963–1965), Argentina (1973–1975), Argentina (1983–2002), Armenia (1991–1994), Benin (1991–2002), Bolivia (1979), Bolivia (1982–2002), Brazil (1946–1960), Brazil (1963), Brazil (1979–2002), Burundi (1993–1995), Chile (1946–1972), Chile (1990–2002), Colombia (1946–1948), Colombia (1958–2002), Costa Rica (1946–1947), Costa Rica (1949–2002), Cuba (1946–1951), Cyprus (1983–2002), Dominican Republic (1966–2002), Ecuador (1948–1962), Ecuador (1979–1999), El Salvador (1984–2002), Ghana (1979–1980), Ghana (1993–2002), Guatemala (1946–1953), Guatemala (1958–1962), Guatemala (1966–1981), Guatemala (1986–2002), Guinea-Bissau (2000–2002), Guyana (1992–2002), Honduras (1957–1962), Honduras (1971), Honduras (1982–2002), Indonesia (1999–2002), Ivory Coast (2000–2002), Kenya (1998–2002), Malawi (1994–2002), Mexico (2000–2002),

Micronesia (1991–2002), Namibia (1990–2002), Nicaragua (1984–2002), Nigeria (1979–1982), Nigeria (1999–2002), Palau (1994–2002), Panama (1949–1950), Panama (1952–1967), Panama (1989–2002), Peru (1946–1947), Peru (1956–1961), Peru (1963–1967), Peru (1980–1990), Peru (2001–2002), Philippines (1946–1965), Philippines (1986–2002), San Marino (1992–2002), Sierra Leone (1996), Sierra Leone (1998–2002), South Korea (1988–2002), Sri Lanka (1989–2002), Suriname (1988–1989), Suriname (1991–2002), Switzerland (1946–2002), Uganda (1980–1984), United States (1946–2002), Uruguay (1946–1972), Uruguay (1985–2002), Venezuela (1946–1947), Venezuela (1959–2002), Zambia (1991–2002).

Appendix 2.2: Government Formation and Assembly Dissolution in Three Mixed Constitutions – Weimar (1919), Iceland (1949), and France (1958)

Definition of the Government

Weimar Article 52: The Reich government consists of the chancellor and the Reich ministers.

Iceland Article 2: Althingi and the President of Iceland jointly exercise legislative power. The President and other governmental authorities referred to in this Constitution and elsewhere in the law exercise executive power. Judges exercise judicial power.

Article 16: The State Council is composed of the President of the Republic and the Ministers and is presided over by the President. Laws and important government measures shall be submitted to the President in the State Council.

France Article 21: The Prime Minister directs the operation of the Government. [Government is not explicitly defined.]

President's Power to Dissolve Assembly

Weimar Article 25: The Reich president has the right to dissolve the Reichstag, but only once for the same reason. New elections are held no later than sixty days after the dissolution.

Iceland None.

France Article 12: The President of the Republic, after consulting the Prime Minister and the Presidents of the Assemblies, can declare the National Assembly dissolved. General elections take place not less than twenty days and not more than forty days after the dissolution. The National Assembly convenes as of right on the second Thursday following its election. If it convenes outside the period prescribed for the ordinary session, a session is called by right for a fifteen-day period. No new dissolution can take place within a year following this election.

Appointment of the Government

Weimar　Article 53: The Reich chancellor, and, at his request, the Reich ministers, are appointed and dismissed by the Reich President.

Iceland　Article 15: The President appoints Ministers and discharges them. He determines their number and assignments.

Article 20: The President appoints public officials as provided by law. The President may remove from office any official whom he has appointed.

France　Article 8: The President of the Republic appoints the Prime Minister. He terminates the functions of the Prime Minister when the latter tenders the resignation of the Government. On the proposal of the Prime Minister, he appoints the other members of the Government and terminates their functions.

Operation of the Government

Weimar　Article 55: The Reich chancellor presides over the Reich government and conducts its affairs according to the rules of procedure, to be decided upon by the Reich government and to be approved by the Reich president.

Article 56: The Reich chancellor determines the political guidelines and is responsible for them to the Reichstag. Within these guidelines every Reich minister leads his portfolio independently, and is responsible to the Reichstag.

Iceland　Article 13: The President entrusts his authority to Ministers.

France　Article 9: The President of the Republic presides over the Council of Ministers.

Article 13: The President of the Republic signs the ordinances and decrees deliberated on in the Council of Ministers.

Assembly Confidence

Weimar　Article 54: The Reich chancellor and the Reich ministers, in order to exercise their mandates, require the confidence of the Reichstag. Any one of them must resign if the Reichstag votes by explicit decision to withdraw its confidence.

Iceland   Article 14: Ministers are accountable for all executive acts. The accountability of the Ministers is established by law. Althingi may impeach Ministers on account of their official acts. The Court of Impeachment has competence in such cases.

France   Article 49: The Prime Minister, after deliberation by the Council of Ministers, may make the Government's program or possibly a statement of its general policy an issue of its responsibility before the National Assembly. The National Assembly may question the responsibility of the Government by the vote on a motion of censure. Such a motion shall be admissible only if it is signed by at least one-tenth of the members of the National Assembly. The vote may only take place forty-eight hours after the motion has been filed; the only votes counted shall be those favorable to the motion of censure, which may be adopted only by a majority of the members comprising the Assembly. Except in the case specified (prévu) in the paragraph below, a deputy cannot be signatory to more than three motions of censure in the course of the same ordinary session and more than one in the course of the same extraordinary session. The Prime Minister may, after deliberation by the Council of Ministers, make the passing of a bill an issue of the Government's responsibility before the National Assembly. In that event, the bill shall be considered adopted unless a motion of censure, introduced within the subsequent twenty-four hours, is carried as provided in the preceding paragraph. The Prime Minister may ask the Senate to approve a statement of general policy.

Article 50: Where the National Assembly carries a motion of censure, or where it fails to endorse the program or a statement of general policy of the Government, the Prime Minister must tender the resignation of the Government to the President of the Republic.

3

---

*Are the Incentives for Coalition Formation
Different in Parliamentary and
Presidential Democracies?*

As discussed in Chapter 1, the prevailing argument about the alleged inferiority of presidentialism with respect to governance and survival of a democratic system runs as follows.

1. Parliamentarism and presidentialism are different in their structures: the former is a system of "mutual dependence" and the latter of "mutual independence" between the executive and the legislature (Stepan and Skach 1993:17–18; Linz 1994:64; Linz and Stepan 1996:181).
2. Institutions shape incentives: presidentialism generates fewer or weaker incentives to form coalitions (Mainwaring 1990; Stepan and Skach 1993:20; Mainwaring and Scully 1995:33; Linz and Stepan 1996:181; Huang 1997:138).
3. Coalitions are difficult to form and rarely, "only exceptionally," do they form under presidentialism (Linz 1994:19).
4. When no coalition is formed under presidentialism, a "long-term legislative impasse" ensues (Linz and Stepan 1996:181), "there is no alternative but deadlock" (Mainwaring and Scully 1995:33), and "the norm is conflictual government" (Jones 1995:38). As a result, "the very notion of majority government is problematic in presidential systems without a majority party" (Huang 1997:138), "stable multi-party presidential democracy ... is difficult" (Mainwaring 1990), and "presidential systems which consistently fail to provide the president with sufficient legislative support are unlikely to prosper" (Jones 1995:38).

Parliamentarism and presidentialism are indeed different, and institutions do shape incentives. But which institutional features of the two systems shape the incentives relevant for coalition formation? What are these incentives? Most importantly, is the difference in incentives sufficient to impede coalitions in presidential systems?

The goals of this chapter are to isolate the institutional features that are relevant for coalition formation under parliamentarism and presidentialism, to postulate identical actors under the two systems, and to study the effect of these features on coalition formation. In this I follow Diermeier and Krehbiel's (2003) prescriptions for institutional analysis in that I keep behavioral postulates fixed and vary the institutional setup in order to examine the implications for the outcome of interest: coalition formation. However, I do not claim to be building an institutional theory of coalition formation in democratic regimes, as my goal is not to explain why coalitions emerge in parliamentary and presidential democracies. Rather, my strategy is to start from existing models of coalition formation under parliamentarism, an area of research sufficiently advanced to offer a variety of plausible and well-studied choices, and then extend them to presidential systems. In this way, we can address the issue of whether the opportunities offered and constraints imposed by presidentialism are such that coalition formation will rarely occur.

As we shall see later in this chapter, coalitions form less frequently in presidential than in parliamentary democracies – which could be taken as confirmation of what, in Chapter 1, I called the Linzian view of presidentialism. Yet, as demonstrated by the quotations cited at the start of this chapter, the claim that is often made about coalition propensities in parliamentary and presidential systems is a strong one. It is not simply that coalition governments will be more frequent in parliamentary than in presidential systems but rather that the structure of presidentialism is such that actors will not find it in their interest to form coalitions at all. Consequently, the difference in coalition propensities between the two systems should be qualitative and not simply a difference of degree. In this chapter I demonstrate that this is not the case. Although there are conditions under which minority governments emerge in presidential democracies when a coalition government would have emerged under a parliamentary system, these conditions do not necessarily predominate under presidentialism. There is a range of possible scenarios in presidential systems where presidents will make coalition offers and parties will find it in their interest to accept them. Hence coalition governments in presidential systems are not aberrations – odd occurrences that cannot be accounted for by the structure of the system. To the contrary, they occur because actors find it in their best interest to share participation in the government.

Preliminaries

In order to compare incentives for coalition formation under parliamentary and presidential regimes, we need to identify the actors, their preferences, the outcomes of their interaction, and the institutional features relevant for coalition formation. These institutional features are the rules that specify who can make coalition offers and what happens when no coalition is formed.

Actors

Consider a legislature composed of $j \in \mathcal{J}$ political parties who care about the number of portfolios they hold, the policies the government implements, and their performance in the next election.[1] The parties' policy preferences concern a single policy dimension on which they are characterized by ideal points x^j. Parties derive transferable utility from portfolios (and associated perks) as well as nontransferable utility from policy:

$$V_t^j(g, x) = g_t^j - (x_t - x^j)^2 + \rho V_{t+\delta}^j,$$

where g denotes the share of portfolios, $\sum_j g^j = G$ is the value (for any party) of holding all the portfolios, x is the actual policy outcome, $V_{t+\delta}$ is the continuation value, and $0 < \rho \leq 1$ is the discount rate. The quadratic form of policy in the utility function, although standard, is not innocuous; it implies that, if the policy were to deviate far from the ideal point of the party in charge of forming the government, then this party would be willing to give up portfolios in exchange for bringing the policy closer to its preferred point. One justification for this formulation is that, whereas parties are certain about the distribution of portfolios, they (are risk averse and) cannot completely assure themselves of policy outcomes.

Observe that the period before the next election, δ, is endogenous under parliamentarism while (with some exceptions) it is fixed under presidentialism.[2] Hence, under presidentialism, waiting for the next election is unpleasant for the opposition parties because in the meantime they may hold no portfolios. But if parties believe that they would benefit electorally from opposing the president, they may be willing to wait. Note that the continuation value can be quite large: if a party expects to win an absolute majority in the next election, it can be as large as G.

---

[1] This analysis follows the methodology, but not all of the assumptions, in Austen-Smith and Banks (1988), who analyzed coalition formation in parliamentary systems.

[2] In some presidential systems, the president can dissolve one or both houses of the legislature under qualified conditions, such as failure to pass the budget. Note that this does not make the system any less presidential. As discussed in Chapter 2, what matters from the point of view of characterizing presidential systems is the dependence of the government on the legislature, not the converse.

I assume throughout that no party holds a majority in the legislature and that, in a legislature composed of three parties A, B, C, the share of seats held by $A >$ $B > C$. I also assume that $x^C > x^B > x^A$ in the policy space, normalized between 0 and 1.[3]

Outcomes

Given that no party holds a majority of seats in the legislature, the outcome of the government formation game can be either a minority government composed of a single party or a coalition government composed of at least two parties.

There are two kinds of coalitions, and distinguishing them is important for understanding the implications of each of these outcomes. A *government* (portfolio) coalition is a set of legislators belonging to parties that hold cabinet posts, whereas a *legislative* (policy) coalition is a set of legislators from different parties who vote together. If parties are disciplined, then every government coalition is a legislative coalition. Legislative coalitions may vary from one issue to another; such variation may arise from the fact that parties may vote together on some but not all issues or from a lack of party discipline among members.[4] Moreover, the two coalitions need not be coextensive. A party may be outside a portfolio coalition and yet vote with the government (or at least not vote against it) on some or all issues. This was true, for example, of the French Communist Party after it left the Socialist government in 1983: positioned to the left of Socialists, the PCF's only alternatives were either to vote for Socialist proposals or to abstain, giving Socialists a majority in either case. Finally, it is possible that a majority legislative coalition may oppose the portfolio government (such as in Chile under Salvador Allende, to invoke a dramatic example).

It is worth noting that the distinction between government and legislative coalitions – standard in studies of parliamentary regimes – has not always been recognized when the focus of analysis is presidential systems. This distinction

---

[3] The case where $x^C < x^B < x^A$ is identical. Austen-Smith and Banks (1988) analyze other cases and show that the results do not change. See also Laver and Schofield (1998) for a discussion of the situations in which the party that forms the government occupies the median position in the policy space.

[4] Mainwaring (1993) and Amorim Neto (2002) claim that participation in a portfolio government under presidentialism, as distinct from parliamentarism, does not bind legislators to support the president. Presumably, under parliamentarism parties can use the vote of no confidence to discipline their own members, a device not available under presidentialism. Yet even if party discipline were lower under presidentialism – an issue I discuss in Chapter 5 – the effect on presidential coalitions would be indeterminate: it would depend on which parties (government or opposition) are less disciplined.

was crucial for Strøm's (1990) pathbreaking analysis of minority governments in parliamentary democracies, where he showed that such governments emerged as a result of parties' calculations about the costs and benefits of participating in government and that, although a minority in terms of the number of parties holding portfolios, they were able effectively to build legislative majorities. Indeed, the fact that minority governments survive under parliamentarism constitutes prima facie evidence that no majority wants to replace them: if it wanted to, it could and it would.[5] Under presidentialism, however, the implicit assumption has been that a minority government coalition is necessarily a minority legislative coalition – hence the expectation of catastrophic consequences when minority governments emerge.

Institutions

There are important differences between parliamentary and presidential regimes when it comes to institutions relevant for coalition formation. One difference is obvious, indeed, definitional: under parliamentarism, every government must enjoy the support of a parliamentary majority because the legislature can dismiss the government if it so wishes; under presidentialism, it cannot. A prime minister can change at any time, with or without elections. This is not just an abstract possibility: in a previous study, I found that 163 out of 291 prime ministers in OECD parliamentary democracies left office without elections between 1946 and 1995 (Cheibub 1998). In contrast, a president remains the head of government even when he or she is opposed by a majority in congress. Hence, as Linz (1994) emphasized, parliamentary systems enjoy a flexibility not available to presidential ones.

Yet one should not jump from chief executives to governments. Presidents serve fixed terms independently of their legislative support, but they are free to form and to change government coalitions. President Sarney of Brazil, for example, ruled with the support of two different coalitions. His successor, Fernando Collor, formed three coalitions; when he was impeached his vice-president, Itamar Franco, completed the term with the support of three distinct coalitions. The next president, Fernando Henrique Cardoso, assembled four different coalitions during his eight years in office.[6] Even if they do not include the chief executive, government reshuffles are not infrequent under presidentialism. Examples can be found in Benin, Burundi, Chile, Colombia, Ecuador,

---

[5] See Laver and Shepsle (1996).
[6] Based on the author's data set.

Guatemala, Panama, and Venezuela. Indeed, Stepan and Skach (1993) report that ministers change more frequently under presidentialism than under parliamentarism. The rigidity of presidential systems need not extend to the composition of governments.

A second difference between parliamentary and presidential systems arises because the party charged with forming a government – the *formateur* – is not fixed in parliamentary regimes but is always the party of the president under presidentialism. In parliamentary systems the rules for identifying the *formateur* are often the result of convention – the party that obtains a plurality of seats in the election is normally the first called to form a government – although more recently such a rule has been written into the constitutions.[7] In models of coalition formation in parliamentary systems, these rules specify a bargaining protocol, that is, the order in which parties attempt to form coalitions. In our analysis here, a fixed protocol is assumed such that, given $A > B > C$, first A is identified as the *formateur* followed by B and then C if A fails.[8] Under presidentialism, the *formateur* is always the president (or the party of the president). Thus, whereas under parliamentarism every coalition is, in principle, possible and any party can be excluded from a coalition, under presidentialism every government coalition must include the party of the president. As a consequence, the possible set of coalitions is smaller under presidentialism than under parliamentarism. Given our three parties A, B, C (and assuming that party A is the party of the president in a presidential system), there are four possible coalitions under parliamentarism and three under presidentialism.[9]

The two systems differ also in terms of what happens when no coalition is formed. Except in Norway, parliamentary systems facing a government crisis can revert to early elections. They may also tolerate nonpartisan governments of "caretakers" or "experts" (Austen-Smith and Banks 1988; Kalandrakis 1999).

---

[7] For instance, article 96 of the 1998 Albanian constitution states that "the President of the Republic, at the beginning of a legislature, as well as when the position of Prime Minister remains vacant, appoints the Prime Minister on the proposal of the party or coalition of parties that has the majority of seats in the Assembly." Likewise, article 99 of the 1993 Bulgarian constitution states that, "following consultations with the parliamentary groups, the President entrusts the candidate for the Prime Minister nominated by the largest parliamentary group with the formation of the Government."

[8] A bargaining protocol is *fixed* if it is determined by some rule, such as the one specified in the text; it is *random* if this rule specifies only the probabilities of this sequence. Whether the protocol is fixed or random makes a difference for the kind of coalitions that will be formed but not for whether they actually will be formed (see Kalandrakis 1999).

[9] Under parliamentarism, the following governments are possible: *AB, AC, BC,* and *ABC.* Under presidentialism, only *AB, AC,* and *ABC* are possible.

Under presidentialism, an instantaneous election is virtually impossible and, when it happens, is for the legislature and not for the presidency. In this system, when no government coalition is formed, the party of the president holds all portfolios and remains in office until the next election. The resulting policy, in turn, will depend on the legislative powers of the executive. If the president has little power and the legislature can legislate unencumbered (e.g., the congress can initiate and the president cannot veto legislation, or the veto can be overridden), then the policy adopted when no coalition has been formed is the one preferred by a majority of the legislature. If the president has the monopoly of legislative initiative or can veto without being overridden, then the reversion outcome is some kind of status quo. Note that, contrary to a view widely accepted by those who operate from within the Linzian framework, it is not necessarily true that failures to pass legislation in presidential systems entail the invocation of extra-constitutional mechanisms; most presidential constitutions, as we will see in Chapter 4, specify what should happen in this eventuality.

Coalition Formation in Parliamentary and Presidential Democracies

Parliamentarism

In parliamentary systems, every portfolio government – minority or coalition – enjoys the support of a legislative majority. If it does not, then an election occurs. Outcomes in this system depend on the parties' continuation or reservation value (their expectation regarding their performance in the next election) and on the policy distance between the *formateur* and the party next to it in the policy space.

The first statement in the previous paragraph has been proven by Austen-Smith and Banks (1988, Prop. 1) under the assumption that the reversion outcome is a particularly defined caretaker government. Defining the reversion outcome as an early election makes no difference, and the proof that this is so can be found in Appendix 3.1.

The intuition is as follows. Consider a legislature composed of three parties, $j \in \{A, B, C\}$, where these letters also denote the cardinality of the legislative seats controlled by each party. Remember that, in this setup, no party holds a majority and there is a fixed bargaining protocol such that: if $A > B > C$, then A is the *formateur* first; if A fails to form a coalition, then B is the *formateur*; if B fails to form a coalition, then C tries; and if C fails, then some reversion outcome ensues.

Party A considers whether to make an offer that would induce one of the parties to enter into a portfolio coalition. Party A, which moves first, anticipates the entire process: A knows that no reversion outcome will occur at the last stage if B and C can form a coalition that will make both at least as well off as under the reversion outcome; A also knows that if it fails to form a coalition with C then it will (at the second stage) want to accept an offer by B, which will not accept A's offer at the first stage. Hence, if A and B are distant in policy space, so that a {CB} coalition[10] would be costly to A in policy terms, then A offers portfolios to C in exchange for bringing the policy closer to A's ideal point. If B is close to A in policy space (or if A is the center party), then A forms a minority portfolio government and enjoys a legislative majority by setting the policy at B's (or its own) ideal point. Now suppose A knows that a {CB} coalition will not be formed and that A would accept the offer of B if A fails to coalesce with C. If A and C prefer a policy at the midpoint between them to the reversion outcome, then A forms a minority portfolio government, moves the policy toward C, and enjoys a legislative majority. Finally, suppose that the values of the reversion outcome are such that neither the {CB} nor the {BA} coalition will be formed. Then, if an {AC} coalition can be formed, it will be both a portfolio and a legislative coalition. Otherwise, the reversion outcome will occur.

In a way this conclusion is obvious, for with whom can a party coalesce if no one else wants to enter a coalition? So the question is simply how to view the reversion outcomes. The reversion outcome in the Austen-Smith and Banks (1988:407) model is artificial and poorly motivated. All they say is: "In the event that no government is able to form, a 'caretaker' government forms that is assumed to make the choice of legislative outcomes 'equitably'," where "equitably" is interpreted to mean that the portfolios and the policy are allocated in such a way that each party's utility is zero. Yet it is the value these authors attach to the reversion outcome that drives their conclusion that either portfolio or legislative coalitions are always formed. More reasonably, Kalandrakis (2000) takes as the reversion outcome a "technical" government, in which none of the parties hold portfolios ($g^j = 0$ for all $j \in \mathcal{J}$) and the policy is midway between extreme positions. But this assumption also makes some coalition inevitable, since now the reversion outcome takes all the portfolios away from the general pie to be distributed.

As Diermeier and Merlo (2000) show, however, coalitions are not inevitable if the reversion outcome is a new election. Think of the reversion outcome as an almost instantaneous early election, in which case the value of the reversion outcome depends on the expectations of parties with regard to the outcome of this election. If at least two parties believe that they will do well in the election,

---

[10] The *formateur* of each coalition is always listed first.

then no coalition will be formed. In Spain, for example, the Izquierda Unida (IU) and the Socialist Party (PSOE) may think they will gain against the Popular Party (PP), or the IU and the PP may think they will gain against the PSOE. Hence, if the reversion outcome is an unscheduled election, then it may occur when at least two parties expect that they will improve their situation as the result of this election.

In conclusion, then: under parliamentarism, portfolio minority governments survive only if they enjoy a legislative majority. For suppose a government does not enjoy a legislative majority; then there exists a combination of portfolios and policy that is better for some majority. But a defining feature of parliamentarism is that a majority can vote the incumbent government out of office at any time. The government may be a portfolio minority, and the opposition may defeat the government on particular issues. Even so, if there is a government then no majority wants to replace it. Hence the two possible outcomes under parliamentarism are either that the portfolio government (whatever its composition and size) enjoys legislative majority or that new elections are held almost instantaneously.

Presidentialism

There are competing models of coalition formation under parliamentarism – Austen-Smith and Banks (1988) initiated one line of analysis and Laver and Shepsle (1996) proposed an alternative view – but studies of coalitions under presidentialism remain largely descriptive. It is therefore necessary to analyze the logic of coalition formation under presidentialism.

To fix ideas, consider a legislature composed of three parties: P (for "presidential") B, and C. As before, the policy line is normalized with $x^P = 0 < x^B < x^C = 1$, and $V_{t+\delta}^B$ (party B's continuation value) is not much larger than $V_{t+\delta}^C$ (that value for party C), so B is cheaper for the president to buy than C. The ideal position of party B and the status quo policy can be anywhere between x^P and x^C.

Consider now the process of coalition formation. Under parliamentarism, coalitions result from formal negotiations among parties. These negotiations entail a distribution of portfolios and often commit parties to an explicit program, "a platform of the government," like the Programme du Gouvernement Commun of the Socialist Party, the Communist Party, and the Left Radicals in France.[11]

---

[11] Strøm and Müller (1999) studied coalition agreements in thirteen European countries between the end of World War II and 1996. Of the 223 coalition governments in their sample, 136 were based on an identifiable coalition agreement. The authors also found that this proportion increased with time.

Under presidentialism, this process is more unilateral: the president may appoint cabinet members from any party, although (as will be discussed in Chapter 4) it is generally fair to say that participation in the government formally commits parties to cooperate with the president on important issues.

Since what matters here is only whether coalitions are formed, rather than which particular ones, we need not enter into the details of the process by which governments are formed. In parliamentary and presidential systems both, some party – typically the largest one under parliamentarism and always the president's party under presidentialism – considers whether or not to invite another party (or parties) into a government coalition. This *formateur* party offers portfolios and policy, so that the offers are $\{g^J, x\}$. The recipient party then decides whether or not to accept. Under parliamentarism, if the current *formateur* fails to form a coalition then another party gets a chance; under presidentialism, the process ends if no party accepts the president's offer.

As shown in Appendix 3.2, the outcomes under presidentialism depend on the allocation of legislative powers – that is, they depend on whether or not the government monopolizes legislative initiative. There are four possibilities, which we describe next.

(1) The legislature can initiate legislation, the president has no veto power (or not enough votes to exercise the veto), and x^B is far from x^P. In this case a $\{PB\}$ majority portfolio coalition is formed with policy at x^{PB} (panel A in Figure 3.1). The intuition is as follows. If the legislature can legislate then the opposition can set policy at some point $x^B \leq x^{BC} \leq x^C$, which is far away from the president's ideal point. Even if party C is willing to set policy at x^B, the president does not like this outcome. Hence, to achieve preferred policies, the president offers portfolios to party B in such a way that it weakly prefers policy x^{PB} with portfolios to policy x^B without them.

(2) The legislature can legislate and x^B is close to x^P; then a minority government is formed and the policy is x^B. When x^B is close to x^P, the president does not mind policy x^B and offers this policy (panel B in Figure 3.1). In turn, party C cannot induce B into a legislative coalition at any point other than x^B, so the policy is x^B while the government is a presidential minority. As under parliamentarism, this minority government is in no sense a "failure": although the government is a portfolio minority, it enjoys a legislative majority and the equilibrium policy is to its liking.

Thus, given presidential systems characterized by de facto or de jure strong legislatures, the outcomes of the coalition formation process will be identical to the ones in parliamentary systems: majority portfolio coalitions will be formed when the policy distance between the *formateur* and the party closest to it in

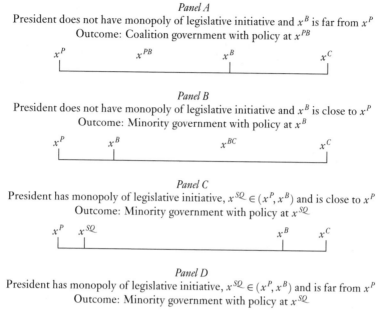

Panel A
President does not have monopoly of legislative initiative and x^B is far from x^P
Outcome: Coalition government with policy at x^{PB}

$x^P \qquad\qquad x^{PB} \qquad\qquad\qquad x^B \qquad\qquad\qquad\qquad x^C$

Panel B
President does not have monopoly of legislative initiative and x^B is close to x^P
Outcome: Minority government with policy at x^B

$x^P \qquad\qquad x^B \qquad\qquad\qquad x^{BC} \qquad\qquad\qquad\qquad x^C$

Panel C
President has monopoly of legislative initiative, $x^{SQ} \in (x^P, x^B)$ and is close to x^P
Outcome: Minority government with policy at x^{SQ}

$x^P \quad x^{SQ} \qquad\qquad\qquad\qquad\qquad\qquad x^B \qquad x^C$

Panel D
President has monopoly of legislative initiative, $x^{SQ} \in (x^P, x^B)$ and is far from x^P
Outcome: Minority government with policy at x^{SQ}

$x^P \qquad\qquad\qquad\qquad\qquad x^{SQ} \qquad x^B \qquad x^C$

Figure 3.1 Government Formation in Presidential Systems by the Legislature's Relative Power.

policy space is large, and minority portfolio coalitions will be formed when this distance is small. In either case, the government will be supported by a majority legislative coalition.

(3) The president has a monopoly on legislative initiative with regard to major policies (e.g., the budget, internal security, foreign affairs) or can sustain a veto, so that the reversion outcome is the status quo x^{SQ} with $x^{SQ} \notin (x^P, x^B)$; then the outcomes are the same as when the legislature can legislate (just replace x^{BC} by x^{SQ} in (1)). If x^B is distant from x^P, which implies that x^{SQ} is even farther away, then the president wants to avoid the status quo policy. The president must compensate B for preventing an x^{SQ} policy outcome and for party B's continuation value. Hence, the president sets policy at x^{PB} and offers sufficient portfolios for B to join the portfolio coalition. On the other hand, if x^B is close to x^P then a presidential minority government again enjoys the support of a legislative majority. Indeed, if the status quo policy is sufficiently distant from the ideal policy of B, then the president's party gains legislative support for its ideal point x^P.

(4) The president has a monopoly on legislative initiative with regard to major policies or can sustain a veto, so that the reversion outcome is the status quo x^{SQ}, where now $x^{SQ} \in (x^P, x^B)$; then a minority government is formed and the policy is x^{SQ} (panel C of Figure 3.1). In this case the president is defeated in the legislature and no legislation is passed, resulting in "legislative paralysis." However, the political consequences differ depending on the location of the status quo. If x^{SQ} is close to the president (in the limit it may be the president's ideal point) then the president's party governs as a minority and is defeated in the legislature, but it enjoys the policy outcome. And when party B also likes the status quo (say, the previous year's budget), it votes against the president's proposals if it expects to gain electorally by showing itself to be in opposition – even as it likewise enjoys the x^{SQ} policy. Hence, ardent speeches are just a smoke screen to cover an underlying consensus. Not every outcome that looks like legislative paralysis actually is so.

Yet it is possible for the status quo to be far from the president's ideal policy and still prevail (panel D in Figure 3.1). Here the president wants to alter the status quo but cannot. Both B and C prefer the status quo to any policy closer to the president's ideal, and both parties may suffer electoral costs by cooperating with the president. Hence, either B does not accept any portfolio offer that leaves the president in office or its portfolio price for entering a coalition is too high for the president. This is a true impasse: the president would like to alter the status quo, but his proposals are defeated and the government is supposed to implement policies that it does not like. Note that this situation could not transpire under parliamentarism, where parties B and C could form a majority portfolio coalition without P and legislate to their liking.

To conclude, we should expect that some minority governments occur under presidentialism for the same reason as under parliamentarism: no majority wants to replace them because enough parties get policies they like. Nonetheless, some minority governments survive under presidentialism when a portfolio coalition would have been formed under parliamentarism. Controlling for the distribution of seats and policy preferences, we therefore conclude that government coalitions should occur in both systems but should be more frequent under parliamentarism. We should also expect parliamentary governments to be more successful legislatively than presidential ones. If we assume complete information on the part of all actors, then bills proposed by parliamentary governments should never be defeated. Under presidentialism, in contrast, government proposals may be defeated in the legislature even if all actors know they are being rejected only because a majority likes the status quo policy.

Conclusion

What do we learn from this analysis? One view is that it confirms what many analysts of presidential democracies have emphasized over the years: that under presidentialism – a system in which the president and the legislature are independently elected for fixed terms in office – a minority portfolio government may face a hostile legislative majority, resulting in a legislative paralysis that could not emerge under parliamentarism. But we can also view this analysis as demonstrating that, in presidential systems, not all minority governments face a hostile legislative majority. Some minority presidential governments occur under presidentialism for the same reason that they occur under parliamentarism: no majority wants to replace them because enough parties get policies they like. Moreover, the analysis in this chapter shows that there will be conditions under which coalition governments in presidential democracies will emerge because it is in the interest of presidents to make portfolio offers to nonpresidential parties and it is in the interest of these parties to accept them. Thus, it is not the case that presidential systems lack incentives for coalition formation. Only when one specific set of conditions materializes – conditions involving the relative power of the legislature and the location of the status quo with respect to the parties' policy preferences – do we observe the kind of paralysis that, according to the literature developed within the Linzian framework, could cause the death of presidentialism. Of course, it could be that these conditions characterize most presidential democracies or that, even if they do not, they lead to the breakdown of democracies whenever they transpire. But as we shall see in Chapter 4, this does not seem to be the case. For the moment, what needs to be emphasized is that the institutional framework of presidentialism does not itself preclude actors' self-interest in coalition making – either by acquiring portfolios or by supporting the president in the legislature.

There are three empirical predictions that follow from the analysis presented here and that will guide our investigation in Chapter 4.

1. Controlling for the distribution of seats and of policy preferences, government coalitions should occur in both parliamentary and presidential systems. Coalitions should be more frequent in the former because there is one configuration – unique to presidentialism – of legislative powers that generates minority governments.
2. Parliamentary governments should be more successful legislatively than presidential ones, although minority governments in both systems should

not necessarily be less successful than coalition governments. There are minority governments in both systems that are supported by a legislative majority and, in this respect, will be at least as successful legislatively as governments based on a portfolio coalition. It follows from this that minority governments in presidential systems should not lead inevitably to the breakdown of democracy.

3. Coalition governments should be less frequent in presidential systems that are characterized by a relatively weak legislature (i.e., where the president has either a monopoly on important legislative initiatives or veto power and enough votes to sustain a veto). But given that what looks like paralysis may actually be a preference for the status quo, and given that presidential institutions often specify what should happen in case of failure to pass legislation, these situations will not necessarily result in the breakdown of democracy.

Appendix 3.1: Government Legislative Support in Parliamentary Democracies

In this appendix I show that a reversion outcome, interpreted as an election, occurs under parliamentarism and that it occurs whenever a legislative majority coalition cannot be formed. Hence, no portfolio minority government survives under parliamentarism unless it enjoys a *legislative* majority. Therefore, under parliamentarism, all governments are supported by a legislative majority.

There are three parties, $A > B > C$, and no party holds a majority. Each party associates the value U_O^j to the reversion outcome, where $\sum_j U_O^j \leq G$. For convenience, the analysis here covers only the case where $x^C > x^B > x^A$ (the case where $x^C < x^B < x^A$ is identical; other cases are analyzed in Austen-Smith and Banks 1988).

Suppose that previous attempts at coalition formation have failed and that C is the current *formateur*. Party C, like the other parties, wants to maximize its utility at the lowest cost in terms of portfolios and policy; toward this end, C makes an offer such that party B is indifferent between entering into a coalition with C and B's reservation utility. This offer, $\Omega_{CB} = \{x^{CB}, g_{CB}^C, g_{CB}^B\}$, is a solution to

$$\max_{x, g} g^C - (x - x^C)^2,$$

subject to

$$G - g^C - (x - x^B)^2 \geq U_O^B \quad \text{and} \quad g^C \geq 0.$$

The solution is

$$x^B \leq x^{CB} \leq \frac{x^C + x^B}{2},$$

where the second inequality holds if

$$G - \left(\frac{x^C - x^B}{2} \right)^2 - U_0^B \geq 0,$$

$$g_{CB}^C = G - (x^{CB} - x^C)^2 - U_0^B,$$

$$g_{CB}^B = G - (x^{CB} - x^B)^2 + U_0^B.$$

The associated utilities are

$$U^A = -(x^{CB} - x^A)^2,$$

$$U^B = U_0^B,$$

$$U^C = G - (x^{CB} - x^C)^2 - U_0^B - (x^{CB} - x^B)^2.$$

It is immediately apparent that C will make this offer only if it can gain more from Ω_{CB} than what it would have gained from its reservation utility – that is, only if $U_0^C + U_0^B \leq G - [(x^{CB} - x^C)^2 + (x^{CB} - x^B)^2]$. Otherwise, the reversion outcome of new elections ensues.

At the previous stage, party B made a proposal to party A. If at the next stage a coalition $\{CB\}$ will be formed, then party A will accept a proposal that makes party B first-best, $\Omega_{BA} = \{x^B, G, 0\}$, since this proposal gives A utility of $-(x^B - x^A)^2$, which is higher than $-(x^{CB} - x^A)^2$, the utility it would obtain under a $\{CB\}$ coalition. The utilities associated with Ω_{BA} are thus

$$U^A = -(x^B - x^A)^2,$$

$$U^B = G,$$

$$U^C = -(x^B - x^C)^2.$$

Since $G \geq U_0^B$, it follows that B will always make this offer.

However, if the reversion outcome will occur at the last stage, then B must offer A utility $U^A = U_0^A$, so that $\Omega_{BA} = \{x^{BA}, G - (x^{BA} - x^B)^2 - U_0^A, (x^{BA} - x^A)^2 + U_0^A\}$. The utilities associated with this offer are

$$U^A = U_0^A,$$

$$U^B = G - (x^{BA} - x^B)^2 - U_0^A - (x^{BA} - x^A)^2,$$

$$U^C = -(x^{BA} - x^C)^2.$$

Again, B makes this offer only if

$$U_0^B + U_0^A \leq G - [(x^{BA} - x^B)^2 + (x^{BA} - x^A)^2].$$

Finally, consider the first stage, at which A anticipates what will happen if it fails to form a coalition. There are several cases, as follows.

(A) The reversion outcome is inferior for both B and C to the coalition $\{CB\}$. Then party A cannot offer party B more than G and still be better-off. In turn, party A can offer party C the following proposals, which are a function of the policy distances among the parties.

(A.1) If parties A and B are distant enough in policy terms that $x^B - x^A \geq x^C - x^B$, then the optimal policy proposal from party A will be

$$x^{AC} = \frac{x^A + x^C}{2}$$

with the portfolio allocation

$$g_{AC}^A = G - [(x^{AC} - x^A)^2 - (x^B - x^C)^2],$$
$$g_{AC}^C = (x^{AC} - x^C)^2 - (x^B - x^C)^2.$$

The utilities associated with this outcome are

$$U^A = G - 2[(x^{AC} - x^A)^2] + (x^B - x^C)^2,$$
$$U^B = -(x^{AC} - x^B)^2,$$
$$U^C = -(x^{AC} - x^C)^2.$$

Hence, a portfolio and a legislative coalition will be formed – both, of course, majoritarian.

(A.2) If parties A and B are close enough in policy terms that $x^B - x^A < x^C - x^B$, then the optimal policy proposal from party A will be

$$x^{AC} = x^B$$

with the portfolio allocation

$$g^A = G,$$
$$g^C = 0.$$

The utilities associated with this outcome are

$$U^A = G - (x^B - x^A)^2,$$
$$U^B = 0,$$
$$U^C = -(x^B - x^C)^2.$$

Hence, a portfolio coalition will not be formed and the government of party A will be a portfolio minority government. But a legislative coalition will be formed, and it will be majoritarian.

(B) The reversion outcome is superior for parties B and C to the coalition $\{CB\}$ but it is inferior for parties B and A to the coalition $\{BA\}$. Now party A knows that, if party C becomes the *formateur*, the reversion outcome will occur. Party A also knows that party B knows that, if it rejects A's offer at the first stage, then at the second stage B will be able to make an offer giving A the reversion utility U_0^A, which A will accept. Suppose party B becomes the *formateur* and turns to party A. We know from the foregoing that A will accept an offer Ω_{BA}, which gives party C utility $U^C = -(x^{BA} - x^C)^2$. Hence, C will also accept an offer $\Omega_{AC} = \{x^{BA}, G, 0\}$, which is associated with an identical utility to C, and party A will always make this offer. Thus, once again, the government will be a portfolio minority government of party A that is supported by a legislative majority coalition.

(C) The reversion outcome is superior for parties B and C to the coalition $\{CB\}$ and for B and A to the coalition $\{BA\}$, so that

$$U_0^C + U_0^B \geq G - [(x^{CB} - x^C)^2 + (x^{CB} - x^B)^2]$$

and

$$U_0^B + U_0^A \geq G - [(x^{BA} - x^B)^2 + (x^{BA} - x^A)^2].$$

Now party A must guarantee C the reversion utility U_0^C. Party C will accept an offer $\Omega_{AC} = \{x^{AC}, G - (x^{AC} - x^A)^2 - U_0^C, (x^{AC} - x^C)^2 + U_0^C\}$, which would give party A the utility

$$U^A = G - (x^{AC} - x^C)^2 - U_0^C - (x^{AC} - x^A)^2.$$

Hence, an $\{AC\}$ portfolio coalition will be formed if

$$U_0^A + U_0^C \leq G - (x^{AC} - x^C)^2 - (x^{AC} - x^A)^2.$$

Otherwise, a reversion outcome will occur.

In summary, for parliamentary systems with no majority parties, there are three possible coalition outcomes. First, if some of the parties expect that they will do well by provoking an election, a reversion outcome may occur. Second, if a reversion outcome does not occur and if the second-largest party is far in policy terms from the largest one (i.e., from the party that will be first identified as the *formateur*), then the largest party will form a portfolio coalition government with the smallest party in order to avoid an undesired policy. Finally, if a reversion outcome does not occur yet the second-largest party is close in policy terms to the largest one, then the largest party will hold all the portfolios but a minority government will enjoy the support of a legislative majority. Thus, although parliamentary governments may be minority or majority portfolio governments, they will also enjoy the support of a legislative majority. If they do not, then a new election occurs.

Appendix 3.2: Coalition Formation under Presidentialism

The purpose of this appendix is to extend the model of Austen-Smith and Banks (1988) to presidential systems.

Consider a three-party legislature $j \in \{P, B, C\}$, where P stands for the president's party. No party holds a majority, but no other assumption is made about their legislative size. As a notational convention, party B is closer than C to P in policy terms.

What B and C can agree on depends on the agenda powers of the president. Hence, we need to distinguish two situations as follows.

1. If the legislature can legislate, then nonpresidential parties can form a legislative coalition $\{CB\}$ with the policy set at some point x^{CB} such that $x^B \leq x^{CB} \leq x^C$.
2. If the legislature cannot legislate, then the president makes a proposal that is voted up or down by the legislature. In this case, all that nonpresidential parties can achieve by uniting against the president is some status quo, x^{SQ}, which is different across presidential systems and policy areas.

Since the algebra is the same, let the policy outcome when the president fails to form a portfolio coalition be $x^* \in \{x^{CB}, x^{SQ}\}$. Suppose no government coalition is formed. Then, at the second stage, the portfolio allocation is

$$g^C = 0,$$
$$g^B = 0,$$
$$g^P = G,$$

and the policy outcome is x^*.

Assume that nonpresidential parties that vote against the president will receive, after the next election, a utility with present value $\rho V^k > 0$ and that otherwise each such party receives $\rho V^k = 0$ ($k \in B, C$). Then the utilities of parties at this stage are

$$U^P = G - (x^* - x^P)^2,$$
$$U^B = -(x^* - x^B)^2 + \rho V^B,$$
$$U^C = -(x^* - x^C)^2 + \rho V^C.$$

Consider now the problem of the president at the first stage. The president considers whether to make an offer that would induce one of the parties to enter into a portfolio coalition. For simplicity, assume that offers made to party C will be more costly to the president, so that the president's problem is to maximize $g^P - (x - x^P)^2$ subject to

$$G - g^P - (x - x^B)^2 \geq \rho V^B - (x - x^B)^2, \quad 0 < g^P \leq G$$

(G large).

If $\rho V^B - (x - x^B)^2 \leq (x^P - x^B)^2$ then the first constraint does not bind, since B will support x^P even when $g^B = 0$. Hence, the president forms a minority government, $g^P = G$, with $x = x^P$. Otherwise, the solution is[12]

$$x^{PB} = \frac{x^P + x^B}{2},$$
$$g^P = G - (x^{PB} - x^B)^2 - \rho V^B + (x^* - x^B)^2,$$
$$g^B = (x^{PB} - x^B)^2 - \rho V^B + (x^* - x^B)^2,$$

with utilities

$$U^P = G - 2(x^{PB} - x^B)^2 - \rho V^B - (x^* - x^B)^2,$$
$$U^B = \rho V^B - (x^* - x^B)^2.$$

However, we must check whether the president will want to make this offer – that is, whether

$$G - 2(x^{PB} - x^P)^2 - \rho V^B + (x^* - x^B)^2 \geq G - (x^B - x^P)^2,$$

which implies that the president will want to form a portfolio coalition if

$$[(x^P - x^*) + (x^B - x^P)]^2 > 2\rho V^B.$$

Otherwise, the government will be a minority and the policy will be set by the legislative coalition of the opposition at x^*.

---

[12] The assumption that G is large guarantees that $g^B < G$.

4

Are Coalitions Rare in Presidential Democracies?

Recall from Chapter 1 that, in the Linzian framework, presidents do not have an incentive to form coalitions while parties have an incentive to decline any coalition offers that are made. Thus the failure to form coalition governments is chronic in presidential systems and implies legislatively ineffective governments, deadlocks, and the eventual breakdown of the democratic regime. Our analysis in the previous chapter, however, suggested a different picture whereby: coalition governments are not uncommon in presidential democracies; there are conditions in presidential systems that will lead to the emergence of either a coalition government or a minority government supported by a legislative majority; and these conditions are identical for presidential and parliamentary systems, which means that minority governments in presidential systems – just as in parliamentary systems – do not necessarily spell disaster.

What do the data say? In this chapter I examine the patterns of coalition formation in both presidential and parliamentary democracies. I start by discussing the criteria used to observe coalition governments in democratic regimes. I then examine the actual pattern of coalition formation in democratic regimes and show that, although more frequent in parliamentary systems, coalition governments are not uncommon in presidential ones. I proceed to study the impact of the government status on the government's legislative effectiveness as well as on the probability of democratic breakdown. From this analysis it becomes clear that the status of the government – whether minority or majority, single-party or coalition – has no impact on its ability to govern. The reason was presented in Chapter 3: some minority presidential governments are supported by legislative majorities and, for this reason, should not be any less effective in approving legislation than majority/coalition governments. I also show that the failure to form a coalition or achieve majority status in presidential democracies, just as in parliamentary ones, does not increase the likelihood that democracy will break down. Thus, the chain of events that the Linzian view predicts when minority presidential governments emerge (i.e., legislative ineffectiveness, deadlock, and appeals to extra-constitutional means of resolving the conflict) is not observed among the presidential democracies that have existed between 1946 and 2002. Finally, I isolate the institutional configuration under which, according to the analysis in Chapter 3, presidential governments should be less successful in legislative terms. If most presidential democracies are characterized by this institutional configuration, and if this configuration is indeed associated with less successful governments, then it could be that this is what makes presidential democracies collapse with more frequency than parliamentary ones. Yet, as we shall see, this is not the case.

Overall, then, the analysis in this chapter shows that – contrary to the Linzian framework and consistent with the framework developed in Chapter 3 – coalition governments are rather frequent in presidential democracies, minority governments are not disastrous for the government's capacity to rule or for the survival of democracy, and presidential democracies characterized by institutionally strong presidents are not more likely to become a dictatorship. Whatever makes presidential democracies vulnerable has nothing to do with the alleged structure of incentives that follow from the separation of executive and legislative powers that defines these regimes.

Observing Coalition Governments

Unit of Analysis

The first task in the study of coalition formation in presidential and parliamentary democracies is to identify the presence of a coalition as opposed to a single-party government. Even though this is fairly unproblematic – coalition governments are those consisting of two or more parties – such a simple definition raises at least two important issues of measurement that must be addressed before we can proceed. The first concerns government composition: How can one determine whether a party is a member of the government? The second concerns the level at which observations are made: What is the temporal framework used for determining the frequency of coalition governments? Let us start with the latter issue.

The need and opportunity for coalition formation depend on the partisan distribution of seats in the legislative assembly. The question is whether, given a distribution of legislative seats, a portfolio coalition is formed. The most natural way to approach this issue would be to collect information for as many countries during as many years as possible, organize it into a database where the country-year is the unit of analysis, and then compute the frequency of coalition governments in each type of democratic regime. Although this chapter implements such an approach, we need to recognize a potential bias that these procedures may introduce in the counting of coalition governments.

Is a country-year the appropriate unit for estimating the frequency of coalition governments across democratic regimes? Since the issue that matters is whether a coalition government was formed given a set of opportunities (represented by the distribution of legislative seats), one could argue that the correct unit of analysis should be these opportunities, regardless of how long they last. For example, if elections take place so that legislative seats are distributed across political parties, and if this distribution remains unaltered for the length of the legislative term, then we have observed one opportunity – call it a *situation* – for the formation of coalitions. In the course of this situation we may observe one of three possible outcomes: a coalition government that lasts the whole term, a single-party government that lasts the whole term, or alternation between coalition and single-party governments.

Were it not for this third possibility, counting on the basis of situations versus country-year observations would yield virtually identical results. Consider the hypothetical country represented in panel A of Table 4.1, which was observed for 35 years between 1970 and 2004, with 19 (i.e., 54%) of these years spent under coalition governments. This same country experienced nine legislative elections during the same period and so produced nine different distributions of legislative seats – that is, nine different situations of which five (or 55%) led to the formation of coalition governments. In this case, the frequency of coalition government is the same whether our observations are made in terms of country-years or in terms of situations.

However, if the coalition status of the government had changed in the middle of a situation, then the rate of coalition formation would differ significantly depending on the level at which observations are made. This is indicated in panel B of Table 4.1. In this case, the number of years spent under a coalition government is the same as before: 19 out of 35 years, or 54% of the time. But here the status of the government changed in the middle of the legislative term twice: first, a coalition government that was formed after new elections became a single-party government (situation 3); second, a single-party government became a coalition government (situation 6). Now six of the nine observed situations (67%) were spent under a coalition government for at least some of the time, a figure that is quite different from the 54% obtained when counting country-years spent under a coalition government.

Are Coalitions Rare in Presidential Democracies?

Table 4.1. *Counting Coalition Governments in a Hypothetical Country: Country-Years and Situations*

Year	Situation #	Government status	
		Panel A	Panel B
1970*	1	Coalition	Coalition
1971	1	Coalition	Coalition
1972	1	Coalition	Coalition
1973	1	Coalition	Coalition
1974*	2	Single-party	Single-party
1975	2	Single-party	Single-party
1976	2	Single-party	Single-party
1977	2	Single-party	Single-party
1978*	3	Single-party	Coalition
1979	3	Single-party	Coalition
1980	3	Single-party	Single-party
1981	3	Single-party	Single-party
1982*	4	Coalition	Coalition
1983	4	Coalition	Coalition
1984	4	Coalition	Coalition
1985	4	Coalition	Coalition
1986*	5	Coalition	Coalition
1987	5	Coalition	Coalition
1988	5	Coalition	Coalition
1989	5	Coalition	Coalition
1990*	6	Coalition	Single-party
1991	6	Coalition	Single-party
1992	6	Coalition	Coalition
1993	6	Coalition	Coalition
1994*	7	Single-party	Single-party
1995	7	Single-party	Single-party
1996	7	Single-party	Single-party
1997	7	Single-party	Single-party
1998*	8	Single-party	Single-party
1999	8	Single-party	Single-party
2000	8	Single-party	Single-party
2001	8	Single-party	Single-party
2002*	9	Coalition	Coalition
2003	9	Coalition	Coalition
2004	9	Coalition	Coalition

* New elections.

Thus, observations made at the country-year level may underestimate the frequency of coalition governments: they may fail to capture all the instances in which coalitions were formed for at least some of the time during which the distribution of legislative seats remained constant. This bias may be severe if the number of situations during which we observe changes in the coalition status of the government is large; it will be even worse if the changes in the coalition status of the government during a situation are significantly different across democratic systems.

Fortunately, neither possibility is evident in the data for democratic systems that existed between 1946 and 2002: about 7% and 13%, respectively, of the situations under presidential and parliamentary (combined with mixed) regimes led to the formation of more than one type of government. In the remainder of the cases, the coalition status of the government remained the same throughout the situation. For this reason, the difference between the two ways of counting is small; given that observations at the country-year level are easier to manipulate and to merge with external information (which is necessary for the multivariate analysis performed later in the chapter), this is what I use here and throughout the book. Appendix 4.1, however, counts coalition governments on the basis of situations and then compares the probability of coalition and majority governments computed on the basis of situations and country-years. The reader can thus see that the two methods, given the way things actually are in the world, do indeed yield results that are virtually indistinguishable.

Operational Criteria

Having established the unit of observation, the next task is to define a coalition government and to develop criteria for observing it. Since the central interest is on the legislative support of the government (i.e., coalition or single-party), we also need to define and empirically identify the government legislative support.

A coalition government exists when portfolio positions are held by at least two political parties. When only one party holds all portfolio positions, we observe a single-party government. The following five operational rules were adopted in the process of identifying governments as single-party or coalition types.

1. Only top ministerial positions were considered. Although sometimes relevant for the process of coalition formation (Mershon 1996), lower-level positions such as "deputy minister" or "undersecretary" do not matter for deciding the status of a government. The reason is mostly practical: whether these positions exist is rarely reported, let alone the partisan affiliation of those who hold them. Substantively, however, there is no significant loss in ignoring lower-level

positions because it is reasonable to assume that what parties really care about is control over an entire area of the government, which is achieved by occupying the top ministerial position.

2. Legislative support expressed by the vote of its members is not sufficient for a party to be considered a member of the government. To use the distinction made in Chapter 3, membership in a *legislative* coalition does not imply membership in the *government* or *portfolio* coalition. Thus, even when members of some party vote in favor of every project of interest to the government, if no one from that party has a ministerial position then that party is not a member of the government. This criterion is standard in cross-national studies of coalition governments under both parliamentary and presidential systems.[1]

3. Only parties with legislative representation count as members of a government coalition. There are cases in which governments include members of political parties that do not have legislative representation, either because they failed to obtain it in the most recent election or because they have not yet participated in an electoral contest. Since (as discussed in Chapter 2) coalition governments are seen as solutions to a bargaining situation in which the parties' strengths are determined by the share of legislative seats under their control, parties that control no seats may not be considered full participants in this bargain. Such parties may be relevant for the government in a number of ways (see Zelaznik 2001), but not in providing the necessary support to approve legislative bills.

4. Unless additional information exists, participation in the government of individuals from a party other than the *formateur*'s indicates that other party's membership in the government. We know, for example, that participation of the occasional Republican in Clinton's administration did not commit the Republican Party as a whole to cooperating with the executive on important issues. And when Francisco Weffort accepted an invitation to join the Cardoso administration in

---

[1] For parliamentary regimes, see Strøm (1990), Woldendorp, Keman, and Budge (1993), Warwick (1994), Lane, McKay, and Newton (1997), and Laver and Schofield (1998). For presidential systems see Deheza (1997), Amorim Neto (1998), and Zelaznik (2001). The exception to this way of determining membership in the government is the Database of Political Institutions assembled by a World Bank team, which adopts an asymmetrical criterion for parliamentary and presidential systems. For parliamentary systems, parties in government are those holding portfolio positions. For presidential systems, parties are (in addition) considered as being in the government when they "1) ... are listed in our sources as in the government; 2) are supportive of the president on substantial issues; or 3) take seats in the legislature but do *not* run a candidate for the presidency" (Keefer 2002:11). Not only is this an inadequate criterion for government membership, but the asymmetry in the coding for parliamentary and presidential systems renders the data set unusable for cross-system analysis.

Brazil, he had to resign from the Worker's Party (PT) after it formally and publicly expressed its disapproval of the party's participation in the government. Although Weffort's presence may have extended the government's political base, it did not imply PT's cooperation with Cardoso. Thus, individuals may join a government without committing the support of the party to which they belong.

Virtually all students of coalition governments, and especially those who focus on presidential regimes, recognize this fact and try to distinguish the two types of participation in government. The difficulty comes in establishing empirically whether participation is individual or partisan. The rule adopted here is first to assume that participation in government implies participation of the individual's party and then, recognizing that this is not always the case, to use whatever additional information is available and decide on a case-by-case basis. The alternative – to require that there be positive evidence of partisan support of the government before deciding that holding of a cabinet position commits the individual's party – could lead to serious underestimation of the occurrence of coalition governments, particularly in presidential democracies.[2]

5. Contrary to the practice in several existing studies of government coalitions in presidential systems, I do not assume that *electoral* coalitions automatically translate into *portfolio* coalitions. Mainwaring and Shugart (1997:402), recognizing the difficulty of identifying the partisan composition of presidential cabinets, decide to equate coalitions for presidential elections with government coalitions. However, even if we accept that all electoral coalitions become governing coalitions in presidential regimes, this procedure would not capture the cases in which coalitions are formed after the election. It would also fail to capture the cases in which coalitions, and perhaps the status of the government, change during the presidential term. Zelaznik (2001) uses the existence of pre-electoral coalitions as one of several criteria for identifying government coalitions. For him, "partnership at the electoral level is taken as proof that the allied parties are willing to enter a governing coalition even if it is unclear whether an agreement took place after the electoral victory" (p. 132). This, however, is also inadequate. The willingness to enter into an electoral coalition is, of course, not the same as the actual formation of a government coalition. As discussed in Chapter 3,

---

[2] The view that presidential governments are not partisan is widespread. Even Keesing's Contemporary Archives – the most complete and consistent source on government information for a large number of countries, and the main source I used to identify a government's partisan composition – suffers from a reporting bias against presidential democracies. Reports on new governments in parliamentary democracies always include the partisan affiliation of cabinet members; however, reports for presidential democracies are inconsistent, with the partisan information of cabinet members being provided for some countries but not others.

in a presidential system only the president can offer portfolio positions; and the president may very well choose not to make any offers to some of the parties that supported her during the campaign.[3] Assuming that presidential and legislative elections were concurrent, the president may discover after the election that her party can itself provide the legislative support needed to approve legislation. The president may also decide that the cost of ignoring a pre-electoral ally is smaller than the cost of allowing that party to control a portfolio; conversely, the president may decide that higher benefits will accrue to including in the government a party that did not support her during the elections than to excluding that party. Hence there is no reason for us to assume that coalitions that are formed to support a candidate in presidential elections always will become a government coalition; that is, information about pre-electoral coalitions has no bearing on government coalitions.

In addition to the coalition status of the government, we shall also need a measure of the government's legislative support. Here I follow standard practice and consider a government's legislative support to be the sum of the share of legislative (lower-house) seats held by all parties in the government. The main issue that arises with respect to this measure is the error that is necessarily introduced by our not knowing the partisan distribution of legislative seats for all countries at all times. Here again I follow standard practice by taking the distribution of seats immediately following an election as indicating the distribution of seats during the legislative term; yet I deviate from standard practice by allowing the distribution of seats in the legislature to change with known mergers and splits of political parties that occur during the legislative term.

Thus, to cite one example, the legislative strength of the South Korean government changed dramatically in 1990 when the opposition Reunification Democratic Party (RDP) and the New Democratic Republican Party (NDRP) merged with the ruling Democratic Justice Party (DJP) (Kim 1997). Even though no election took place, the government – while retaining its status as a single-party government – went from a minority to a majority legislative position. Although South Korea is probably the most dramatic example (there were two additional party mergers, in 1999 and 2002), changes in the distribution of seats without the occurrence of elections appear in the data for countries as diverse (in terms of

---

[3] In the presidential election of 1989, Fernando Collor was the candidate of the PRN, the PST, and the PSL. The PSL did not obtain legislative representation until the 1990 election, which occurred after the government was formed; the PST had a small legislative contingent in 1989. The government that was formed, however, did not include the PST; it was composed of the PRN (Collor's party) together with the PDS and the PFL, two right-wing parties that had presented independent candidates in the first round of elections but supported Collor in the second round.

income, democratic experience, and geographic location) as Albania, Belgium, Brazil, Ecuador, Finland, Honduras, Italy, Latvia, Luxembourg, the Netherlands, New Zealand, Norway, the Philippines, Portugal, the Slovak Republic, Spain, Sudan, Thailand, and Turkey.

Mergers and splits are not the only sources of nonelectoral changes in the partisan distribution of legislative seats. The party switching that occurs in many systems is also a source of change, albeit one that has not been incorporated into the data set for this book. The decision to ignore party switching was made on two grounds. In the first place, information on party switching exists only for a handful of countries and cannot be easily acquired. Second, the effect of any one party switch on the overall distribution of legislative seats is, in itself, small; party switching matters only when it cumulates over time or when it occurs *en masse*. Mass exoduses are rare and (when they do occur) are likely to take the form of party splits, the information about which is incorporated here. Moreover, a small number of switches is unlikely to have a significant impact on the distribution of legislative seats, but the costs of searching for them would be high. My guess is that the bias introduced by not incorporating information about party switching is small. Such bias would be serious if switches were systematically correlated with regime type – for example, if they were more frequent under presidentialism than under parliamentarism. I consider the existence of a correlation between switches and regime type to be unlikely. Although there are well-known cases of presidential democracies in which party switching is pervasive, as in Brazil, it would be a mistake to assume that this well-known case is typical under presidentialism. As a matter of fact, recent research has shown that the migration of legislators from one party to another during the legislative term also occurs with nontrivial frequency in several parliamentary democracies.[4] Thus, until we are able to rely on studies that systematically assess the frequency of party switching across democratic regimes, it seems prudent to assume that switches are not systematically distributed across regime type.[5]

---

[4] See the Party Switching Research Group, led by William B. Heller and Carol Mershon, ⟨http://faculty.virginia.edu/partyswitching/index.html⟩. See also Heller and Mershon (2005) and Turan (1985) for a study of Italy and Turkey, respectively.

[5] Note that, from the point of view of defining situations, what matters is not the absolute number of switches but the distribution of seats that results from party switching. Even in a case as extreme as Brazil (Desposato 2005), the high rate of switching does not necessarily affect the government's status. Mainwaring (1999:143) reports the occurrence of 197 instances of party switching in the Brazilian lower house based on observations made in February 1987, September 1988, January 1990, and October 1990. In spite of the high rate with which legislators changed parties, the status of the government remained unchanged through this period: it was still a government composed of two parties that together controlled a majority of seats in the lower house.

There are circumstances in which determining the partisan composition of the legislature, let alone of the government, is impossible; therefore, these cases are simply treated as missing information. Just as with party switches, missing information might be a problem if it is systematically correlated with the form of democratic government. However, this does not seem to be the case. The rate of missing data is virtually identical for parliamentary and presidential systems: about 10% of all country-years. It is higher (16%) for mixed systems but is less than 11% when mixed and parliamentary regimes are combined.

Coalition Governments in Democratic Regimes

Figures 4.1, 4.2, and 4.3 summarize the information about coalition formation in democracies. It is clear from these figures that coalitions are more frequent in mixed and parliamentary than in presidential democracies. Yet it is also clear that coalition governments are by no means rare in the latter. Contrary to the lore about presidential democracies, coalitions are a common occurrence and so indicate that, more often than not, a president builds legislative support by offering ministerial positions to parties other than his or her own. Here are the details supporting this assertion.

The rate of coalition formation is lower in presidential democracies, 40% of all country-years versus 43% for parliamentary and 70% for mixed democracies. These numbers, however, include the cases where coalitions are virtually unnecessary because there is a party that holds more than half of the legislative seats. These are majority situations, and the formation of coalition governments entails the formation of oversized coalitions. In majority situations, as one would

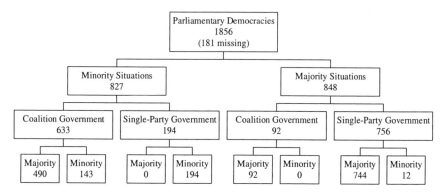

Figure 4.1 Coalition and Majority Government, Parliamentary Democracies (country-years).

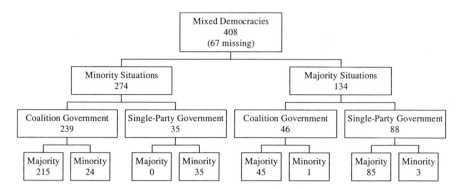

Figure 4.2 Coalition and Majority Government, Mixed Democracies (country-years).

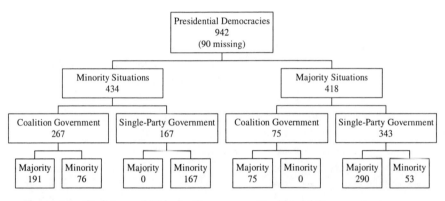

Figure 4.3 Coalition and Majority Government, Presidential Democracies (country-years).

expect, coalitions are relatively infrequent: they occur in 18% of the cases under presidentialism, 11% under parliamentarism, and 34% under mixed institutions (which underlies what emerges very clearly in these data, namely, that of all democracies and under all conditions, mixed systems have the greatest propensity toward coalition formation). In the vast majority of these cases, the party of the *formateur* – the head of the government – is also the party that controls more than half of the legislative seats;[6] so naturally, in all these cases the government

---

[6] The few instances in which this is not the case include situations when the head of the government is nonpartisan. Rarely do we observe coalition governments in majority situations in which the party with more than half the seats is not the party of the head of the government (e.g., Turkey in 1971–1973, Colombia in 1982–1985, and Senegal in 2000).

that was formed was a majority government.[7] The norm, however, is for the formation of a single-party majority government when there is a party that holds more than half of the seats. Only in presidential democracies do we observe the formation of single-party *minority* governments in majority situations; these are the cases of divided government, in which the party of the president faces a majority opposition party.

Of course, coalitions matter the most in minority situations – that is, when no party commands a majority of seats in the legislature. These situations are relatively common, occurring 67% of the time in mixed, 51% in presidential, and 49% percent in parliamentary democracies. Under these circumstances, the formation of coalition governments is the norm, even in presidential systems: given a minority situation, coalitions emerge 87% of the time in mixed, 77% of the time in parliamentary, and 62% of the time in presidential democracies. Once formed, such coalitions are also likely to reach majority status: 72% of the coalitions formed in minority situations under presidentialism reached majority status, while 77% did so under parliamentarism and 90% under mixed institutions. It is thus clear that coalition governments emerge quite frequently in presidential democracies. They are not as frequent as they are in parliamentary and especially in mixed systems. Nonetheless, they occur in over three fifths of the country-years – hardly a rare phenomenon that is observed only under exceptional circumstances.

The relatively high rate of coalition formation in presidential democracies could be masking a pattern of high coalition instability. As a matter of fact, those who believe that the form of democratic government radically affects the incentives for coalition formation assume that, if they emerge, coalitions in presidential democracies will be unstable (Mainwaring and Shugart 1997:397; Altman 2000; Amorim Neto 2002). Yet, as Table 4.2 demonstrates, this is not what we observe in the data.

The figures in this table indicate first the number of governments we observe in each regime ("coalition spells") and second the number of years during which each regime was observed. A coalition spell, in line with our previous discussion, is defined in terms of the parties that hold portfolio positions. Thus, there is a new government any time that, for whatever reason, the composition of the

---

[7] The exception occurred in Senegal, a mixed democracy, when the opposition candidate won presidential elections in 2000 and survived for a year (until legislative elections in 2001) with a legislature that had been composed in 1998. Upon assuming office, the new president appointed a prime minister out of that legislature, wherein (what was now) the opposition party (the incumbent until 2000) commanded a majority of seats.

Table 4.2. *Coalition Duration in Democratic Systems*

Type of democracy	Coalition spells	Years	Average duration
All cases			
Parliamentary	430	1718	4.00
Mixed	144	414	2.88
Presidential	182	915	5.03
Presidential[a]	181	858	4.74
Minority situations			
Parliamentary	289	839	2.90
Mixed	103	274	2.66
Presidential	100	436	4.36
Presidential[a]	99	379	3.83

[a] Excludes Switzerland.

parties holding portfolio positions changes. As we can see, the average coalition in presidential democracies lasts more than a year longer than the average coalition in parliamentary systems and more than two years longer than the average coalition in mixed systems. Even after we exclude Switzerland, where the same coalition has been governing regardless of electoral results for the past several decades, we find that presidential coalitions last on average three quarters of a year longer than coalitions in parliamentary systems.

According to the Linzian framework, the difficulties of coalition formation that are generally present in presidential systems will become even more manifest when the legislature is fragmented (Mainwaring 1993; Mainwaring and Scully 1995:33; Mainwaring and Shugart 1997; Valenzuela 1998:124). Theoretically, however, the effect of increased fractionalization on coalition formation depends on the distribution of policy preferences of the parties that compose the legislature (Cheibub, Przeworski, and Saiegh 2004, Apx. I). Recall the results presented in Chapter 3, according to which the emergence of a government coalition depends on the distance between the party of the *formateur* and the next party in the policy space. Thus, as we have seen, if the party of the *formateur* (the largest party in parliamentary and mixed systems, or the president's party in presidential systems) has policy preferences that are distant from the party closest to it in the policy space, then a coalition government will emerge. In turn, if the *formateur* party is close in policy to some other party (or parties) with which it together holds a majority, then it has no incentives to offer portfolios to other parties and so a minority, single-party government will emerge.

Table 4.3. *Proportion of Coalition and Majority Governments (country-years) by Legislative Fractionalization*

Seat share of largest party	All	Parliamentary	Mixed	Presidential
Coalition governments				
>0.50	0.1305	0.1052	0.3145	0.1462
≤0.50	0.7270	0.7523	0.8662	0.6169
>0.33/≤0.50	0.6601	0.6885	0.8544	0.4895
≤0.33	0.8953	0.9689	0.8974	0.8239
Majority governments				
>0.50	0.9629	1.0000	0.9919	0.8795
≤0.50	0.5808	0.5884	0.7817	0.4610
>0.33/≤0.50	0.5427	0.5618	0.7767	0.3531
≤0.33	0.6793	0.6788	0.7948	0.6364

Given this, it is not hard to see that the impact of more political parties will depend entirely on where in that policy space the new parties locate themselves.

Assuming that new parties will occupy "empty" spaces in the policy dimension, coalition governments will become less frequent as a legislature fractionalizes if the distance between the *formateur* and the other parties is large; new parties will appear between them, and the possibility increases that a supported minority government will emerge. If the distance between the *formateur* and the other parties is small and if there is a policy "void" between two of these other parties, then fragmentation will make it attractive for the president to offer portfolios to the pivotal party in order to bring it closer in policy space. The point is that increasing legislative fragmentation may or may not lead to more coalition governments: it all depends on where the new parties are located in the policy space. Thus, unless one assumes that legislative fragmentation invariably implies more polarization, there is no reason to believe that it will necessarily affect coalition formation one way or another.[8]

Empirically, it turns out that legislative fragmentation actually strengthens the incentive for coalition formation, and more so in presidential than in parliamentary or mixed democracies. As Table 4.3 demonstrates, the frequency of

---

[8] This seems to be precisely what Mainwaring (1993:220) assumes when he states that "intense ideological divisions increase the stakes of the political game, serve as an incentive to polarization and, consequently, are less favorable to stable democracy. Such ideological divisions are unlikely in the context of a two-party system. This is one of the reasons why two-party democracies have been less prone to breakdown."

coalition governments is higher when no party holds more than a third of the seats than when some party does hold at least a third of the seats. Although weak in mixed systems, this effect is strong in both parliamentary and presidential democracies – sufficiently so that *majority* coalitions are also more likely when the legislature is more fragmented.

Table 4.4 presents the estimates of this effect for each form of government separately in a multivariate context. The first two models use the seat share of the largest party as the indicator of legislative fragmentation, whereas the last two models use the effective number of legislative parties. Models 1 and 3 are based on all the data and include a variable indicating whether no party controls more than half of the seats. Models 2 and 4 are based only on those cases where no party controls more than half the legislative seats and thus exclude the cases in which coalition governments are unnecessary for the emergence of a majority government. All models control for per capita income, the age of the democracy, and unobserved country characteristics.

The results are unambiguous: An increase in the share of seats held by the largest party (i.e., a decrease in legislative fragmentation) is associated with a decrease in the likelihood that a coalition government will emerge; an increase in the effective number of political parties (i.e., an increase in legislative fragmentation) is associated with an increase in the likelihood that a coalition government will emerge. The effect is substantively quite strong. On the basis of the parameters estimated in models 2 and 4 of Table 4.4, we find that the probability of a coalition government when there is a minority situation in a ten-year-old parliamentary democracy (in a country with average per capita income) increases by 0.20 when the share of seats of the largest party drops from 48% to 30%. In a presidential democracy under identical circumstances, the probability increases by 0.46 when the share of seats of the largest party suffers the same drop. As for the effective number of parties, the probability of a coalition government in a democracy increases by 0.17 in parliamentary systems and by 0.29 in presidential systems when the number of parties increases from 2.5 to 4.5. Thus, legislative fragmentation exerts a strong pressure on political parties – in parliamentary and presidential systems both – to form a coalition government.

One final point involves the fact that, under presidentialism, the party of the president – regardless of the share of seats it holds in the legislature – is the government *formateur*. As a consequence, the number of possible coalitions in presidential regimes is necessarily smaller than the number of possible coalitions in parliamentary regimes. This may become a serious problem when the president is an "outsider" who does not have or does not care to have

Table 4.4. *Legislative Fragmentation and Coalition Formation in Parliamentary and Presidential Democracies: Probit Analysis*

	Model			
	1	2[a]	3	4[a]
Parliamentary and mixed democracies				
Seat share of largest party	−2.1574	−3.5176		
	(0.001)	(0.001)		
Effective number of parties			0.3086	0.2548
			(0.000)	(0.005)
Minority situations	0.7679		0.8356	
	(0.000)		(0.000)	
Per capita income	−3.23e-6	3.10e-5	−1.45e-5	2.25e-5
	(0.862)	(0.130)	(0.505)	(0.272)
Age of democracy	0.0037	8.26e-5	0.0055	0.0022
	(0.369)	(0.984)	(0.280)	(0.625)
Constant	0.5222	1.8193	−1.3296	−0.4622
	(0.226)	(0.000)	(0.000)	(0.172)
N	1642	887	1642	877
Wald χ^2	54.88	17.17	66.9	13.14
Probability > χ^2	(0.000)	(0.001)	(0.000)	(0.004)
Presidential democracies[b]				
Seat share of largest party	−5.5364	−6.8190		
	(0.000)	(0.000)		
Effective number of parties			0.3472	0.3676
			(0.007)	(0.018)
Minority situations	0.0224		0.5385	
	(0.922)		(0.065)	
Per capita income	4.63e-5	−1.11e-5	−3.80e-5	−4.86e-5
	(0.370)	(0.856)	(0.500)	(0.470)
Age of democracy	−0.0144	−0.0003	−0.0157	0.0029
	(0.121)	(0.970)	(0.094)	(0.770)
Constant	2.3901	2.8385	−1.3399	−1.0128
	(0.000)	(0.000)	(0.002)	(0.096)
N	677	331	677	331
Wald χ^2	29.84	18.49	24.5	6.39
Probability > χ^2	(0.000)	(0.000)	(0.000)	(0.094)

Notes: Population-averaged models with robust standard errors; *p*-values in parentheses. Dependent variable is coalition government. "e-5" denotes "$\times 10^{-5}$".

[a] Majority situations excluded.

[b] Excludes Switzerland.

Table 4.5. *Relative Size of Government Head's Party in the Lower (or only) Legislative House*

Relative size	Parliamentary and mixed	Presidential
Largest	0.8288	0.7337
Second largest	0.0841	0.1663
First or second largest	*0.9130*	*0.9000*
Third largest	0.0218	0.0629
Fourth largest or smaller	0.0653	0.0371
TOTAL	1.0000	1.0000

Note: Entries are the proportion of country-years observed in each category.

support in congress. In these cases the president's power will be magnified by the institutional fact that his party must be a member of the government. To the extent that the emergence of outsiders is to be expected in presidential democracies, there may exist a "governability" problem.[9] But an outsider president is not the norm. As we can see in Table 4.5, it is simply not the case that presidents tend to be outsiders in the sense that they belong to small parties: the probability that the head of government will belong to one of the two largest parties is almost identical in both parliamentary (including mixed) and presidential regimes. Furthermore, as Figure 4.4 shows, the overall distribution of seats held by the party of the president and of the prime minister is similar under the two systems. There is nothing in this distribution suggesting that presidential regimes are more likely than parliamentary regimes to produce governments headed by outsiders.

Thus, presidential regimes are not particularly prone to producing governments headed by outsiders. Moreover, they are not necessarily more constrained than parliamentary regimes in the process of coalition formation. According to a study of 21 OECD parliamentary democracies over the 1946–1995 period (Cheibub 1998), for only 7.6% of the 290 changes in the partisan composition of

[9] For Linz (1994), there are structural reasons why presidential systems foster the presidential candidacies of outsiders: "If the purpose of a presidential election is to elect the 'best' woman or man to the office and the individual voter has to make the choice, why should he or she think of parties? If voters can get sufficient information, or think they have gotten it, to make up their minds about the 'personal' qualifications and positions of the candidates, they are presumably right in voting for a *candidate* irrespective of his links with a party. Voters feel that they do not need a party to tell them how to vote" (p. 27). Amorim Neto (2005) observes a tendency for presidential systems to alternate between coalition governments and governments led by outsiders.

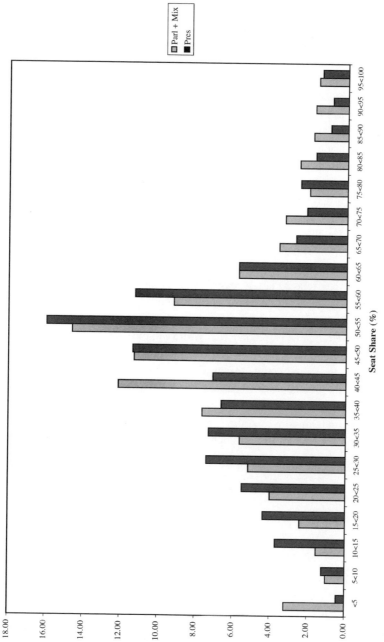

Figure 4.4 Share of Seats Held by the Party of the Head of Government.

the government did the new government exclude the party of the previous prime minister. The process of government formation in parliamentary democracies is constrained by the political reality that parties that were strong yesterday will continue to be strong today and hence will have a claim to participating in the government. Thus, in both parliamentary and presidential democracies, the government tends to be headed by the largest party, and this political factor – rather than any formal rule – is apparently sufficient to constrain the process of government formation so that the two systems look alike in practice.

In conclusion, there is no doubt that the frequency of coalition formation is lower in presidential democracies than in parliamentary democracies. This, however, is not what is under dispute. The prevailing claim, as demonstrated in Chapter 1, is that coalitions are infrequent and that they occur only in exceptional circumstances under presidential institutions. The data are unambiguous about this: Coalitions in presidential democracies are common; they occur in about three fifths of the cases in which no party commands a majority of legislative seats; in almost three fourths of these cases the coalition reaches majority status; and they tend to last at least as long as the coalitions formed in either parliamentary or mixed systems. This, of course, is not sufficient to conclusively refute the traditional view about presidentialism. It could be that coalitions, although relatively frequent (i.e., relative to the expectations derived from the Linzian framework), are not formed when most needed. The lower rates of coalition formation could still be what accounts for the higher death rates of presidential democracies. This will be the subject of the next section, but for now I have established that the theoretical discussion presented in Chapter 3 does find support in reality: in spite of the institutional dissimilarities between parliamentary and presidential democracies, the differences in these systems' propensities toward coalition formation is one of degree, not a difference in kind.

Does the Failure to Form Government Coalitions Spell Disaster for Democracies?

Coalition governments are less frequent in presidential than in parliamentary democracies, but this is not evidence that presidential institutions provide no incentives for cooperation. Chapter 3 has demonstrated that, under most circumstances, incentives for coalition formation are the same under both parliamentary and presidential institutions. Thus, the difference in coalition formation in the two systems is really not one of kind: coalitions in presidential systems are still formed in well over half of the instances when they are most needed – that is, when no party controls a majority of seats in the legislature. The logical next question, of course, is whether the difference in the frequency with which coalitions are formed across types of democratic regimes matters. Recall that, under the Linzian view summarized in Chapter 1, the lack of incentives for coalition formation in presidential systems was the main factor leading to government paralysis and the eventual breakdown of democracy. In this section I examine the effect of the government coalition (and majority) status on the government's legislative effectiveness and also on the survival of the democratic regime itself.

The crucial step in the chain of reasoning that leads from separation of powers to the breakdown of democracy is the claim that legislative paralysis will result from the chronic failure of presidential governments to form coalitions and reach majority status. It is at this juncture that the crucial difference between parliamentary and presidential systems – the existence of the vote of no confidence in the former but not in the latter – becomes most relevant: in parliamentary systems, the majority can use the vote of no confidence to remove the government and, with it, the source of the paralysis; in presidential systems, however, the only way to deal with the paralysis would be to wait for the next election ... or to enlist the help of actors who will use extra-constitutional means to help resolve the conflict. This view correctly characterizes the main institutional difference between parliamentary and presidential governments, but the question is whether this difference does, in fact, lead to the lower rates of democratic survival we observe for presidential democracies.

In order to address this issue, I first examine the available data regarding government legislative effectiveness in parliamentary and presidential democracies, conditioned on the status of the government. Ideally, the next step would be to study the death of democratic regimes conditioned on the form of government and on the government's legislative effectiveness. Unfortunately, however, data on government effectiveness are sparse, and the study of the direct impact of legislative effectiveness on democratic survival is not viable. For this reason, I proceed by studying the impact on a democracy's survival of the conditions that, according to the Linzian view, are likely to reduce the government's legislative effectiveness. These include the (coalition and majority) status of the government as well as the nature of the party system.

Legislative Ineffectiveness

By *legislative effectiveness* I mean the proportion of government-initiated and/or government-sponsored projects that become law. This is what Saiegh (2004) calls the government's "batting average" and is defined as the ratio of the number of executive proposals approved to the number of such proposals introduced in the lower house of the national legislature.[10]

Table 4.6 summarizes the information about government legislative success in parliamentary and presidential democracies by the type of legislative situation (i.e., whether there is a party that holds more than half of the legislative seats in the lower or only house) and by the type of government (coalition or single-party, majority or minority). I use the data collected by Saiegh (2004), which covers 604 democratic country-years since 1946.[11] It is apparent from the table that parliamentary governments are always more legislatively effective than presidential ones: the share of government bills approved in the legislature

---

[10] This is a measure of government legislative success or effectiveness. It is distinct from the government's legislative dominance (ratio of government-initiated laws to total laws) and government legislative output (absolute number of government-initiated laws); see Saiegh (2004:6). This measure of legislative effectiveness is not universally accepted. Samuels (2003:2), for instance, claims that success rates are inadequate because "they do not account for the process that filters potential proposals to actual proposals to proposals that are put to a vote." For Samuels, a more adequate procedure would be the one adopted in a study of Brazil by Ames (2001), who identifies the "genuine" presidential agenda on the basis of statements reported by the press and then compares it with what the president actually sends to congress and with what congress ultimately approves. He concludes that "very few legislative proposals have emerged from Congress unscathed since 1988" (p. 36). Yet it is unclear why this is a superior procedure. First, public presidential statements are hardly the best indicator of true preferences. Second, press reporting can be biased. Third, the president strategically crafts the bills he sends to congress, and their modification in the process of being approved does not in itself constitute evidence that the president's preferences have not prevailed. One good example is given by Figueiredo and Limongi (2005): one of the bills that Ames considers to have been modified beyond the president's preferences was the minimum wage bill, which was approved at R$77.00 (where R denotes "real" dollars in Brazilian currency) – higher than what the president had proposed (R$66.00) but much lower than what the opposition wanted (R$149.00). According to Desposato and Samuels (2003:4), assessing the degree to which presidents are legislatively effective hinges "on identifying the extent to which presidential proposals are modified both before and after submission." In effect, however, this calls for nothing short of reading the president's mind and discovering what he would like to have approved if he lived in a world unconstrained by legislators and the like. This is not only impossible but also, I would claim, irrelevant. What matters is not what the president wants in such an improbable world; what matters is what he wants given what he can get. This is best assessed by his preference as revealed by the projects sent to congress. See Figueiredo and Limongi (2005) for development of this point.

[11] This is a slightly expanded version of the data set used in Cheibub et al. (2004), and it contains information for 37 countries. As explained there, the data on government legislative success are sometimes given on an annual basis, sometimes for a particular coalition, and sometimes for the entire term of a president or a legislature. To create annual observations, longer periods were apportioned to specific years, taking as the criterion the state of affairs as of December 31 of each year.

Table 4.6. *Government Legislative Success in Parliamentary and Presidential Democracies by Legislative Situation and Government Status*

	All	N	Parliamentary	N	Presidential	N
Overall	73.43	610	80.99	372	61.63	238
Coalition status						
Single-party	75.81	316	85.70	165	65.00	151
Coalition	70.88	294	77.23	207	55.78	87
Majority situations[a]	78.64	254	89.12	137	66.36	117
Supermajority	77.68	44	86.57	23	67.94	21
Single-party majority	83.47	170	89.63	114	70.93	56
Divided[b]	59.14	40	—	0	59.14	40
Minority situations[a]	69.72	356	76.25	235	57.05	121
Coalition	69.68	250	76.06	184	51.91	66
Majority coalition	70.66	201	76.04	155	52.54	46
Minority	68.51	155	76.65	80	59.83	75
Minority coalition	65.68	49	76.17	29	50.47	20
Single-party minority	69.82	106	76.92	51	63.23	55

Note: Entries represent the average annual percentage of government bills approved.

[a] Majority situations are those in which there is a party that holds at least 50% of the seats in the lower (or only) house; minority situations are those in which no party holds more than 50% of the seats in the lower (or only) house.

[b] Divided governments are those in which there is a majority party that is not part of the government.

is higher under parliamentarism than under presidentialism, regardless of government coalition or majority status.[12]

To a certain extent, this difference should come as no surprise. The data on legislative success are subject to a form of selection bias that favors parliamentary systems and is induced by the institutional differences between presidential and parliamentary constitutions. Because of their fixed term in office, for presidents the consequences of legislative defeats are not the same as for prime ministers. If the former find the status quo acceptable, they can initiate bills they know will

---

[12] The arguments about government legislative success depend on whether governments serve a fixed term or are subject to a binding vote of no confidence, so here I collapse parliamentary and mixed democracies (as they are identical in this respect). Thus "parliamentary democracies" here refers to both pure parliamentary and mixed systems. Every analysis was replicated for pure parliamentary systems only, with no substantive change in any of the results reported in this chapter.

be defeated in order to embarrass the opposition. In contrast, prime ministers must be careful about what they send to the parliament because a legislative defeat may result in the end of the government.[13] Thus, since presidents may be "reckless" in a way that prime ministers cannot,[14] we should expect to see governments losing more frequently in presidential than in parliamentary systems, even if we assume identical legislative effectiveness.

In spite of the higher rate of legislative success of parliamentary democracies, governments in such systems do not always have their proposals approved in the legislature even when they hold a majority of seats. Therefore, the question of whether the coalition and majority status of the government makes them more or less successful is pertinent for both parliamentary and presidential systems. As we can see in Table 4.6, governments in both systems are more effective in a majority situation. In these circumstances, single-party majority governments are the norm, which means that governments can formulate legislative proposals – unhindered by negotiations with coalition partners – that will be supported by their own party in the legislature. The exception, of course, is when there is a divided government, which occurs only in presidential democracies. In these cases the government faces a majority opposition party and hence is more likely to be defeated. But even when the government faces a majoritarian and unified opposition, the rate of legislative success is close to 60%.[15]

When there is a minority situation – that is, when no party controls more than half the seats in the legislature – the situation is different across systems. Under

---

[13] A government defeat on a legislative vote does not always require the government's resignation in parliamentary democracies. According to Damgaard (1992:32), in Denmark after 1973, but in particular in the 1980s, "the government accepted numerous defeats in more or less important matters without resigning or calling elections." During the "four-leaf clover" governments of 1982–1988, the government lost 108 final divisions (every twelfth taken during the period), but in 105 of them "it decided to accept the defeat without applying sanctions in order to stay in office" (p. 34). Even in England, the least likely place for this to occur, we observe government legislative defeats that are not followed by the government's resignation. According to Boothroyd (2001; cited in Saiegh 2004), the increase in defeats observed during the Heath government (1970–1974) led to the realization that the government need not resign unless it loses an explicit vote of confidence.

[14] Although Jones (1995:40), who believes that presidents "are unlikely to submit bills to congress which they expect will be rejected," would disagree.

[15] This is not inconsistent with Mayhew's (1991) findings for the United States, which indicate that there is no difference in the rate with which "divided" and "unified" governments approve major legislation. Although Mayhew's finding that divided government does not significantly affect U.S. legislative output has generally survived intense scrutiny (see Fiorina 1996 for a summary), the issue is far from being settled in the literature; see Binder (1999) and Coleman (1999) for two examples of work in this area. Note that the dependent variable in this debate is "major proposals" or the "government political agenda," and much of the disagreement hinges on how these are measured.

Table 4.7. *Determinants of Legislative Effectiveness in Democratic Regimes*

	Model			
	1	2	3	4
Presidential system (PS)	−19.9233	−20.3180	−18.9817	−18.4137
	(0.000)	(0.000)	(0.000)	(0.000)
Single-party minority government (SPMG)	−4.6673	−4.3357	−4.3152	−3.5456
	(0.062)	(0.066)	(0.075)	(0.155)
PS × SPMG	6.2278	5.8524	4.8387	2.5327
	(0.082)	(0.083)	(0.169)	(0.474)
Effective number of parties		−3.6751	−3.5313	−3.4535
		(0.000)	(0.000)	(0.000)
Per capita income			0.0002	0.0004
			(0.531)	(0.202)
Age of democracy			−0.0058	−0.1166
			(0.854)	(0.013)
Constant	81.5902	93.8541	92.1371	94.6196
	(0.000)	(0.000)	(0.000)	(0.000)
N	604	604	567	567
Adjusted R^2	0.2368	0.3239	0.3029	87.44[a]
Probability $> \chi^2$				(0.000)

Notes: Dependent variable is government legislative success; *p*-values in parentheses. Models 1–3, ordinary least squares; model 4, population-averaged with robust standard errors.
[a] Wald χ^2.

parliamentarism, governments obtain a success rate of about 76%, regardless of their coalition and majority status. Under presidentialism, on the contrary, the coalition status and majority status of the government seem to matter: the most effective governments are precisely those that the traditional view of presidentialism considers to be doomed, namely, single-party minority governments. Under these circumstances, presidential governments approve 63% of the bills sent to the legislature, versus 53% for majority coalition governments.

However, we should be conservative when interpreting these differences. Once per capita income and the age of democracy are held constant, as they are in Table 4.7, the coalition and majority status of the government do not matter for its legislative effectiveness, regardless of whether the system is parliamentary or presidential. According to the coefficients produced by models 3 and 4 in that table, the difference in legislative effectiveness between single-party minority presidential governments and other types of presidential governments is at most

1% (i.e., statistically no different from zero). What this means substantively is that minority governments in presidential democracies, just like minority governments in parliamentary democracies, are not *any* less effective legislatively than majority coalition governments. Clearly, legislative paralysis must be a relatively rare phenomenon: among the countries for which there is information, single-party presidential governments in minority situations – that is, minority presidential governments – failed to pass half or more of their proposals only in Argentina (1999), Costa Rica (1996–1998), Ecuador (1979–1980 and 1990–1991), and Uruguay (1988–1989). The implication, of course, is that most single-party minority presidential governments appear to be supported by a majority of the legislature. Their portfolio minority status does not necessarily carry over to their legislative capacity.

It is clear, therefore, that the existing data do not support the view that presidents in minority situations who fail to form coalition governments are less able to govern than those who either belong to a majority party or bring other parties into the government. It is interesting to note that, since Strøm's (1990) seminal book, the standard wisdom regarding parliamentarism has been that minority governments are often supported by legislative majorities. Somehow the possibility that this may also occur under presidentialism has eluded those who study this system. Yet the numbers in Table 4.7 indicate that, when no party holds a majority in the legislature in presidential democracies, single-party minority governments are at least as effective legislatively as coalition or majority governments. Hence, the very motivation for the concern with coalition formation and minority governments in presidential democracies appears to be misplaced. Minority governments legislate no less successfully than majority coalitions in both parliamentary and presidential democracies, so minority governments cannot be viewed as failures of coalition formation. Indeed, governments are least successful legislatively when partisan policy positions are so polarized that portfolios must be traded in exchange for policy compromises and when the resulting government coalitions are internally divided in their policy preferences.

Breakdown of Democracy

Do presidential democracies die when their governments are legislatively ineffective? Unfortunately the available data do not allow us to answer this question directly; there are simply too few instances of democratic breakdowns in the set of cases for which information on the government's legislative success is also available. We can only address this issue indirectly, that is, by examining

Table 4.8. *Transition Probabilities of Parliamentary and Presidential Democracies by Legislative Situation and Government Status*

	Parliamentary[a]	N	Presidential	N
Panel A: Government status				
Single-party	0.0096	1042	0.0285	491
Coalition	0.0092	973	0.0365	329
Majority	0.0081	1614	0.0297	538
Minority	0.0150	401	0.0355	282
Panel B: Government status given minority situations[b]				
Single-party	0.0134	224	0.0316	158
Coalition	0.0071	843	0.0391	256
Majority	0.0044	682	0.0380	184
Minority	0.0156	385	0.0348	230
Panel C: Government status by legislative situation				
Supermajority	0.0232	129	0.0274	73
Single majority	0.0087	803	0.0249	281
Divided			0.0385	52
Coalition majority	0.0044	682	0.0380	184
Coalition minority	0.0186	161	0.0417	72
Single minority	0.0134	224	0.0316	158

Note: Transition probabilities are defined as TJK_i/J, where TJK is the number of transitions away from democracy and J is the number of democracies.
[a] Includes mixed systems.
[b] Minority situations are those in which no party holds more than 50% of the seats in the lower (or only) house.

whether the coalition and/or majority status of the government affect the survival of democracy.

Table 4.8 presents the necessary information for such an analysis. What becomes apparent from this table is that the expected effect of the government's coalition and majority status on the survival of democracies is simply not there. As panel A indicates, in both parliamentary and presidential democracies, coalition governments are more likely to die (to become a dictatorship) than single-party governments. In presidential democracies, minority governments face higher risks of turning into a dictatorship than majority governments. These differences, however, disappear (or are reversed) once we condition the probability of a democratic breakdown on the existence of a minority situation. A minority situation refers to the distribution of seats in the legislature; it exists when no one party holds more than half of the seats. When this is the case, as panel B in Table 4.8 indicates, minority presidential governments face slightly lower risks of breakdown than majority governments, whereas the reverse is true for parliamentary governments. Finally, once the legislative situation *and* the status of the government are taken into consideration, as in panel C, we find that single-party minority presidential governments have lower chances of breaking down than either coalition majority or coalition minority governments.

These differences, however, are not statistically significant. Probit analyses of the survival of democracy for parliamentary and presidential systems (not presented) consistently indicate that the status of the government does not matter for the survival of democracy. Whether the government is single-party, minority, single-party and minority, or multiparty and minority – conditions that are allegedly difficult for the government to manage – does not affect the probability that a transition to dictatorship will occur. This is true if we control for the cases where no party holds a majority of seats in the legislature (the situation in which forming a coalition and/or reaching majority status matters the most) and also if we control for per capita income, the number of past transitions to democracy, the number of other democracies in the world, measures of religious fragmentation, or the age of the current democratic regime. It is also true if, in addition, unobserved country effects are controlled for by estimating models that correct for the panel structure of the data. None of these cases exhibits statistical significance for the effect of variables indicating the majority and/or coalition status of the government on the probability of a transition away from democracy. Finally, the estimation of a survival model – which also takes into consideration the effect (if any) of time on the survival of democracy – corroborates these conclusions: the political conditions under which governments exist do not matter for the survival of democracy. It is therefore safe to conclude that the risks faced by democratic regimes, presidential and parliamentary alike, are not affected by whether the government includes one or many parties or by whether it holds more or less than half of the legislative seats.

A look back at Table 4.8 reveals something else: No matter what the political conditions under which their governments exist, presidential democracies always face higher risks than their parliamentary counterparts of becoming a dictatorship. Remember that, according to the view of presidentialism presented in Chapter 1, it is the lack of incentives for coalition formation and the pervasiveness of minority governments in presidential democracies that lead to their higher rate of breakdown into authoritarianism. Yet controlling for these conditions does not equalize the risks faced by the two types of democratic regimes, which implies that these conditions cannot be causing the observed differences in their propensity to collapse.

Legislative Fragmentation and Democratic Breakdown

The relationship between multipartism and democratic breakdown deserves some detailed consideration. One thing that stands out from the figures presented in Table 4.7 is that governments are less effective legislatively when legislatures are more fragmented. The estimates in Table 4.7 suggest – with a high degree of confidence and stability across different models and estimating techniques – that one extra "effective" party implies a reduction of about 3% in the number of government-initiated bills approved in the legislature. If legislative paralysis is what causes presidential democracies to crumble into dictatorships then we should observe, as Mainwaring (1993) proposed, that presidential democracies and multipartism constitute a difficult combination; democracy should become increasingly threatened as the number of political parties increases.

The general wisdom seems to be that it does. Golder (2006), for example, starts his analysis of the effect of presidential elections on legislative fragmentation by stating: "considerable evidence suggests that legislative fragmentation has a deleterious effect on the survival of presidential regimes." The evidence he refers to is provided, among others, by Mainwaring (1993:212), who finds a "virtual absence of multiparty systems" among stable presidential democracies (which are defined as those systems that experienced at least 25 years of uninterrupted democracy), and by Stepan and Skach (1993), who conclude that parliamentarism is a constitutional framework more supportive of democracy because, in part, of "its greater ability to rule in a multiparty setting" (p. 22).[16]

However, Przeworski et al. (2000) and Cheibub (2002) present evidence that the relationship between the number of legislative parties and transitions to authoritarianism, if it exists at all, is different in parliamentary and presidential regimes. In particular, they argue that the risks of democratic breakdown in presidential systems do not increase steadily with the number of political parties. In presidential democracies, higher risks are associated with situations of low pluralism or with situations conducive to moderate pluralism – which, as Sartori (1976) suggests, are those in which there are more than two but fewer

---

[16] For Stepan and Skach, "East European or Latin American political leaders who believe that their countries, for historical reasons, are inevitably multiparty in political representation are playing against great odds if they select a presidential system" (1993:20). Other studies that postulate – either theoretically or on the basis of empirical analysis – that multiparty systems are less conducive to the survival of democracy include Jones (1995:10), for whom "high levels of multipartism most often lead to disastrous consequences" in presidential systems, as well as Lawrence and Hayes (2000), Pérez-Liñán (2003), and Valenzuela (2004:13).

Table 4.9. *Transition Probabilities of Parliamentary and Presidential Democracies by Effective Number of Parties (ENP)*

	Presidential		Presidential[a]		Parliamentary	
All	0.0319	(816)	0.0342	(760)	0.0094	(2015)
ENP < 2	0.0289	(173)	0.0289	(173)	0.0102	(490)
2 < ENP ≤ 3	0.0311	(322)	0.0311	(322)	0.0142	(703)
3 < ENP ≤ 4	0.0472	(127)	0.0472	(127)	0.0023	(434)
4 < ENP ≤ 5	0.0444	(90)	0.0580	(69)	0.0049	(203)
ENP ≥ 5	0.0096	(104)	0.0145	(69)	0.0108	(185)
2 < ENP ≤ 5	0.0371	(539)	0.0360	(518)	0.0090	(1340)

Notes: Transition probabilities are defined as TJK_i/J, where TJK is the number of transitions away from democracy and J is the number of democracies; number of country-years in parentheses.
[a] Excludes Switzerland.

than five relevant political parties. Indeed, as we can see in Table 4.9, presidential democracies with more than five effective parties – the cases conducive to "polarized pluralism" in Sartori's typology – have a considerably longer expected life span than those in which the effective number of parties is fewer than five: 71 against 29 years.[17]

The evidence presented by Przeworski et al. (2000) and Cheibub (2002) is disputed by Samuels and Eaton (2002). They object, first, to the use of "effective number of political parties" as a measure of legislative fragmentation, a measure that (they argue) is too blunt to be of any use. Second, Samuels and Eaton claim that the predicted probability of a transition away from presidentialism increases steadily with the number of parties (2002, p. 28). The bluntness of the effective number of parties as a measure of legislative fractionalization is well known and is not subject to dispute. It is, however, the measure used by all sides in the debate about the relationship between multipartism and democracy and hence is justifiable at this level. Regarding the steadily increasing effect of the number of parties on the probability of collapse of a presidential democracy, Samuels and Eaton (2002) neglected to include in their logit estimation a term – the square of the effective number of parties – that would allow them to adjudicate between the competing hypotheses.[18] It is not surprising, then, that they find the probability

[17] This excludes Switzerland. If it is included, then the expected lives are 106 years when the effective number of parties is greater than five and 30 years when this number is less than five.

[18] Contrary to what Samuels and Eaton (2002) repeatedly assert throughout the text, the claim made by Przeworski et al. (2000) and Cheibub (2002) is not that there is *no* relationship between

Table 4.10. *Effect of Effective Number of Parties on Democratic Breakdown: Probit Estimates*

	Type of democracy	
	Presidential	Parliamentary
Effective number of parties (ENP)	0.0197	0.0001
	(0.037)	(0.659)
$(ENP)^2$	−0.0022	3.91e-6
	(0.074)	(0.808)
Per capita income	−7.27e-6	−2.64e-7
	(0.000)	(0.413)

Notes: Dependent variable is transition to dictatorship; entries are marginal effects. Population-averaged model with robust standard error; *p*-values in parentheses.

of democratic collapse in presidential democracies to be steadily increasing with the number of parties; given their specification, it could hardly be otherwise.

Table 4.10 presents the estimates of the effect of party fragmentation on the probability of a transition to dictatorship for presidential and parliamentary democracies, controlling for the level of economic development (as indicated by per capita income). It is apparent from this table that party fragmentation matters for democratic collapse only in presidential democracies and that the effect is curvilinear: the probability that a democracy will die increases with up to about four effective parties and then declines markedly.[19] Figure 4.5 illustrates this relationship when per capita income is held at the mean for each regime (7,039 1985 Purchasing Power Parity – PPP – dollars for parliamentarism and 4,582 1985 PPP dollars for presidentialism). It is only in parliamentary democracies that an increase in the number of legislative parties leads to a steady increase in the probability that democracy will die. This effect, however, is so small as to be virtually nonexistent.

---

multipartism and the survival of presidential democracies but rather that this relationship is curvilinear.

[19] This, of course, is in marked contrast to Mainwaring and Shugart (1997:399), who state that "in general, ... presidentialism is likely to function better if party system fragmentation is moderate (effective number of parties up to about 3.5), such that presidents are likely to find a significant bloc of legislators to support their initiatives or sustain their vetoes so that presidents are not marginal to lawmaking." It also contrasts with the opinion of Jones (1995:7) that countries that desire stable democracy but have presidential systems should "ensure a moderate level of multipartism" (given that the better alternative – the adoption of parliamentarism – is not available).

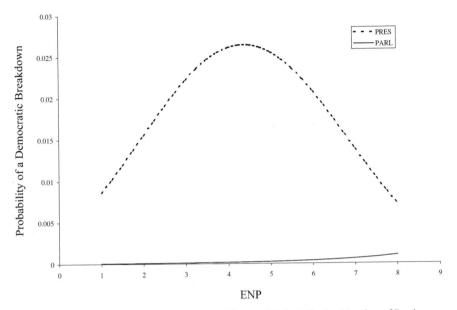

Figure 4.5 Probability of Transitions to Dictatorship by Effective Number of Parties: Parliamentary and Presidential Democracies.

Let me summarize what we have learned so far from the examination of democracies between 1946 and 2002. We have seen that coalitions are more frequent in parliamentary than in presidential regimes. We also have seen that parliamentary governments are, in general, more effective legislatively than presidential democracies. Although the data are incomplete, we have some indication that the status of the government does not matter for its ability to propose bills that the legislature actually approves. And we know with a high degree of certainty that the status of the government has no bearing on the survival of democracy.

Now it is true that there remains the possibility that presidential democracies – unlike parliamentary ones – face much higher risks of falling into dictatorship when their governments are legislatively ineffective. This is the claim of the traditional view of presidentialism, for when there is legislative paralysis there are no constitutional mechanisms (such as parliamentarism's vote of no confidence) to resolve the impasse. The scarcity of data does not allow us to examine this proposition directly. Even so, the findings reported in the previous section allow us to conclude that, if presidential democracies die when they experience legislative paralysis, this paralysis is not generated by the institutional setup inherent to presidentialism. This, we will recall, is another claim of the traditional view of presidentialism. In sum, we cannot say whether legislative ineffectiveness (paralysis) is what kills presidential democracies. But whatever the answer, we do know that the causal steps in the story that traces the fragility of presidential democracies to the incentives it generates are not supported by the data.

Strong Presidents and Democratic Performance

Our analysis in Chapter 3 identified the institutional conditions under which legislative paralysis in presidential systems may occur. Such paralysis will be possible if the president has a monopoly on legislative initiative with regard to important policies or if the president can sustain a veto. In other words: under presidentialism, paralysis is possible when the president dominates the legislative process.

The logic is simple. When the president does not dominate the legislative process, governments will always be supported by a *legislative* majority regardless of their coalition or majority status; when the president does dominate the legislative process, there will be governments that are not supported by a legislative majority. In particular, when the status quo is located between the policy preference of the president's party and that of the next party in the policy space, no coalition government will emerge and the policy will remain at the status quo. Since the president controls the legislative process, in these cases, all that the nonpresidential parties can achieve by uniting against the president (and pushing a bill that he opposes) is to keep the status quo. There is, in this sense, a stalemate between congress and the president – a stalemate to which, it is alleged, there is no automatic solution given that the executive and the legislature have independent bases of authority. This is the situation that should make presidential regimes most vulnerable, since both the president and the opposition have an incentive to seek extra-constitutional solutions to the stalemate (Linz 1994). Thus, although we cannot observe the occurrence of deadlocks directly, we are able to observe the institutional setup that is more likely to generate deadlocks. We are also able to observe the consequences that, in the Linzian view, should follow from these deadlocks: a reduction in the government's capacity to approve legislation and an increase in the likelihood of a democratic breakdown.

In this section I thus examine whether presidential democracies that are characterized by an institutional and political situation compatible with the emergence of deadlocks do in fact generate governments that are less effective as well as whether these democracies are more likely to collapse into a dictatorship. I define presidential dominance of the legislative process in terms of two dimensions: the president's control over the budget process and the president's ability to effectively veto legislation.[20] In the remainder of this chapter, I first define and operationalize presidential control over the budget process and effective presidential veto; I then show that, contrary to the expectation derived from the Linzian framework, the chances of survival of presidential democracies are not affected by the extent to which presidents control the budget or are capable of exerting their veto powers. I show that, instead, the chances of a democratic presidential regime surviving actually *increase* with some aspects of the president's institutional strength.

Presidential Control of the Budget Process

Although legislatures can initiate legislation in all democracies, in many of them – both presidential and parliamentary – legislatures are limited in their ability to initiate and amend some of the most important laws they have to vote on, including the budget law. For example, the 1980 Chilean constitution states: "The President of the Republic has the exclusive initiative for legal projects related to the alteration of the political or administrative division of the country or with the financial or budgetary administration of the State, including the amendments to the Budgetary Law" (article 62). It also states that "The National Congress may not increase nor diminish the estimation of revenues [contained in the project of Budgetary Law presented by the President]: it may only reduce the expenditures contained in the project of the Budgetary Law except those established by permanent law" (article 64). We therefore need a procedure for characterizing empirically the different ways in which legislative power is distributed between the executive and the assembly with respect to important legislation.

---

[20] A third dimension would be presidential decree powers, which – as defined by Carey and Shugart (1998:9) – means "the authority of the executive to establish law in lieu of action by the assembly." However, decree powers are pervasive: virtually all presidential constitutions grant some degree of such powers to the president, though the form in which they do so varies. Decree powers can be constitutionally granted, either in the form of authority to act in areas not covered by legislation or in the form of emergency powers, or they can be delegated by the legislature with explicit substantive or temporal limitations (see Carey and Shugart 1998 for a discussion of these distinctions). But in all cases the president has the power to legislate unilaterally and thereby place the congress in a position either to accept the presidential action or to try reverting to the status quo. This is true even in the United States, where presidents are generally believed to have no or only weak powers to act unilaterally (Mayer 2001). There is considerable variation with respect to the actual scope of presidential use of decree powers, but this variation is a function not so much of specific constitutional provisions as of specific historical and political circumstances (Carey and Shugart 1998; Pereira, Power, and Rennó 2005).

I develop this procedure by focusing on the budget, with the plausible assumption that it is the most important law a legislature must pass as part of its routine activities. The goal is to use information about the budget process to separate presidential democracies into those where the president dominates the legislative process from those where the president does not.

Presidential dominance over the budget process can be characterized in terms of three aspects: the power to initiate budget laws, the power to amend the budget proposal, and the default position – that is, the situation that would prevail if no budget law is approved. In combination, these three variables define an institutional setup that either favors the president in the budget process or does not.

Power of Initiation   In some presidential countries, such as Chile under the 1980 constitution and Brazil under the 1988 constitution, the president has the exclusive power to initiate budget legislation. In others – such as the United States, Sri Lanka, Cyprus, and Chile under its 1925 constitution – there is nothing specifying that the executive has the exclusive power to propose budget law.[21]

Power of Amendment   With one exception to be noted shortly, there are no cases of presidential democracies in which the constitution forbids the legislature to amend the budget proposal. In the vast majority of cases, however, the legislature's power of amendment is limited in scope and/or substance.

To determine whether the legislature is restricted in its capacity to amend the budget proposal, information on three aspects of the budget process needs to be considered simultaneously: whether the budget proposal can be amended at all, whether amendments are restricted in terms of areas, and whether amendments can entail an increase in expenses. On the basis of these three aspects it is possible to characterize the degree to which the legislature's capacity to amend is limited.

Thus, if the constitution simply forbids the budget proposal from being amended, then obviously the legislature is totally restricted in its capacity to amend the budget proposal. The only country in which the constitution prevents autonomous legislative amendment of the budget is Armenia. After transition

---

[21] For example, article 62 of the 1980 Chilean constitution states that "the President of the Republic has the exclusive initiative for legal projects related to the alteration of the political or administrative division of the country or with the financial or budgetary administration of the State, including the amendments to the Budgetary Law and with the matters specified in numbers 10 and 13 of Article 60." Article 165 of the 1988 Brazilian constitution states that "laws initiated by the Executive shall establish: I – the multi-year plan; II – the budgetary directives; III – the annual budgets."

to democracy in 1991, Armenia operated under the Soviet-era constitution until a new constitution was approved in 1995. Article 75 of the former constitution states that the government is to initiate budget legislation and that "the government shall stipulate the sequence for debate of its proposed draft legislation and may request that they be voted on only with amendments acceptable to it." In effect, then, legislative amendments had to be approved by the executive. The 1995 constitution adopted a mixed form of democratic government and, as a result, Armenia fell out of the sample of presidential democracies. However, the provision about legislative amendment of the government's budget law remained in place.

If the proposal may be amended but amendments are restricted in terms of substantive areas, then the legislature is constrained, though not entirely, in its capacity to amend the budget. For example, in the 1988 Brazilian constitution, paragraph 3 of article 66 precludes amendments that affect expenditures related to appropriations for personnel and their indirect costs, for debt servicing, and for constitutional tax transfers to the states, counties, and federal district. If amendments pertaining to any area of the budget are possible yet amendments cannot imply increased expenses, then the legislature is similarly restricted in its capacity to amend the budget. In these cases, which are the most common in presidential democracies, congress is free to act on any aspect of the budget as long as the changes it proposes do not imply new expenditures or expenditures not funded by new taxes. Finally, in an arrangement that is fairly common in presidential constitutions, the legislature's capacity to amend the budget proposal may be completely unrestricted. This is, of course, what the U.S. constitution prescribes; it is also prescribed by the constitutions of Argentina (1853 and 1994), Benin (1990), Brazil (1946), Burundi (1992), Chile (1925), Guatemala (1945, 1957, 1965, and 1985), Guinea-Bissau (1984), Honduras (1957 and 1982), Namibia (1990), Nigeria (1979 and 1999), Peru (1933), Sierra Leone (1991), South Korea (1987), and Uganda (1967).

An indicator of the existing limitations to the legislature's power of amendment may be constructed in two ways. The first and more restrictive one registers only the situations in which amendments by the assembly are not allowed (i.e., either the legislature is forbidden to amend the budget proposal or the legislature's power to amend is restricted in terms of both area *and* income). There are only three countries (four constitutions) with such an arrangement: Brazil (1988), Colombia (1886 and 1991), and Malawi (1994). They represent 81 of the 942 presidential country-years observed between 1946 and 2002. The second, less restrictive way, and the one that will be adopted here, adds to these cases those in which there are *some* restrictions (in terms of area *or* income) to the assembly's capacity to amend the budget proposal. When this is done, the number of country-years increases to 528, spread over ten different countries.

Default Situation (Reversal Point)   Life goes on even if no budget is approved, and many constitutions specify exactly how life must go on in such circumstances. Cases such as that of the United States, where there are no provisions for when a budget law is not passed, are less frequent than cases in which the constitution specifies what should transpire in the absence of a budget law; they are also more frequent in earlier presidential constitutions. Thus, whereas the current constitutions of Ecuador, Guatemala, Peru, the Philippines, Uruguay, and Venezuela contain explicit provisions for what happens when a budget law fails to be approved, their previous constitutions (designed in the 1930s, 1940s, and 1950s) were silent in this respect.

Identification of the reversal point in the budget process – that is, of the constitutional default position in case of failure of the budget process – requires first identifying *whether* the constitution explicitly specifies what should transpire in case the budget is not approved, and second, if it does, identifying *what* it specifies should happen in such circumstances. When constitutions do specify what happens in case of failure to approve the budget, they tend to adopt one of three solutions: the budget proposed by the assembly is adopted, the executive proposal is adopted, or the previous year's budget is adopted (usually in some restricted way, such as the adoption of monthly installments equal to a twelfth of the previous year's budget until the current year's budget is approved).

This information allows us to identify the cases in which the default position prescribed by the constitution under budget process failure favors the president. There are only two cases that clearly favor the president. The first is obvious enough: when the constitution explicitly says so (e.g., article 198 of the 1979 Peruvian constitution stipulates that the executive's proposal is to be adopted if the budget law is not approved before December 15). The second case is when the constitution stipulates that the previous year's budget is to be adopted if a new budget is not approved *and* the legislature is limited in its power to amend a budget proposal initiated by the president. In all other cases, the failure of the budget process in the legislature does not favor the president; either it is neutral, favoring neither the president nor the legislature, or it favors the legislature.

To summarize, the budget initiative may or may not be an exclusive presidential power. The legislature, in turn, may or may not be restricted in its ability to amend the budget. Finally, if the budget law is not approved in time, the default situation may either favor the president or not. Taken together,

Table 4.11. *Institutional Configurations Resulting from the Combination of Three Characteristics of the Budget Process in Presidential Democracies*

Does the president have exclusive power to initiate budget law?	Is congress limited in its capacity to amend the budget proposal?	Does the default situation favor the president?	Does the president dominate the budget process?
Yes	**Yes**	**Yes**	**Yes**
Yes	**Yes**	**No**	**Yes**
Yes	No	Yes	No
Yes	No	No	No
No	**Yes**	**Yes**	**Yes**
No	Yes	No	No
No	No	Yes	No
No	No	No	No

Notes: Boldface denotes cases where the president is coded as dominant (see text). The presidential dominance variable is coded 1 when the last column = **Yes**.

these three variables generate eight possible institutional arrangements, which are summarized in Table 4.11. Three of these configurations indicate presidential dominance of the budget process. In the first two instances, the legislature is limited in its capacity to amend a budget proposal that is exclusively initiated by the president. The difference between the two is that in the first instance the constitution clearly and explicitly favors the president when the budget is not approved, whereas in the second it does not (invariably because, as in the 1949 Costa Rican and 1988 Brazilian constitutions, they provide no guidance for when the budget law is not approved). Because the president proposes the law and the legislature is limited in its power to amend it, I consider this a case of presidential dominance. The third configuration indicating presidential dominance of the budget process is the one where no single actor has the exclusive power to initiate the budget proposal, the legislature has limited amendment power, and failure to pass the budget law implies the adoption of the executive's proposal. Presidential dominance of the budget process exists whenever one of these three configurations is present; the remaining configurations do not favor the president when it comes to the budget and so the president does not dominate the budget process in those cases.

Effective Presidential Veto

The vast majority of presidential democracies grant presidents the power to veto legislation and thus the power to exert a significant level of influence over the

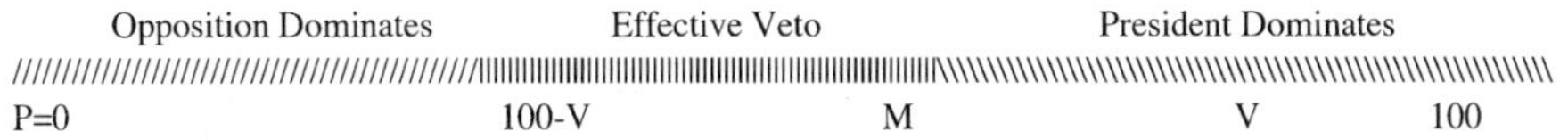

Are Coalitions Rare in Presidential Democracies?

Opposition Dominates	Effective Veto	President Dominates

```
//////////////////////////////////////////////|||||||||||||||||||||||||||||||||||||||||||||||||||||||||\\\\\\\\\\\\\\\\\\\\\\\\\\\\\\\\\\\\\\\\\\\\\\\\\\\\\
```

P=0   100-V   M   V   100

P = Share of seats held by the government coalition
President has veto powers and a majority of V votes is required to override the presidential veto

Figure 4.6   Zone of Effective Presidential Veto.

legislative process (Cameron 2000), but it is not always the case that such power can be effectively exercised. Since most constitutions allow the legislature to override the presidential veto, effective presidential veto depends both on the constitutional provisions granting the president that power *and* on the distribution of seats in the legislature. Hence we must identify the situations in which presidential veto power is effective.

Consider the case of only two parties, that of the president and that of the opposition: P is the share of seats held by the party of the president and O is the share of seats held by the opposition. Legislation is passed by votes of at least M members of congress and, in the case of bicameral systems, bills have to be approved in both houses. Under these conditions, we can distinguish the situation in which the party of the president controls a majority of seats in congress (so that congress passes bills preferred by the president) from that in which the party of the president does not control a majority of seats in congress. When the latter obtains, congress approves bills that are not the ones preferred by the president. In these instances the president vetoes the bill if constitutionally empowered to do so. Presidential vetoes can be overridden by at least V members of congress. Thus, $0 < M \leq V < 100$.

This setup defines three possible situations with respect to executive–legislative relations, which are illustrated in Figure 4.6. One situation is defined by $P < 100 - V$ and $O \geq V$. In these cases, congress passes bills preferred by the opposition and these bills are likely to become law: even if the president vetoes the bill, the opposition has the votes to override the presidential veto. We can say that in these cases the opposition rules. Another situation is defined by $P > M$, where congress passes bills preferred by the president, the president signs the bills, and they become law. In these cases we can say that the president rules. It is only when $100 - V \leq P < M$ and $M \leq O < V$ that the presidential veto will be effective; then congress passes bills preferred by the opposition, the president vetoes these bills, and the opposition does not have enough votes to override the presidential veto. Legislative action by the legislature is thus curbed by the president's ability to block unwanted bills. As discussed in Chapter 3, all that the nonpresidential parties can achieve by uniting against the president is to maintain the status quo. Hence we have a stalemate (between congress and the president) that supposedly cannot be resolved because the executive and the legislature are independently elected. The result is a vulnerable presidential regime, because the president and the opposition would each have an incentive to seek an extra-constitutional resolution.

Empirically, the effective presidential veto depends on the combination of institutional and political factors. On the one hand, it depends on the distribution of seats in congress or, more specifically, on the share of seats held by the party of the president. On the other hand, it depends on the following institutional provisions regarding the presidential veto:

- whether the president has veto power;
- the type of congressional majority necessary to override the presidential veto (the location of V with respect to M in Figure 4.6);
- whether the system is unicameral or bicameral;
- whether (in bicameral systems) veto override is by a vote in each chamber separately or in a joint session of both chambers.

Table 4.12 presents the distribution of cases (country-years) of presidential systems according to these institutional factors. Note, to begin with, that the vast majority of presidential democracies grant the president the power to veto legislation. In only about 4% of all cases are presidents deprived of the right to at least force the legislature to reconsider a bill that it has approved. Over half of these cases come from Switzerland, by no means a typical presidential democracy; the others are found in Indonesia, Peru (prior to its 1980 constitution), Sri Lanka, and Suriname. Nonetheless, in all systems (except for Micronesia) the legislature is allowed to override the presidential veto. In a significant portion of the cases, it is sufficient that a majority similar to the one that approved the bill in the first place reaffirms its desire to make it into law (this rule obtains in about 18% of the unicameral cases and 12% of the bicameral cases). But usually a presidential veto can be overridden only by a larger (e.g., three-fifths or two-thirds) majority than the one that initially approved the bill.

In some of the configurations shown in Table 4.12, it is possible to determine whether the president has effective veto powers regardless of the share of seats that the president's party controls in congress. This is obviously the case when the president has no constitutional veto powers. It is also the case when the president has veto power that cannot be overridden by the legislature; in this event, the president's preference regarding legislation will prevail even if the party of

Table 4.12. *Distribution of Presidential Democracies (country-years) by Institutional Features Related to the Presidential Veto*

UNICAMERAL (379)	BICAMERAL (563)
Missing (3)	Missing (11)
No veto (32)	No veto (70)
Veto (344)	Veto (482)
No override (12)	No override (0)
Override (332)	Override (482)
Majority of present (29)	Majority of present (9)
	Override by lower house only (9)
Majority of members (34)	Majority of members (48)
	Override by joint session of both houses (34)
	Override by separate session of each house (14)
Three fifths of members (5)	Three fifths of present (45)
	Override by joint session of both houses (45)
Two thirds of present (48)	Two thirds of present (240)
	Override by joint session of both houses (56)
	Override by separate session of each house (184)
Two thirds of members (216)	Two thirds of members (140)
	Override by separate session of each house (127)
	Override by lower house only (13)

Note: $N = 942$ total presidential democracies.

the president holds a very small share of seats in the legislature. Similarly, when the president can veto legislation but the veto can be overridden by an absolute majority in congress, the situation is functionally equivalent to that when the constitution does not give the president veto power. In these cases (using our previous notation) $V = M$: whoever controls the congress, whether the president or the opposition, dominates; that the president can veto legislation is of no consequence. If the president's party does not hold a majority in congress, the same majority that approved a bill in the first place may override the presidential veto.[22]

---

[22] There are a few cases in which the president can veto a bill either partially or totally, with a different majority required to override each type of veto. The 1983 constitution in El Salvador requires an absolute majority of chamber members to override a partial veto and a two-thirds majority of members to override a total veto. Since 1943, the Uruguayan constitutions have required a majority of those present to override a partial veto and three fifths of those present to override a total veto. Finally, the 1979 constitution of Ecuador requires a two-thirds majority of members to override a partial veto and an absolute majority of members to override a total veto. In these cases I took the larger majority as the requirement for legislative override.

In all other cases, it is the combination of rules regarding presidential veto and the share of seats held by the president's party that determines whether the president has effective veto powers. Thus, when veto override is by a majority vote in each house of a bicameral system, the president will have effective veto power even if his party controls a majority of seats in only one of the houses. Hence the president will veto the legislation and the opposition, lacking control in one of the houses, will be unable to override the veto.

When veto override is by a majority vote in a joint session of both houses, the president will have effective veto only if his party holds more than half the seats in the joint congress. When the president's party holds fewer than half of the seats in a joint meeting of both legislative houses, the veto will be ineffective even if the party of the president controls a majority in one of the houses. In these cases, the opposition dominates.

When veto override is by a two-thirds majority in a unicameral system, the presidential veto will be effective only if the party of the president controls between a third and a half of the seats. When veto override requires a two-thirds majority and the system is bicameral, effectiveness of the presidential veto will depend on the share of seats held by the president's party and also on whether the vote is to be taken in each chamber or in a joint session of both chambers. Table 4.13 illustrates the possible scenarios when the vote is to be taken in each chamber separately. Here the presidential veto is widely effective; it is ineffective only if the opposition holds more than two thirds of the seats in both houses. When the party of the president holds more than half the seats in both houses, the president is likely to favor legislation approved in them and no veto will occur. All the other cells in Table 4.13 represent situations in which the presidential veto is effective.

If the system is bicameral and if veto override requires a two-thirds majority in a joint session of both houses, then the presidential veto will be effective when the party of the president does not control a majority in either house as long as it does control more than a third of the votes in the joint congress. In these cases the president will veto legislation, and the opposition will not control enough votes in the joint congress to override the presidential veto.

Finally, the cases in which veto override requires a three-fifths majority are the same as those in which the requirement is a two-thirds majority, except that now the cutoff points change from 33.3% to 40%.

Thus we have listed all the cases in which the presidential veto is effective. The president's power to veto legislation approved by congress is obviously necessary but does not in itself make the veto effective. The president's capacity

Table 4.13. *Effectiveness of Presidential Veto in a Bicameral Setting with a Two-Thirds Veto Override Requirement to Be Voted Separately in Each Chamber*

	Share of seats held by the president's party in the:		
	Lower house		
Upper house	0–33.3%	33.3–50%	>50%
0–33.3%	President likely to veto; Opposition overrides; Veto ineffective (opposition rules)	President likely to veto; Opposition cannot override in the lower house; Veto effective	President likely to veto; Opposition cannot override in the lower house; Veto effective
33.3–50%	President likely to veto; Opposition cannot override in the upper house; Veto effective	President likely to veto; Opposition cannot override in either house; Veto effective	President likely to veto; Opposition cannot override in either house; Veto effective
>50%	President likely to veto; Opposition cannot override in the upper house; Veto effective	President likely to veto; Opposition cannot override in either house; Veto effective	No presidential veto (president rules)

to veto legislation also depends on the number of legislative chambers and the distribution of seats in congress.

Strong Presidents, Legislative Effectiveness, and Survival of Democracy

Presidential dominance of the legislative (budgetary) process and effective veto power were coded for all presidential democracies that existed between 1946 and 2002 and for which information was available. Overall, 82 constitutions or constitutional amendments were consulted. The resulting variables – presidential dominance and presidential effective veto power – differ from existing indices of presidential power (Shugart and Carey 1992; Frye 1997; Metcalf 2000; Johannsen and Nørgaard 2003; Krouwel 2003) that assign an arbitrary value to a series of presidential functions, which are then aggregated into an overall index. Such a procedure does not distinguish specific configurations of presidential powers (very different powers may yield identical scores) and assumes that each "power" contributes equally to the overall power of the president. The interval index of presidential power it generates thus provides an artificial sense of precision in measurement.

In contrast, our variables indicating presidential dominance of the budget process and effective veto power are based on the notion that what matters is the specific configuration of relevant attributes, not the mere addition of a series of attributes. The difference that our procedure makes for the final assessment of presidential powers can be clearly seen with respect to the effectiveness of the presidential veto. Although we observe that presidential democracies have existed under constitutions that grant the president *formal* veto powers in 89% of the country-years observed between 1946 and 2002, the president had *effective* power in only 23% of these country-years. With respect to presidential dominance, what matters is not simply the presence or absence of one of the relevant constitutional provisions but rather the combination of these provisions, which (as I have argued) come together to characterize a budget process that favors the president over the legislature. Thus, 74% of the country-years of presidential democracies occurred under constitutions that granted the president initiative with respect to the budget; 57% limited the legislature's ability to amend the budget proposal; and 34% specified a default situation that favored the president when the budget process failed. However, when combined according to the rules summarized in Table 4.11, these three features yield a "rate" of presidential dominance equal to 54%.

Therefore, given these instruments for observing presidential powers, the question is whether institutionally strong presidents matter for the emergence of coalition governments, for the government's legislative effectiveness, and for the survival of democracy. There are two alternative stories. In the Linzian framework, strong presidents – even more so than regular presidents – will have no incentive to form coalitions. Such presidents will use their legislative powers to impose their preference over that of the legislative majority and thus will be ineffective in gaining approval for their proposals in congress; ultimately, their actions will lead to a breakdown of democracy as actors seek the support of extra-constitutional forces to resolve their conflicts.

By our discussion in Chapter 3, coalition governments will, indeed, be less frequent when presidents are institutionally strong. Yet this will not necessarily lead to legislative paralysis, since there will also be circumstances in which a coalition or minority government will be supported by a legislative majority. Similarly, there are no reasons for us to expect that the rate with which democracies break down will be higher when presidents are institutionally strong than when they are not. Although a deadlock may emerge, one attribute of this deadlock (as we saw in Chapter 3) is that it is actually pleasing to some of the actors

Table 4.14. *Effect of Presidential Dominance of the Budgetary Process and Effective Veto on the Probability of Coalition Government*

	Model	
	1	2
Presidential dominance	−0.1368	
	(0.728)	
Effective veto		−0.4103
		(0.113)
Effective number of parties	0.3146	0.2498
	(0.007)	(0.038)
Minority situation	0.5672	0.7121
	(0.051)	(0.015)
Per capita income	0.0001	0.0001
	(0.333)	(0.156)
Age of democracy	−0.0173	−0.0212
	(0.081)	(0.028)
Constant	−1.2394	−1.1645
	(0.012)	(0.004)
N	675	677
Groups	34	34
Wald χ^2	27.97	35.47
Probability $> \chi^2$	(0.000)	(0.000)

Notes: Population-averaged models with robust standard errors, adjusted for clustering on countries; p-values in parentheses. Dependent variable is coalition government.

involved. Thus, institutionally strong presidents will not necessarily act against the preferences of the legislative majority.

Table 4.14 presents estimates of the effect of presidential dominance of the legislative process and of presidential effective veto power on the probability that a coalition government will be formed, controlling for the same variables introduced in Table 4.4: the effective number of parties, whether there is a minority situation, real per capita income, and age of the democracy. When this is done we find that both variables (presidential dominance and effective veto) have a negative impact on the probability that a coalition government will be observed, although the effect of presidential dominance of the budgetary process cannot be safely distinguished from zero.

Yet the lower propensity for coalition formation when presidents are strong does not necessarily lead to conflict between the president and the congress – expressed in deadlock, legislative paralysis, and the ultimate breakdown of democracy. Keeping in mind our caveats regarding the data on legislative effectiveness, we find that the difference, though slight, is in favor of "strong" presidents: 58% of the bills initiated by the executive are approved in the legislature when presidents dominate the budgetary process, versus 54% when they do not; and 60% of executive bills are approved when presidents have effective veto, versus 55% when they do not. Most importantly, institutionally strong presidents do not make presidential democracies more likely to collapse. When the president controls the budgetary process, presidential democracies are about 3% less likely to collapse into a dictatorship than when he does not. But whether or not the president can effectively veto legislation has no impact on the survival of democracy.

Thus, all in all, there seems to be no support for the Linzian story about the incompatibility between institutionally strong presidencies and the survival of democracy. Given the premise of inherent conflict that underlies the Linzian view of presidentialism, it is understandable that strengthening the presidency is seen as a source of increased conflict with the legislature. Mainwaring and Shugart (1997:436), for example, "believe that presidential systems tend to function better with limited executive powers over legislation, mainly because a weaker executive means that the congress has more opportunity for debating and logrolling on controversial matters." "Having weaker executive powers," they continue, "also means that cases in which presidents lack reliable majorities are less likely to be crisis-ridden, since the president has fewer tools with which to try to do an end run around the congress." Likewise, Shugart and Carey (1992, Chap. 8) find that presidential systems with institutionally weak presidents are more likely to last than those granting the head of the government extensive legislative and nonlegislative powers. For them, the usual criticisms of presidential regimes "apply with greatest force to strong presidents" (1992:165). This observation is, of course, bolstered by the fact that the only long-lasting presidential democracy in the world also has one of the weakest presidencies from an institutional standpoint. The implicit message, it seems, is that presidential democracies that deviate from the U.S. model are doomed to fail.

Coalitions are frequent in presidential democracies. They are more common in parliamentary systems, but the frequency with which they occur under presidentialism indisputably denies the notion that they are uncommon, rare, or exceptional. There is nothing in the structure of presidential institutions that makes it in the actors' interests to always adopt a strategy of noncooperation. The notion that conflict, as opposed to cooperation, is dictated by the structure of the system and is thus a dominant strategy for politicians in presidential democracies conveys an extremely simplified (if not entirely erroneous) view of politicians' behavior in these systems. Once it is accepted that politicians in both parliamentary and presidential democracies care about being in office and seeing the policies they like being implemented, the contrast between parliamentary and presidential democracies fades considerably while the similarities between the two systems become more pronounced. Most importantly, it becomes clear that the absence of government coalitions does not imply the absence of legislative support for the existing government, whether parliamentary or presidential. Given this, it comes as no surprise that minority governments are found to be no less effective than coalition and/or majority governments when it comes to passing their legislative programs. And given that they work as well as any other government, minority governments should not be, as indeed they are not, associated with the breakdown of presidential or parliamentary democracies. Finally, presidential systems that provide for institutionally strong presidents – that is, presidents who control the legislative process, either because they have the monopoly to set the budget or are able to veto legislation they dislike – are not plagued by conflict, inaction, and eventual devolution into an authoritarian system.

The framework developed in Chapter 3 suggests that there may be two reasons for the harmonious operation of a system that could, at least at first sight, be prone to conflict and paralysis: the distribution of policy preferences across political parties and the location of the status quo. Given the lack of data on these components, there is not much I can say about either. Still, they call attention to our claim that the effects of the institutional setup on the behavior of actors should not be evaluated in isolation; noninstitutional factors (e.g., the preferences of politicians over important policy issues and the point of departure for any policy change) play a crucial role in determining what will actually transpire under specific institutional configurations. Presidential democracies will be brittle when they exist in countries where the distribution of preferences and the policy status quo are such that conflict becomes the norm, yet this does not mean that we should blame presidential institutions. The general point is this: Paralysis may emerge in presidential democracies in a way that they cannot emerge in parliamentary democracies, but it does not follow that presidential democracies provide no incentives for actors to cooperate with one another and hence must be plagued by governability problems, even if the government is composed by a single party that lacks a majority in congress. Whatever makes

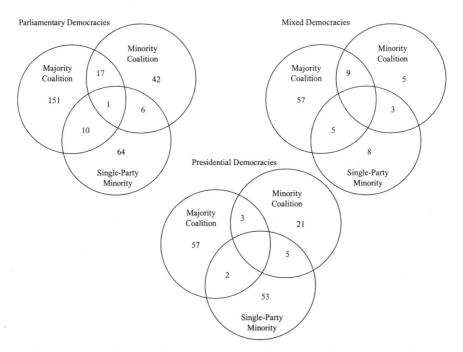

Figure 4.7 Distribution of Coalition and Majority Governments Computed on the Basis of Situation (No Party Holds More than 50% of the Seats).

presidential democracies more brittle, it is not the inability of minority governments to govern.

Appendix 4.1: Frequency of Coalition and Majority Governments Computed on the Basis of Situations and Country-Years

Figure 4.7 presents the distribution of governments according to their coalition and majority status when no party controls more than half of the seats in the lower legislative house. The unit of observation is a *situation*, that is, any period in which the distribution of legislative seats remains the same. This differs from Figures 4.1–4.3, where the unit of observation was a *country-year*.

Observations at the country-year level may underestimate the frequency of coalition governments, since they may fail to capture all the instances in which coalitions were formed for at least some of the time during which the distribution of legislative seats remained constant. This bias may be severe if the number of situations during which we observe changes in the coalition status of

Table 4.15. *Distribution of Democratic Regimes According to Situations and Country-Years*

	Type of democracy			
	Parliamentary + Mixed		Presidential	
	Situations	Country-years	Situations	Country-years
Minority situation	0.5502	0.5286	0.4796	0.5094
Coalition government given a minority situation	0.8095	0.7920	0.6241	0.6152
Majority government given a minority situation	0.6614	0.6403	0.4397	0.4401
Majority government given a coalition government	0.8170	0.8085	0.7045	0.7154

Note: Entries are the proportions in each category.

the government is large or if the changes in the coalition status of the government during a situation are significantly different across democratic regimes. I argue in the body of the chapter that neither seems to be the case in the data on democratic systems between 1946 and 2002: about 8% and 11%, respectively, of the situations under presidential and parliamentary (plus mixed) regimes led to the formation of more than one type of government. As a consequence, counting on the basis of either situations or country-years yields similar results and, for convenience, I use the latter throughout the book. Table 4.15 allows the reader to compare the distribution of governments according to their coalition and majority status when these two methods are employed.

5

Party Discipline and Form of Government

According to the views summarized in Chapter 1, parliamentary regimes are supposed to foster cooperation whereas presidential ones are not. In the former, political parties have an incentive to cooperate with one another; parties in government will support the executive, and parties out of the government will refrain from escalating conflicts owing to the possibility that they may, at any time, become part of the government. Individual members of parliament will also align themselves with their parties. As a consequence, parliamentary governments will be supported by a majority in the legislature, composed of highly disciplined parties that are inclined to cooperate with one another. Presidentialism, in turn, is characterized by the absence of such incentives. Because coalitions are unlikely to emerge, it will frequently generate minority governments. In the rare occasions in which coalitions do form, they will be based on parties that are themselves incapable of inducing cooperation from their members. Thus, coalitions in presidential democracies are rare and are unreliable when they emerge.

We have already examined the incentives for coalition formation under parliamentary and presidential regimes. We saw in Chapter 3 that, once we assume that politicians in both regimes care about being in office *and* passing policies they like, the incentives for cooperation across regimes are not that much different. In spite of important institutional differences between parliamentary and presidential democracies, the conditions under which governments will be supported by a legislative coalition are almost the same in the two regimes. Even when institutional conditions are such that unsupported minority governments might emerge, there is no evidence that governments are paralyzed or that democracy is at higher risk.

Party Discipline and Form of Government

In this chapter I move from the consideration of *inter*party to a consideration of *intra*party cooperation under different forms of government. Specifically, I discuss the view that party discipline is inherently lower under presidentialism than under parliamentarism. This is the last aspect to be addressed in the chain of reasoning presented in Figure 1.1.

Let me anticipate the general argument in this chapter. It is not a matter of arguing that party discipline is higher, or at least as high, in presidential as in parliamentary democracies. I grant from the start that, if we were able to compare the two systems (something that is inherently problematic, as we shall see), we would probably find that average levels of party discipline are higher under parliamentary than under presidential democracies. By design, the former have an instrument for fostering discipline that the latter do not have: the possibility of a vote of confidence or no confidence in the government. But this is not really what matters. We care about party discipline primarily because it is considered to be one of the main mechanisms through which governments are able to obtain consistent and predictable legislative support for their policies – in other words, because it is one of the ways by which governments are capable of governing. Yet the fact that parties in presidential democracies cannot be disciplined via the confidence mechanism, and hence probably have lower overall levels of party discipline, does not imply that presidential governments are inherently less able to obtain such legislative support. It is this particular step in the discussion of party discipline across democratic systems – that is, the step that goes from recognizing that party discipline may be (on average) higher in parliamentary democracies to concluding that, for this reason, presidential governments have a hard time eliciting the consistent support of a legislative majority – that I find fault with and against which I want to argue here.

As I will show, informal arguments about party discipline across systems are theoretically inconsistent, and formal arguments suggest that what matters for party discipline is not the vote of confidence itself but rather the government's control of the legislative agenda, something that presidential governments may also have. Hence, party discipline is not invariably tied to the form of government. It follows that sufficient levels of party discipline may be obtained through mechanisms that are available to presidential governments, such as the president's legislative power and the way in which the legislative body is organized. The presence of these instruments, as I will show, may increase discipline in presidential democracies, just as their absence may decrease discipline in parliamentary democracies. I hope in this way to refocus the research question about party discipline across political systems.

Regime Type and Party Discipline

Informal Arguments

There are formal and informal arguments relating regime type to party discipline (i.e., to cohesion in legislative voting).[1] The informal arguments originated with Juan Linz and, as discussed in Chapter 1, are reproduced by most critics of presidentialism. According to these arguments, the very existence of governments in parliamentary regimes depends on their parties' capacity to impose discipline in order to approve their agenda. Undisciplined parties may result in a failure to obtain majority support in parliament, the defeat of government bills, and consequently the fall of the government. In order to remain in government, political parties enforce discipline so that their members in parliament can be counted on to support bills proposed by the government.

Under presidentialism, the government and the legislature are independent and so political parties have no reason to impose discipline on their members: their survival in office does not depend on the result of any particular vote in the legislature. Individual members of congress, in turn, have no incentive to accept the discipline of political parties in order to avoid the fall of the government and risk losing their mandates in early elections. It is for this reason that Linz (1994:35) concludes that party discipline and presidentialism are structurally incompatible.

The fusion of power that characterizes parliamentary regimes should thus produce a convergence of interests among individual members of parliament, their parties, and the government, resulting in high levels of party discipline. The separation of power that characterizes presidentialism, in contrast, should imply very low levels of party discipline. Even a president lucky enough to belong to the party controlling a majority of seats in congress would not necessarily be able

---

[1] Party discipline and cohesion are conceptually distinct (Ozbudun 1970; Hazan 2003). Empirically, however, we can observe only a group of legislators voting together – either as an expression of their true preferences or as the result of disciplinary measures. As noted by Bowler, Farrell, and Katz (1999), this distinction matters only when cohesion is moderate. If cohesion is high, then disciplinary measures are not necessary; if it is low, then such a heterogeneous group of legislators will not likely agree to any measure that will make them vote together. Only when cohesion is high enough that a group of like-minded representatives will accept a common set of constraining rules, yet low enough that they will occasionally find it in their interests to vote against the party's position, do disciplinary mechanisms become relevant. In what follows, discipline and cohesion are treated as synonymous unless explicitly noted otherwise. Our interest is in the extent to which a group of legislators vote together, assuming there is a sufficiently high degree of heterogeneity in preferences to make posing the question meaningful.

to count on the support of that majority when governing. Quite to the contrary, the president should expect – at least under some circumstances – that no support will be forthcoming from that majority.[2] In this view, then, the threat of government dissolution and early elections, which is possible in parliamentary regimes but not in presidential ones, is necessary and sufficient to induce party discipline.

Note, however, that this argument contains an implicit assumption about the motivation of the actors (politicians and political parties) who participate in the political game: that they are motivated exclusively by a desire to remain in office. Yet this assumption is untenable. To see why, consider that if politicians were exclusively office seekers then two things should follow: (i) no minority governments would ever emerge, and (ii) governments would be based on minimum winning coalitions. Minority governments would not emerge because there would always be at least one party that could be lured into the government to compose a majority (Laver and Schofield 1998). Minority governments, in this sense, would represent the failure to produce a "proper" government and should be expected only under adverse conditions, such as when there is excessive political fragmentation. Coalitions would be "minimum winning" because any other way of partitioning the government would imply either a minority status or smaller spoils.

As we have already seen, however, minority governments are not infrequent in democratic regimes. According to Figures 4.1–4.3, 24% of the country-years in all democracies between 1946 and 2002 were spent under a minority government (34% in presidential, 24% in parliamentary, and 15% in mixed democracies). Moreover, Strøm (1990) showed that, for the sample of parliamentary democracies he studied, the hypothesis that minority governments were the product of bargaining failures due to some kind of crisis could be rejected with a high degree of confidence. Finally, oversized coalitions also are not infrequent. Again according to Figures 4.1–4.3, coalition governments were formed in 16% of presidential, 11% of parliamentary, and 34% of mixed country-years *in which at least*

---

[2] This is in reference to the argument often made that, as presidential elections near, members of the president's party will try to distance themselves from him in order to avoid paying for the costs of policies implemented by the government. Altman (2000) finds evidence of this dynamic for Uruguay, and Amorim Neto (2002) claims that something similar occurs in presidential systems in general. True as this may be, one should also consider the possibility that, as elections approach, under some circumstances members of the president's party may want to identify with him in order to share in the benefits of policies implemented by the government. Moreover, the dynamics of association or dissociation from the government that may be prompted by upcoming elections is probably general in the sense that it may also occur in parliamentary democracies, with coalition members leaving the government as the constitutionally mandated election date approaches.

one party held more than half the legislative seats. This, of course, underestimates the frequency of oversized coalition governments, since some are generated when there is a minority situation. Laver and Schofield (1998:70) report that, of 218 governments observed in twelve European parliamentary democracies between 1945 and 1987, 42% were minimal winning coalitions (36% were multiparty coalitions and 6% were single-party governments), 33% were minority governments, and 25% were surplus majority coalitions. Patterns such as these cannot be accounted for if we assume purely office-seeking politicians.

The argument that connects the threat of government dissolution to party discipline is also inconsistent. While recognizing that, under presidentialism, individual legislators may profit electorally from providing specific benefits to their constituencies, it denies that such gains may also occur under parliamentarism. To see this, consider first the case of presidential democracies. Let a key presidential initiative be one that implies losses for a specific group and gains for the whole society (e.g., a measure that cuts special privileges for some constituencies). In the view under discussion, presidents have no means of inducing legislators to support this kind of proposal. Because they are office seekers, legislators will have a clear preference for policies that concentrate benefits on their constituencies and disperse the costs throughout society; consequently, they will vote against the presidential initiative in order to protect their constituencies' narrow interests. Since their actions do not affect the government's survival, legislators bear no costs by following their constituencies' preferences and collecting the benefits of such action at election time. Thus, legislators who face a choice between supporting the government (and their parties) or the specific interests of their constituencies will tend to prefer the latter because, in so doing, they maximize their chances of re-election without imposing any costs on the government (whose existence is determined exogenously).

The same cannot be said of a parliamentary system when legislators face a government initiative that concentrates costs and disperses benefits. Since dissolution and early elections are possible, legislators who behave according to their constituencies' interests are undermining the survival of the government. Hence purely office-seeking legislators will prefer (or will be induced) to follow the party line, to support the government, and in this way to guarantee the government's survival – and, of course, their own survival in office. Thus, by calling (or threatening to call) an early election and thus inviting the electorate to judge the legislator's behavior, parliamentary governments are supposed to be able to effect legislative cooperation.

Note, however, that unlike in presidential systems, there seems to be a presumption that legislators under parliamentarism will not count on obtaining electoral benefits when they act to protect their constituencies' interests. But why would the constituency punish a representative who helped to defeat a government that was pushing for policies it did not like? Thus we can see the limitation of early elections as a mechanism for achieving party discipline. Under some circumstances, representatives will follow the party line because doing so is in the interest of their constituents. Under other circumstances – for instance, when legislators believe that their constituencies will benefit from a government defeat – they can safely buck the party line, since they will be returned to office if new elections are called. Therefore, with purely office-seeking politicians, early elections in themselves are not a credible threat for inducing party discipline; something else is needed if one is to argue that the threat of dissolution leads to party discipline.

This "something else" concerns the nature of the connections between voters and parties in parliamentary and presidential systems (Kitschelt 2000). The standard argument assumes that, in parliamentary regimes, voters care about executive performance and so will base their vote on party labels, not on individual politicians. As Carey (1997:81) puts it, "where cabinet responsibility is clearly the assembly's prerogative, legislators can expect voters to evaluate their performance largely on the basis of the executive's performance, so they are more willing to submit to the discipline of party leaders." In other words, the electoral connection under parliamentarism necessarily differs from the one that prevails in the U.S. Congress, as analyzed by Mayhew (1974).

But whether voters base their votes on party labels or on legislators' personal attributes is not necessarily related to the form of government. As a matter of fact, electoral laws – not the form of government – are usually seen as the main factor determining whether voters will vote according to personal or party attributes in a given system. In Carey and Shugart's (1994) attempt to rank electoral systems according to the kind of incentives they provide, the key factor is party control over a politician's chances of being elected or re-elected (see also Wallack et al. 2003). This control, in turn, depends on access to the ballot, on the rules for transferring votes within party lists, on opportunities for voting below the party level, and on the size of electoral districts. Parties are said to be strong and capable of enforcing discipline if these factors work in such a way that parties can affect the probability that a politician will be elected.

As important as these electoral variables may be in affecting the degree of party discipline in a system – and I do not deny that they are – they cannot be the whole story. Electoral laws may provide the incentives for legislators to cultivate the personal vote (by seeking policies that have concentrated benefits and diffuse costs), but the decision-making process may deny them the means to do so (by centralizing decisions in a way that makes preferences of the individual legislator virtually irrelevant). Indeed, as Mayhew (1974) has shown, the personal vote in the U.S. Congress is closely related to the *decentralized* decision-making characteristic of its committee system. As Cox (1987) demonstrates in his analysis of nineteenth-century England, a centralized decision-making process may neutralize the electoral incentives for cultivating the personal vote. Thus, in spite of single-member districts and a "first past the post" formula for parliamentary elections, the centralization of decision in the cabinet deprived individual legislators of the ability to provide the types of policies necessary for building personal electoral bases. As a consequence, electoral contests became more and more about the policy record of the party in government than about the services provided by individual legislators.

Finally, there are some implications of the standard view of the relationship between the form of government and party discipline that are not supported by the facts. The calculus of the individual legislator under parliamentarism cannot be entirely connected with the risk of election for the simple fact that an early election is not the necessary consequence (or even the most frequent consequence) of a government dissolution. Cheibub (1998) shows that 56% of all prime ministers in 21 industrialized democracies between 1946 and 1995 changed without new elections. In the same data set he finds that 38% of changes in the party of the prime minister, 46% of changes in the partisan composition of the government, and 24% of changes in the major party in the government occurred without elections. Likewise, Cheibub and Przeworski (1999), looking at all parliamentary democracies between 1950 and 1990, find that 48% of changes in prime ministers took place for reasons other than the occurrence of an election. New elections are far from being an inevitable outcome of government dissolution in parliamentary democracies, so the costs (and risks) they represent are not necessarily high and uniformly distributed across these systems. This point is forcefully made by Mershon (1996, 1999) in her studies of coalition formation in Italy and other countries.

On the other hand, as far as presidentialism is concerned, voters are considered to be exclusively concerned with what their representatives can do for them regardless of those representatives' contributions to the success or failure of the executive. If this is true then they should use their two votes – for president and for legislator – independently. Yet there is considerable evidence indicating that voters do tend to associate their vote in presidential and legislative elections; this is why concurrent presidential and legislative elections tend to reduce the number of political parties competing in a given political system (Shugart and Carey 1992; Jones 1995; Shugart 1995; Golder 2006). Hence, if voters connect their votes in executive and legislative elections, then legislators will have incentives to support the executive on some key votes. Their seats may depend on the good performance of the president.

In conclusion, informal arguments that connect the form of government to levels of party discipline are based on an untenable assumption about politicians in presidential systems – that they are purely office seekers. This assumption is untenable because it is incompatible with the emergence of minority governments and oversized coalitions, which are not infrequent in democratic systems. Moreover, the argument is inconsistent because it is based on an asymmetric view about the connections between politicians and voters in each type of democratic system. If purely office-seeking legislators are assumed to populate parliamentary systems as they do presidential ones, then the threat of early elections that might result from a vote of no confidence in the government is not entirely credible: legislators who contribute to bringing down a government while protecting their constituents' interests are not likely to be punished at the polls by those constituents. In order for such a threat to have teeth, something beyond the vote of no confidence per se must also exist – namely, an electoral system that generates partisan (as opposed to individualistic) linkages between voters and legislators. But the electoral system is not endogenous to the form of government; partisan linkages exist in presidential systems in the same way that individualistic linkages exist in parliamentary ones. We must therefore conclude that the form of government is not itself sufficient to drastically differentiate parliamentary and presidential systems when it comes to party discipline.

Formal Arguments

Formal arguments linking parliamentary regimes with legislative vote cohesion have been developed by Huber (1996), Baron (1998), and Diermeier and Feddersen (1998). Huber (1996) develops a spatial model of the interaction between the prime minister, the cabinet, and the prime minister's majority in which he highlights the role of vote-of-confidence procedures in legislative outcomes. Baron (1998) and Diermeier and Feddersen (1998) use a model of legislative bargaining to show how confidence procedures that characterize parliamentary democracies affect legislative cohesion. These papers represent important advances in the understanding of the functioning of parliamentary democracies, but they do not necessarily provide a compelling argument to the effect that levels of legislative cohesion will be higher in parliamentary over presidential democracies.

To begin with, the models proposed by Huber, on the one hand, and by Baron and Diermeier–Feddersen, on the other, differ in at least one important aspect.

Whereas the latter models are explicit in setting up a situation in which there are conflicts of interest among political parties, so that legislative cohesion is not a function of similarity of preferences, this is not the case in Huber's analysis. In his case, there is an area of the policy space in which the preferences of all the actors overlap; the model shows that the agenda power of the prime minister will allow her to pick, in that area, the policy that she prefers. Legislators who go against the government do so in order to signal to their constituents that they are in fact defending their interests. They do so, however, knowing that the prime minister will choose a policy that they prefer over the status quo. The contribution of Huber's model, in this sense, is not to show that vote-of-confidence procedures will induce high levels of party discipline in a context of conflicting preferences but rather to show, as he himself notes (Huber 1996:279), that prime ministers are strategically well positioned to obtain policies that are to their liking and hence that political parties are constrained in their ability to shape policies after the government is formed.

Baron (1998) and Diermeier and Feddersen (1998), in contrast, explicitly model a situation in which the preferences of the party or coalition members are in conflict. The mechanism that drives their model is the control over the legislative agenda that parties have as part of the government. It is because agenda power guarantees future gains, and because the vote-of-confidence procedure allows the government to link votes on policy with the government's survival – and hence to control the legislative agenda – that parties and legislators may find it in their interest to vote against their preferences.

Underlying both models, as well as Huber's (1996:280), is the view of a presidential system such as that in the United States, where agenda-setting power lies with the legislature. However, if presidents can control the legislative agenda in much the same way as prime ministers can, then the mechanism that drives party cohesion in parliamentary regimes can also operate under presidentialism. When considering the full range of existing presidential regimes, we saw in Chapter 4 that the United States is exceptional in granting little or no legislative powers to the executive. Therefore, presidential regimes are compatible with executives that hold a high level of agenda and legislative powers. The specific institutional procedure whereby this is achieved is obviously different from parliamentarism, but the end result may very well be the same.

Finally, as Diermeier and Feddersen (1998) state, the no-confidence procedure may be a sufficient institutional feature to induce legislative vote cohesion, but it is not a necessary one. Other mechanisms may exist, some of which are institutional (e.g., centralized legislative organization and executive agenda and legislative powers) and some of which are not. In this context, Medina's (2001) analysis is particularly relevant since it shows how legislative voting cohesion can emerge from pure congruence of preferences. The implication of his analysis for the discussion here is that it demonstrates how cohesion does not necessarily depend on disciplinary measures (such as the vote of no confidence) and can be obtained under any institutional setup.

It is thus not at all clear that the existence of cohesive legislative blocs is endogenous to the regime type. We should not presume that presidential regimes will invariably generate low levels of party discipline in the legislature, or that presidents will be unable to count on consistent and disciplined majorities in order to govern.

Centralization of the Decision-Making Process

From the constitutional point of view, all legislators – whether in presidential or parliamentary regimes – have the same rights and duties. Their mandates are the same regardless of the number of votes received in the electorate, their party affiliation, their degree of seniority in the legislature, and so on. Each legislator has the same right to propose legislation, to amend propositions made by others, and to participate in the process of deliberation. In addition, each legislator's vote has the same weight. In principle, then, legislatures are egalitarian institutions.

Of course, the reality is quite different. In order to handle its workload, legislatures organize themselves in a variety of ways and adopt internal rules that regulate individual legislative rights and access to resources (Krehbiel 1992:2). Because legislative rights and resources are not distributed in a uniform way, it follows that legislators are not all equal. The chances that individual legislators have to influence the order of business and to have a say in decision making depends upon the legislative rights granted to them by the internal rules of their assembly. Hence, legislative organization affects the structure of the decision-making process and the influence of individual legislators in policy decisions.

Discussions of legislative organization usually make reference to two paradigmatic cases: Great Britain and the United States, with (respectively) a centralized and a decentralized legislature and, as we know, a parliamentary and a presidential form of democracy. Many arguments about decision making in democracies contrast these two systems and assume, often implicitly, that all legislatures (as well as the decision-making process) are centralized under parliamentarism and decentralized under presidentialism.

The British parliament is indeed characterized by the complete control of the cabinet over the legislative agenda. Government bills are considered under a special calendar that gives them priority over bills introduced by individual members of parliament and, as a consequence, parliamentary minorities have no way to "close the gates" to governmental proposals. In addition, individual members of parliament are often restricted in their capacity to amend government bills. For instance, since the beginning of the eighteenth century the government has had the sole prerogative to initiate measures that increase expenditures (Loewenberg and Patterson 1979:249). It is rare nowadays for the budget presented by the cabinet to be modified by the parliament. In fact, given the high expectations that it will be approved as submitted, "a provisional resolution places it into effect on the day it is delivered, though months may pass before its final enactment" (Loewenberg and Patterson 1979:250).

Because of the government's control over the agenda, legislative output is marked by a high rate of success for the executive's initiatives. Propositions made by the cabinet had a 97% chance of being approved for the 1945–1978 period, whereas bills introduced by backbenchers, irrespective of their party affiliation, had virtually no chance of being approved (Rose 1986:11). This means that the cabinet introduces almost all laws that are approved in parliament. The government legislative success rests on disciplined party support, and cabinet defeats are rare events. The cabinet entirely monopolizes the law-making process and, for that matter, all the decisions about policy.

The U.S. Congress, on the contrary, is supposed to be a quite decentralized body, organized as it is around its strong committee system. In this view, the committee system allows legislators to have a say in decisions related to policy areas that are of importance for their electoral survival. The story, or at least one of them, goes like this. Each committee has the monopoly to initiate legislation in its own policy jurisdiction. Committees report bills to the floor and, for reasons that are not entirely clear, the floor accepts the bill as reported by the committee. Political parties do not control the assignment process of legislators to specific committees; rather, the process is described as one of self-selection: legislators pick the committee with jurisdiction over the policy area that will bring them the highest electoral payoff. Electoral considerations dictate that politicians prefer distributive, pork-barrel policies. The committee system in the U.S. Congress provides the organizational means to make these distributive policies possible.

Hence, with Great Britain as the prototype of executive–legislative relations in parliamentary regimes and the United States as the prototypical presidential system, it follows that Tsebelis (1995:325) is correct when he states: "In parliamentary systems the executive (government) controls the agenda, and the legislature (parliament) accepts or rejects proposals, while in presidential systems the legislature makes the proposal and the executive (the president) signs or vetoes them." The prototypical parliamentary regime is thus one in which the government has complete control over the legislative agenda; the rights of the individual members of parliament are "expropriated" and monopolized by the cabinet. All that individual legislators can do is support the party line. Voters know that this is all legislators can do and thus have no incentive to cast their ballots on the basis of a candidate's personal characteristics. Therefore, by control of the legislative agenda, parliamentarism should lead to party votes in the electorate and to party discipline in the parliament.

The prototype of a presidential regime, in turn, is one in which the organization of congress preserves the rights of individual representatives so that they have a say on policy decisions. Separation of power leads to independent legislators who act on the basis of their individual electoral needs; in response to these needs, they build personal ties with their constituencies. One is thus led to expect that legislatures in presidential regimes will have strong committee systems and that representatives will be elected on the basis of the personal ties they build with their constituencies. Consequently, parties will play smaller roles and legislative behavior will be more individualistic.

Yet, as Cox and McCubbins (1993) have demonstrated, the role of the majority party in shaping legislators' behavior is far from trivial. Moreover, as we already know, presidential systems are not all alike in the powers they grant the president. As Shugart and Carey (1992) have demonstrated (and as we saw in Chapter 4), they vary considerably in terms of the degree of legislative powers they grant the president: to use the language of Mainwaring and Shugart (1997), they have both reactive (veto) and proactive (exclusive legislative initiative and decree) powers and thus are able to do much more than simply sign or veto bills proposed by the legislature. Presidents can, in fact, set the legislative agenda and in this way, much like prime ministers in parliamentary systems, protect the cohesion of the government coalition against the opportunistic behavior of its own members. Thus, rather than being a way of creating checks and balances – a mechanism for checking the power of the majority (the interpretation we find in the context of the U.S. constitution) – presidential legislative powers can also be used as a weapon of the majority. In this sense, separation of powers in presidential regimes is not as complete as it is usually considered to be; the fusion of executive and legislative powers is not entirely absent from presidential systems.

Finally, the organization of congress, particularly in conjunction with the degree of control the executive has over the legislative agenda, also influences the behavior of individual legislators in presidential systems. Legislators act in a constrained environment. If they want to influence policy, they must do so

127

according to the rules of procedure of the body they belong to and within the terms set by the president. Thus, the incentives to cultivate the personal vote that stem from the electoral arena may be entirely neutralized in the legislature through a distribution of legislative rights that favors the executive.

In this context Brazil is of central interest, for it provides an example of the far-reaching effects that centralization of decision making has on neutralizing individualistic behavior inside congress. The system produced by its 1988 constitution is frequently cited as the foremost example of bad institutional design. All of the institutional features that are considered to be problematic for governance seem to have been enshrined in the constitution: a strong presidential regime; a proportional representation formula for legislative elections with large districts; permissive party and electoral legislation (e.g., open-list and low party control over access to the ballot). In such a setup, the party system is bound to be fragmented and presidents can be almost certain that their party will not control a majority of seats in both legislative houses. And even if they did, parties would be highly undisciplined – making the majority status of the president a mere formality (Mainwaring 1991; Sartori 1994:113). Hence, in order to gain approval for their agenda, presidents would use their strong legislative powers, which could lead in turn to conflict and paralysis. To paraphrase Sartori (1994), the system created in 1988 was nothing but hopeless.

Yet the performance of the post-1988 Brazilian regime is completely at odds with what we would expect on the basis of this institutional analysis. Brazilian presidents of this period, when compared with prime ministers in parliamentary regimes, have had great success enacting their legislative agenda. Presidents introduced 86% of the bills enacted since 1988, and these bills were approved at a rate of 78%. Presidents have formed coalitions to govern and have been able to reliably obtain the support of the parties that belong to the government coalition in approving its legislation: the average discipline of the presidential coalition, defined as voting in accordance with the public recommendation of the government leader in the floor, was 85.6%. This support is sufficient to make a presidential defeat in a roll-call vote an extremely rare event. Thus, despite the "centrifugal" characteristics of Brazilian presidentialism – as indicated by its permissive party and electoral legislation – presidents have been able to govern by relying on the support of a disciplined coalition (Figueiredo and Limongi 2000a).

This outcome, according to Figueiredo and Limongi (2000a,b), is a result of (i) the way the Brazilian congress is organized and (ii) the president's ability to control the legislative agenda. The Brazilian congress is highly centralized. Legislative rights heavily favor party leaders, who are taken to be perfect agents of their caucuses (*bancadas*) when it comes to most procedural decisions (e.g., the request for roll-call votes, the closing of debates, and most importantly the designation of a bill as urgent for purposes of consideration). The urgency request is a kind of "discharge petition": it removes the bill from the committee and forces its immediate (within 24 hours) deliberation by the floor. Bills that are designated as urgent cannot be freely amended: only amendments signed by 20% of the lower house are accepted, which implies that only those amendments supported by party leaders will be considered. As Figueiredo and Limongi (2000a:157) have shown, the approval of the urgency petition is strongly associated with a bill's success. Centralization thus limits the legislative rights that individual members of congress would need in order to influence legislation.

In turn, the Brazilian presidents – thanks to their constitutional legislative powers – have direct influence over the legislative agenda. Using its decree power, the executive places what it deems to be the most relevant and pressing issues on the agenda. Moreover, the president can influence the pace of ordinary legislation by requesting urgency for the consideration of specific bills (which will give each house 45 days to deliberate on them). The president also has the exclusive right to initiate legislation that concerns the budget, taxes, and public administration. Therefore, the executive monopolizes legislative initiative in the most crucial areas of policy making.

As Limongi and Figueiredo (1998) argue, it is through participation in the government that individual legislators, via their parties, obtain access to the resources they need for political survival: policy influence and patronage. Party leaders exchange political support of the government's legislative initiatives for access to policy influence and patronage. In so doing, the executive provides party leaders with the means to punish backbenchers who do not follow the party line: their share of patronage may be denied. Given the resources it controls, the executive in turn is well positioned to induce the support of party leaders. The latter become, in fact, the main brokers in the bargaining between the executive and the legislators, ensuring that the government will obtain reliable and consistent legislative support. Contrary to the view proposed by Ames (2001), Samuels (2003), and Pereira and Mueller (2004), Brazilian presidents do not need to bargain on a case-by-case basis; they can demand support for their entire legislative agenda. Once the government is formed and benefits are distributed among the members of the coalition, the president – with the help of party leaders – may threaten representatives and actually punish those who do not follow the party line. Hence, we must reiterate that the actual pattern of legislative–executive relations in Brazil's presidential regimes is rather different from the expectation that follows from its electoral and partisan legislation.

It should be clear by now that separation of powers does not necessarily imply decentralized decision making. Institutional analyses that stress the negative effects of separation of powers – and that recommend specific, often restrictive, electoral laws as a corrective to these effects – miss the point entirely. Presidentialism neither implies nor requires decentralized decision making or legislative–executive conflict. Once one allows the possibility of coalition governments existing also in presidential regimes, as we now know they do, the degree of overlap between the executive and legislative majorities must be adjusted. Presidential control over the agenda becomes a weapon to be used by the majority, not against it. Thus we can see that presidents are not necessarily as distinct from prime ministers as is normally assumed. We have shown that the outcomes usually associated exclusively with parliamentarism (e.g., executive success and dominance of legislative output obtained through disciplined parties) can be found even in such "hopeless" presidential regimes as Brazil's.

Now, if presidential regimes are not all alike then neither are parliamentary systems. That the government will control the legislative agenda does not follow from the definition of parliamentarism. Neither is it necessary that the legislative rights of private members will be curtailed in parliamentary regimes. Committees may have considerable powers in parliamentary assemblies and may erect barriers to the executive agenda.[3] The weakness of individual members of parliament that characterizes Great Britain is not inherent to parliamentary governments, as the cases of Italy (after 1945) and France (in the Third and Fourth Republic) amply illustrate. In both cases, the government had no control over the legislative agenda, committees had considerable power, and the rights of individual legislators were not "expropriated."

In France until 1911, it was the Chamber presidents who defined the legislative agenda. After this date, a Conference of Presidents assumed control over the agenda's definition. The government was represented in the Conference, but it was not until 1955 that internal rules were revised so that voting in the Conference of Presidents was weighted by the proportion of seats held by each party. The proposed agendas had to be approved by the Chamber, and this "often became an occasion for a vote of non confidence through a device called 'interpellation'" (Andrews 1978:471). Hence, the government did not have firm control over the legislative agenda. On several occasions, interpellation led to a judgment on the government's legislative agenda and its subsequent downfall.

---

[3] Note that variation in committee structure and power is used by Strøm (1990) to account for the emergence of minority governments in pure parliamentary democracies.

Moreover, committees could act as veto players, since a report from the committee was necessary for consideration of a bill by the floor. The government could expedite a committee report but could not squelch one. Therefore, committees could respond to government pressure with an unsatisfactory report. According to Andrews (1978), the Third and Fourth Republic placed few restrictions on the ability of private members to propose initiatives that would increase expenditures and reduce revenues. Given the absence of serious restrictions, the government's financial projects were often, in his words, "butchered in parliament" (p. 485).

In Italy one finds the same pattern: the parliament's independence to set the legislative agenda, strong committees, and legislative rights that grant individual members of the assembly significant capacity to influence decisions. In the Italian parliament, the president of each house, not the government, defines the legislative agenda. Bills introduced by the government have no special calendar or precedence over private members' bills. Article 72 of the Italian constitution grants standing committees the authority to pass laws, which they have done in profusion. Whether a bill is or is not to be considered by the floor is decided unilaterally by the president of each legislative house; according to Di Palma (1976), bills that were not considered by the floor always had a much greater chance of becoming law than those that were. Hence, in order to defeat a governmental proposition, a house president need only schedule it for the consideration and vote of the whole house.

In addition to being endowed with the power to pass legislation, Italian committees are not subject to having the bills they are considering discharged by the government. The committee chairmen are autonomous in defining their agenda and even in convening their committee. Hence committees are not only important decision-making bodies but also can act as veto players. As for individual members of parliament, roll-call votes (before the 1988 reform) were secret and could easily be requested at any stage of the law-making process (Cotta 1990:77). Governments consequently fell prey to the *franco attiratori,* members of the majority who voted against government bills, who could not be sanctioned by the government or by their parties.

These are obviously not examples of parliamentary regimes at their best; both are often cited as examples of pathological parliamentary systems and have been either reformed or abandoned. However, this serves to underscore the point I wish to make here: that the instability of these systems was a consequence not so much of the form of government as of the way decision making was organized. Although policy performance is important for the survival of a democratic regime, we cannot deduce it from the basic constitutional principle that defines this regime. Policy making under parliamentarism is not necessarily centralized, so the government is not always successful in having its policy proposals approved. Similarly, policy making under presidentialism is not necessarily decentralized, and governments are not invariably immobilized in their capacity to approve their legislative agendas.

Studying Party Discipline across Systems

The question of whether party discipline (or cohesion) is higher in parliamentary than in presidential systems is not well formulated.

First, as the discussion in the previous sections has indicated, there is more than one mechanism for generating equal levels of party discipline. The confidence vote is neither necessary nor sufficient for us to observe a group of legislators with heterogeneous preferences voting together. Thus, although parliamentary systems may, ceteris paribus, have higher levels of party discipline than presidential systems, this does not preclude the existence of other mechanisms that parties and the government may use in presidential systems to foster discipline. Party discipline may be generated in a variety of ways, and the lack of a vote-of-confidence procedure in presidential systems need not handicap them when it comes to eliciting support from legislators and political parties.

A second (and related) point is that the average level of party discipline is not really what matters. We care about party discipline, at least in the context of discussions related to forms of government and governability, because of its role in generating predictable and consistent legislative support for democratic governments. In this sense, what matters is not whether parties in a given system are always disciplined but whether they are sufficiently disciplined to allow governments to govern – that is, to allow a government to count on the support of a sufficient number of legislators to pass and implement its legislative program.

The qualifying "sufficient" is central in this discussion. Discipline, from the point of view of a political party, is not necessarily something it always wants to maximize. Since any vote represents, for an individual representative, a potential source of conflict between her own preferences, the preferences of her constituency, and the preferences of the political party to which she belongs, it follows that maximizing party discipline may be a waste of resources from the leadership's perspective. If a majority sufficient to approve a measure is already forthcoming, it may well be in the party leadership's interest to allow some members to vote against the party line in order to save face with their own supporters. Discipline is something that parties want to be able to impose when needed. Thus, the question is not which system generates higher levels of discipline; the question is whether governments in these systems can count on the support of a consistent and predictable legislative majority. As we have seen in previous chapters, we cannot say that one of these systems is constitutionally handicapped in generating such support.

Moreover, the extent to which individual legislators vote together is not a systemic attribute but rather an attribute of individual parties. The degree of variation across parties is not to be neglected, even in systems characterized by relatively high levels of overall discipline. Davidson-Schmich (2003) reports that the average rice index [4] for the Social Democratic Party in the German Parliament for the period 1953–1957 was 0.99; it was 0.90 for the Christian Democratic Party and 0.80 for the Free Democratic Party. According to Depauw (2003), whereas 99% of the votes taken by the Communist Party in the French Parliament between 1988 and 1993 had no dissent, the rate was only 90% for the Socialist Party (in government throughout the period), 76% for the RPR, 75% for the UDC, and 70% for the UDF. Likewise, the average proportion of Brazilian legislators who voted according to their party's recommendations between 1989 and 1998 varied: 98% for the left-wing PT, 93% for the right-wing PFL, 91% for the centrist PSDB, and 85% for the catchall PMDB (Figueiredo and Limongi 2000a).

Finally, the empirical analysis of party discipline across political systems is plagued with problems that can be resolved (if at all) only with great difficulty. What is the appropriate research design for studying the issue of party discipline across systems? Given that discipline can be observed only through roll-call votes, one might suppose that the best design would be to compare such votes across parties and across systems. This is done by Carey (2004) in the most ambitious project to date that studies this issue. However, it is not clear how great the payoff is from such an effort.

In its most recent version, Carey's analysis investigates two ways that a presidential system could affect levels of legislative party unity. The first way is through the familiar mechanism of a vote of (no) confidence. The second way is through a novel mechanism: the pull that a president can exert over legislators from his own party, which can be in a direction other than that exerted by the party's legislative leadership. Based on roll-call data for seventeen countries and using the party as the unit of analysis, Carey finds that the existence of a vote-of-confidence procedure has no effect on average levels of vote unity. Having a president, however, does make government parties less united in their

---

[4] An index of vote cohesion that is defined as the difference between the percentage who voted Yes and the percentage who voted No in any given vote.

vote, thus providing evidence for what Carey calls the "competing principals" hypothesis.[5]

Even though these results support the notion that the vote of confidence is not necessary for legislative party unity, this conclusion must be taken with a large grain of salt given the inherent difficulties of cross-national analyses of roll-call votes. By this I mean that the rules generating observed roll calls vary considerably across countries, which implies that the set of votes on which the analysis is based may be qualitatively different from one country to another. Thus, in addition to variation in the number of roll calls per country that is due to the difficulty of obtaining data on recorded votes, there is variation in the kinds of votes that are recorded in the first place. This latter variation is not due to bad record keeping; rather, it is due to the fact that the rules requiring that some votes be taken by roll call vary across countries. That this is a nontrivial problem may be inferred from Carey's summary data: whereas vote unity per party is calculated on the basis of 152 roll calls per month for Poland, 136 for the Czech Republic, 77 for Nicaragua, and 47 for the United States, it is calculated on the basis of only 1.5 roll calls per month for Argentina, 1.1 for Uruguay, 0.92 for Guatemala, and 0.31 for Ecuador. It is unlikely that these differences are due entirely to differences in overall legislative activity in these countries. The point here is not to minimize the invaluable effort that was put into assembling this data. Rather, it is to emphasize that the study of party discipline based on a cross-national design may be plagued by so much data heterogeneity as to make inferences practically useless.

Party discipline may be higher, on average, in parliamentary than in presidential democracies. But this hardly implies that presidents are unable to count on the systematic, consistent, and predictable support from a legislative contingent that will allow them to govern. Although deprived of one mechanism that may be used to induce party cohesion – the vote of (no) confidence that characterizes parliamentary democracies – presidents may count on other mechanisms to induce similar levels of cohesion. Thus, the link from separation of powers to low levels of party discipline – which supposedly compounds the problems of

---

[5] In addition to the extent to which parties vote together, Carey analyzes the extent to which they lose a vote owing to dissent among their ranks (RLOSER). This latter measure, however, is not straightforward; it makes sense only if a party is pivotal for a vote, since otherwise it does not matter how its members voted. Moreover, the effect of the confidence mechanism on the probability that a party will lose because of internal dissent is found to be the opposite of what Carey expects: parties in systems with the confidence vote are *more* likely to lose because of dissent than parties in pure presidential systems (Carey 2004:15 and Table 3). Carey offers no explanation for this finding.

governability in presidential systems and leads to the breakdown of democracy – is a false one.

This, then, concludes our examination of the steps that, in the Linzian view of presidential democracies depicted in Figure 1.1, yield higher levels of democratic breakdown when compared to parliamentary democracies. It should be clear by now that presidential institutions (or the incentives and behavior they generate) cannot be singled out as the factor that causes the instability of presidential democracies. As I hope to have demonstrated in this and the previous two chapters, such a view makes sense only if one adopts a rather simplistic conception of politicians' goals and the way politicians respond to institutional inducements.

6

What Makes Presidential Democracies Fragile?

I have argued in the previous chapters that intrinsic features of presidentialism are not the reason why presidential democracies are more prone to breakdown. Little in the chain of reasoning that leads from separation of powers to the instability of presidential regimes can be supported either theoretically or empirically. Yet the fact remains that democracies tend to have shorter lives when they are presidential. Recall that, for the 1946–2002 period, the expected life of a presidential democracy was 24 years versus 58 for parliamentary ones. Why, then, are presidential democracies more likely to die?

In this chapter I argue that the difference in the survival rates of parliamentary and presidential democracies can be accounted for by the conditions under which these democracies have existed. However, these are not the conditions that have been identified by the extant literature. Thus, I first show that the usual suspects – level of economic development, size of the country, geographic location – are not sufficient to account for the differences in survival rates across democratic systems. Although some of these conditions do matter, they do not fully eliminate these differences. I then argue that some democracies emerge in countries where the probability of a democratic breakdown is high, regardless of the type of democracy that exists, and that presidential democracies have emerged more frequently in such countries. Thus, the fragility of presidential democracies is a function not of presidentialism per se but of the fact that presidential democracies have existed in countries where the environment is inhospitable for any kind of democratic regime. Given that countries are mostly "stuck" with their broad constitutional framework, I conclude the chapter with a discussion of easier-to-implement, subconstitutional reforms aimed at improving, rather than abolishing, existing presidential democracies.

Table 6.1. *Characteristics of Parliamentary and Presidential Democracies*

	Parliamentary[a]	Presidential
Per capita income (1995 PPP$)	6,764	4,467
Economic growth[b]	2.48%	1.59%
In small countries[c]	25.40%	8.49%
In Latin America[d]	0.09%	62.30%

[a] Includes mixed systems.
[b] Annual change in per capita income.
[c] Population less than 1 million in 1980.
[d] Nineteen Spanish- and Portuguese-speaking countries.

Income, Growth, Size, and Location

Parliamentarism is more frequent in wealthier countries, where democracy is much more likely, indeed certain, to survive (Przeworski et al. 2000). It is more frequent in countries that generate relatively high rates of economic growth (Alvarez 1997). Shugart and Mainwaring (1997), in turn, suggest that the difference in survival between the two types of regimes may involve location – presidential regimes tend to be located in Latin America and Africa, parliamentary regimes in Europe – and country size: parliamentary regimes tend to exist in small countries. These factors constitute the menu of exogenous conditions that have been invoked to explain why presidential democracies have shorter lives than parliamentary ones.

Such explanations are plausible and, as Table 6.1 indicates, have prima facie empirical validity. The average per capita income is 1.5 times higher in parliamentary democracies, and the average rate of economic growth is nearly 1.5 times higher under parliamentarism than under presidentialism. Parliamentary regimes are more frequent in small countries: about one quarter of them (against 8% of presidential democracies) are in countries that had 1980 populations of less than a million. And about 60% of presidential democracies are located in Latin America, whereas less than 1% of parliamentary ones – specifically, two years of mixed democracy in Brazil in 1961 and 1962 – are in this region.

Even so, none of these factors is sufficient to account for the difference in survival rates across democratic regimes. Descriptive patterns are clear, as Table 6.2 shows. Although the probability that democracy would die falls steadily as per capita income increases under both parliamentarism and presidentialism, presidential democracies are more likely to die than parliamentary ones at all

Table 6.2. *Transition Probabilities in Parliamentary and Presidential Democracies by Economic and Geographic Conditions*

	All	Parliamentary	Presidential
Per capita income (1985 PPP$)			
Less than 3,000	0.0453	0.0402	0.0517
Between 3,000 and 6,000	0.0153	0.0083	0.0311
More than 6,000	0.0009	0.0000	0.0059
Economic growth			
Positive	0.0127	0.0076	0.0264
Negative	0.0434	0.0331	0.0610
Country size (population)			
Small	0.0062	0.0053	0.0137
Large	0.0215	0.0137	0.0373
Location			
Latin America	0.0436	0.0000	0.0438
Outside of Latin America	0.0128	0.0116	0.0210

Note: Transition probabilities are defined as TJK_i/J, where TJK is the number of transitions away from democracy and J is the number of democracies.

income levels. Short-term economic performance also matters, but it does not explain why presidential democracies die more frequently than parliamentary ones: the expected life of presidential democracies when the economy is doing well is not much higher than that of parliamentary democracies when the economy is doing poorly. Although democracies in small countries do indeed have longer expected lives, presidential democracies die more frequently than parliamentary ones in small and large countries both.

Probit analyses confirm these findings, as columns 1–3 of Table 6.3 demonstrate. Per capita income matters for the survival of democracy, as Przeworski et al. (2000) have demonstrated. Economic growth also matters, although this effect should be viewed with caution given that growth may be endogenous to the form of government (Przeworski et al. 2000). Finally, population size has no effect on the survival of democracy. Note that, even after controlling for these factors, presidential democracies are still more likely to become a dictatorship than parliamentary ones. The story with Latin America is more complex and will be the subject of subsequent sections. For the moment, let me say that democracies are considerably more unstable in this region than elsewhere

Table 6.3. *Effect of Presidentialism on Democratic Breakdown*

	Model						
	1	2	3	4	5	6	7
Per capita income	−0.2227 (0.031)			−0.2287 (0.000)	−0.2432 (0.000)	0.9994 (0.003)	−0.2435 (0.000)
Growth		−0.0416 (0.000)					
Population			−0.001 (0.388)				
Presidential democracy	0.2840 (0.030)	0.3944 (0.001)	0.5354 (0.000)	0.0591 (0.691)	0.0518 (0.709)	1.3469 (0.234)	0.0487 (0.771)
Military legacy				0.5386 (0.000)	0.4576 (0.001)	1.7052 (0.021)	0.4570 (0.001)
"Latin America"							0.0048 (0.979)
Constant	−1.4459 (0.000)			−1.5896 (0.000)	−1.4943 (0.000)		−1.4936 (0.000)
N	2446	2386	2530	2446	2446	2446	2446
Log likelihood	−199.76	−220.89	−204.18	−193.13			
Wald χ^2					49.74 (0.000)	26.18 (0.000)	50.36 (0.000)

Notes: Dependent variable is transitions to dictatorship; p-values in parentheses. Models 1–4, pooled probit; models 5 and 7, population-averaged probit with Huber–White variance; model 6, Cox survival model with standard errors adjusted for clustering on countries (entries are hazard rates).

(1 in 19 democracies die if they are in Latin America, versus 1 in 70 elsewhere), although presidential democracies still die more frequently than parliamentary democracies if they are located outside of Latin America: 1 in 55 against 1 in 88.[1]

---

[1] One more possible explanation for the difference between parliamentarism and presidentialism is income distribution. Unfortunately, data on income distribution across countries and time are highly sparse and not entirely comparable. The most comprehensive available data set (Deininger and Squire 1996) covers only 10.3% and 13.6% of the country-years for parliamentary and presidential democracies, respectively. According to these data, incomes are more unequally distributed in presidential democracies (average Gini coefficient is 43.3 against 36 for parliamentary democracies). However, presidential democracies face higher risks of collapsing into a dictatorship regardless of whether the Gini coefficient is below or above the average. Therefore, given the existing data, income inequality is not what generates the difference in survival between presidential and parliamentary democracies.

Military–Presidential Nexus

Consider column 4 in Table 6.3, where a variable indicating "military legacy" is added to a model of democratic survival that also contains variables for per capita income and presidentialism.[2] "Military legacy" is coded 1 if the dictatorship preceding the current democracy was headed by a professional military (see Appendix 6.1 for the coding of types of dictatorships). Once this legacy is taken into account, presidentialism has no effect on the longevity of democracy, and the effect of per capita income remains the same as it was before. If we control for unobserved determinants of the probability of transition to dictatorship (column 5), then the effect of presidentialism remains null and the impact of military legacy is only slightly attenuated. A similar picture emerges if a survival model is used, which accounts for the possibility of time dependency and the fact that democracies were not observed beyond December 31, 2002: as column 6 shows, democracies that follow military dictatorships are 70% more likely to die than those that follow civilian dictatorships; the effect of presidential democracies, in contrast, cannot be safely distinguished from null. Thus, what kills democracies is not presidentialism but rather their military legacy. Since presidential democracies tend to follow military dictatorships more frequently than they follow civilian dictatorships, presidential democracies will die more frequently than parliamentary democracies. Thus there is a military–presidential nexus that accounts for the relatively high level of instability of presidential democracies.

To get the sense of the effect of military legacy on the survival chances of different democratic regimes, consider Table 6.4. This table presents the distribution of democracies, the number of democratic breakdowns, the probability of a democratic breakdown, the expected life of the democratic system (calculated as the inverse of the probability of a democratic breakdown), and its relative frequency – all conditioned on the type of dictatorship that preceded the current democracy. Thus, from panel A in Table 6.4 we learn that there were 133 country-years of parliamentary democracies (during the 1946–2002 period) that were preceded by military dictatorships and that seven of these were cases of democratic breakdown. This means that parliamentary democracies that followed a military dictatorship during this period had a 0.0526 probability of becoming a dictatorship, which is equivalent to an expected life of 19 years. Of

---

[2] Growth of per capita income was not included owing to possible endogeneity; population size was not included because it does not matter for democratic survival.

all parliamentary democracies that existed between 1946 and 2002, 30.23% of them were preceded by a military dictatorship.

Table 6.4 (panel A) shows, to begin with, that the survival chances of democracies of any type differ considerably depending on their origin: the column labeled "all" indicates that those democracies that follow a dictatorship led by civilians are expected to last for 89 years, whereas those that followed a dictatorship led by the military are expected to last for only 20 years. At the same time, presidential democracies are more likely to follow military dictatorships, whereas parliamentary (and mixed) democracies are more likely to follow civilian dictatorships: two thirds of the observed presidential democracies – as opposed to less than a third of parliamentary (and mixed) democracies – follow dictatorships led by the military. The military–presidential nexus is the product of these two facts: that democracies following military dictatorships are more likely to become a dictatorship and that presidential democracies are more likely to follow military dictatorships. It is the concurrence of these facts that accounts for the higher overall regime instability of presidential democracies. As we can see in the table, once the current democracy's authoritarian legacy is held constant, presidential and parliamentary democracies that followed military dictatorships both face relatively short lifetimes: about 19 years for pure parliamentary and presidential democracies, 24 years if we add parliamentary and mixed democracies.

Thus, while democracies that follow military dictatorships have much shorter lives regardless of their institutional form, presidential ones are much more likely to succeed military than civilian dictatorships. Hence, presidential democracies are more likely to become a dictatorship than parliamentary ones. To see this, assume that democratic regimes emerged with equal likelihood from civilian or military dictatorships. To use the figures in panel A of Table 6.4, let the probability that a democracy of any type will follow a civilian (resp., military) dictatorship be 0.5323 (resp., 0.4677). The expected probability of a transition to dictatorship is given by the sum of two products: the transition probability of democracies that follow a military dictatorship times the proportion of democracies that follow a military dictatorship; and the transition probability of democracies that follow a civilian dictatorship times the proportion of democracies that follow a civilian dictatorship. Thus, assuming that democracies emerge with equal likelihood from military and civilian dictatorships, the expected probability that a presidential democracy would die is given by $(0.0537 \times 0.4677) + (0.0162 \times 0.5323) = 0.0337$. The expected probability that a parliamentary democracy would die is given by $(0.0526 \times 0.4677) + (0.0098 \times 0.5323) = 0.0298$. This translates into expected lives of 33 and 30 years for parliamentary and presidential democracies,

Table 6.4. *Probability of Democratic Breakdown by Authoritarian Legacy*

Dictatorships preceding current democracy	Type of democracy (current)			
	Parliamentary	Parliamentary + Mixed	Presidential	All
Panel A: Democracies between 1946 and 2002				
Military				
Country-years	133	218	484	702
Transitions to dictatorship	7	9	26	35
Probability of breakdown	0.0526	0.0413	0.0537	0.0499
Expected life (years)	19	24	19	20
Share (%)	30.23	28.31	66.21	46.77
Civilian				
Country-years	307	552	247	799
Transitions to dictatorship	3	5	4	9
Probability of breakdown	0.0098	0.0091	0.0162	0.0113
Expected life (years)	102	110	62	89
Share (%)	69.77	71.69	33.79	53.23
Total				
Country-years	440	770	731	1501
Transitions to dictatorship	10	14	30	54
Share (%)	100.00	100.00	100.00	100.00
Panel B: Post-1945 democracies only				
Military				
Country-years	122	207	421	628
Transitions to dictatorship	6	8	19	27
Probability of breakdown	0.0492	0.0386	0.0451	0.0430
Expected life (years)	20	26	22	23
Share (%)	29.26	32.60	66.72	49.61
Civilian				
Country-years	295	428	210	638
Transitions to dictatorship	3	5	2	7
Probability of breakdown	0.0102	0.0117	0.0095	0.0110
Expected life (years)	98	86	105	91
Share (%)	70.74	67.40	33.28	50.39
Panel C: Per capita income less than 1995 PPP$10,000				
Military				
Country-years	118	192	423	615
Transitions to dictatorship	6	9	19	28
Probability of breakdown	0.0508	0.0469	0.0449	0.0455
Expected life (years)	20	21	22	22
Share (%)	38.56	34.97	63.99	50.83

Dictatorships preceding current democracy	Type of democracy (current)			
	Parliamentary	Parliamentary + Mixed	Presidential	All
Civilian				
Country-years	188	357	238	595
Transitions to dictatorship	3	5	4	9
Probability of breakdown	0.0160	0.0140	0.0168	0.0151
Expected life (years)	63	71	60	66
Share (%)	61.44	65.03	36.01	49.17
Panel D: Democracies between 1900 and 2002				
Military				
Country-years	213	311	599	910
Transitions to dictatorship	9	12	27	39
Probability of breakdown	0.0423	0.0386	0.0451	0.0429
Expected life (years)	24	26	22	23
Share (%)	39.30	34.29	66.19	50.22
Civilian				
Country-years	329	596	306	902
Transitions to dictatorship	5	8	6	14
Probability of breakdown	0.0152	0.0134	0.0196	0.0155
Expected life (years)	66	75	51	64
Share (%)	60.70	65.71	33.81	49.78
Probability of breakdown regardless of origin	0.0122	0.0115	0.0354	0.0196
Expected life (years)	82	87	28	51

respectively. Thus, had democracies emerged with equal likelihood from civilian and military dictatorships, we would find that the differences in survival would be minimal across forms of government.

Panels B, C, and D of Table 6.4 show that the nexus between dictatorships led by the military and presidentialism is not a consequence of the fact that the sample is composed of democracies observed between 1946 and 2002. Panel B indicates that the survival chances of parliamentary and presidential democracies are about the same even in a sample of democracies that have emerged since 1945 (thus excluding older democracies, which are now considered to be "advanced" or "consolidated"). Panel C shows that authoritarian legacy accounts for the difference in survival rates of democracies even if we consider only those that are relatively poor. This panel excludes democracies that have per capita income above 10,000 1995 PPP$, the point above which no democratic regime has ever collapsed.[3]

Finally, panel D extends the analysis to include regimes that have existed between 1900 and 1945. There were sixteen democratic breakdowns during this period, fourteen of which took place in European countries.[4] It is conceivable that the patterns observed for the post-1945 period might not hold if we also consider these earlier democratic collapses. In fact, however, the same patterns hold, and again we find that the difference in the survival rates of parliamentary and presidential democracies disappears once we consider that presidential democracies more often follow military than civilian dictatorships.

Note that it could be presidential institutions that generate the nexus between military dictatorships and presidentialism. In this case, and in accordance with the Linzian view, presidentialism would lead to frequent political deadlocks and subsequent military intervention aimed at resolving those deadlocks. In this story, the presidential institutions would generate a domestically strong and active military establishment, which would intervene in the political process and so lead to the breakdown of democracy.

However, the military is the main agent of democratic breakdown, regardless of regime type. Table 6.5 portrays the regime transition matrix for the 1946–2002 period. The diagonal entries give the number of years during which each type of regime survived, while the off-diagonal entries count regime transitions. It turns out that when democracies collapse they most likely do so at the hands of the military, regardless of their constitutional framework: 27 out of 32 cases (85%) of breakdown of presidential democracies, and 21 out of 26 cases (81%) of breakdown of parliamentary and mixed democracies, occurred at the hands of the military. The military, it seems, does not discriminate between democracies it chooses to overthrow. Yet when the military departs from the government it generally leaves presidential regimes behind: 40 out of 60 (67% of) transitions to democracy away from military dictatorships led to a presidential democracy and 15 out of 36 (42% of) transitions to democracy away from civilian dictatorships led to a presidential democracy.

Since democracies are much more brittle when they succeed military dictatorships, and since military dictatorships are followed disproportionately often

---

[3] The difference with Przeworski et al. (2000), for whom the threshold of safety was $6,000, is due to their use of 1985 PPP dollars.

[4] They were in Austria (1934), Bulgaria (1934), Estonia (1933), Finland (1930), Germany (1933), Greece (1936), Italy (1922), Latvia (1934), Lithuania (1926), Poland (1926), Portugal (1917 and 1926), Spain (1937), and Yugoslavia (1929). The two breakdowns outside of Europe took place in Argentina (1930) and Chile (1925).

Table 6.5. *Regime Transition Matrix (country-years)*

Past regime	Current regime						TOTAL	First-order transition probability
	Parl.	Mixed	Pres.	Civilian	Military	Royal		
Parliamentary	1780	1	0	4	17	1	1803	0.0128
Mixed	1	445	1	1	4	0	452	0.0155
Presidential	0	2	870	5	27	0	904	0.0376
Civilian	11	10	15	2214	62	2	2314	0.0432
Military	11	9	40	46	1450	0	1556	0.0681
Royal	1	0	0	5	5	649	660	0.0167
TOTAL	1804	467	926	2275	1565	652	7689	0.0365

by presidential systems, presidential democracies have shorter lives. Hence, the reason for the instability of presidential democracies lies not in any intrinsic features of presidentialism but rather in the conditions under which they emerge – namely, the fact that presidential regimes tend to exist in countries that are also more likely to suffer from dictatorships led by the military.

Why a Military–Presidential Nexus?

What we know thus far is that military dictatorships tend to be followed by presidential systems and that democracies following military dictatorships have shorter lives, regardless of their institutional frameworks. Two stories, not necessarily rival, can be constructed to account for these patterns. In one the military–presidential nexus is causal; in the other it is purely coincidental, the product of historical accident. I shall argue here that the first story, while plausible, is not empirically accurate, whereas the second is compatible with empirical evidence.

The causal version of accounting for the military–presidential nexus runs as follows. The military has a preference for presidential institutions. Faced with the prospect of transition to democracy, the military prefers the hierarchical structure and concentration of authority in one national office over the explicitly partisan, contentious, and precarious existence of parliamentary governments, subject as they are to the whims of the current majority. Hence, the argument would go, when the military rules the dictatorship, transitions to democracy are more likely if civilians consent to presidential institutions. In turn, if the military has been in power, neither presidential nor parliamentary systems are able to subject it to civilian control and so reduce its role in politics. Under either system the military retains organizational autonomy and thus its capacity to intervene in politics. And once the military intervenes, neither democratic institutional system can dismantle its capacity to do so again; under this explanation, the military just happens to have an autonomous preference for presidentialism.

However, I do not believe it is historically correct to suppose that different democratic systems resulted from preferences of military dictators over the specific form of democratic government that succeeds them. For one thing, there is no reason for the military to prefer presidentialism on the grounds of preserving their capacity to return to power. Recall that the military is equally likely to overturn presidential and parliamentary democracies: one system is not any easier than the other for it to overthrow; and, per Table 6.4, democracies that succeed dictatorships headed by the military are equally vulnerable to breakdown. This again suggests that the constitutional framework does not matter for the military's ability to suspend democracy.

Moreover, as far as I can tell, there have been few cases where the issue of regime type under democracy was on the agenda during the process of extricating the military from politics and eventual transition to democracy. Suberu and Diamond (2002) report that the military in Nigeria expressed a strong preference for presidential institutions prior to preparations for the 1979 constitution. Likewise, Than (2004) reports that one of the proposals of the military regime in Myanmar is the establishment of a presidential constitution, although this is not yet a case of transition to democracy and the military preference is not conditioned on a regime transition occurring. A case that is sometimes invoked as providing evidence of a military preference for presidentialism is Brazil, where the option of a mixed system (referred to as the "parliamentary" alternative) was seriously considered in 1986–1988, when a new constitution was being written. During this process the military allied itself with the side favoring the preservation of the presidential system (Elkins 2003). However, in 1986 the transition to democracy had already occurred (the first civilian president took office in March 1985), and there is no evidence that the form of government appeared anywhere as an item of negotiation or contention during the long period of liberalization that preceded the military's relinquishing of power in 1985.

Finally, if the nexus between military dictatorships and presidentialism were the product of the preference of incumbent dictators, then we should observe that military dictatorships always leave behind presidential democracies. But this is true only for Latin America, where all transitions to democracy away from a military dictatorship led to presidential democracies. In other areas of the world the military left behind both presidential and parliamentary institutions: of 34 transitions to democracy from a military dictatorship that took place outside of Latin America, 11 were to pure parliamentarism, 9 to mixed systems, and 14 to presidentialism.[5] Thus, whereas the story based on preferences of the military seems to fit the Latin American record, it does not fit transitions that occurred elsewhere. Even in Latin America, it is telling that the transitions occurring from civilian dictatorships also led to the establishment of presidential institutions.

Thus, it is improbable that democratic systems resulted from preferences of dictators over the form of democracies that succeed them. The nexus between the nature of the previous dictatorship and the institutional form of democracy, I argue, is purely accidental – that is, a product of the historical coincidence of two independent processes. The military–presidential nexus exists because the countries where militarism remained strong at the middle of the twentieth century were also countries that had adopted presidential institutions. Had these countries adopted parliamentary institutions, the level of instability of parliamentary democracies would be much higher than what is actually observed.

Given existing professional bias in favor of seeing important outcomes as the product of causal processes, it is rather unorthodox to invoke a historical coincidence when accounting for presidential instability. Yet I believe that this account is plausible – and closer to the truth than one that views the inherent features of presidentialism as causing the instability of presidential democracies.

There are four steps in the argument that the military–presidential nexus is the product of a historical coincidence.

1. Countries vary in their propensity toward military intervention. Militarism may be a function of social structure or a phenomenon that results from exogenous and conjunctural factors, but it is not likely to be a function of presidentialism itself.
2. Countries *adopt* their initial institutions for reasons that are unrelated to the ones that lead to the occurrence of military dictatorships; in other words, whether a country adopts a presidential or a parliamentary constitution has nothing to do with its propensity toward military intervention. This is particularly true for the relatively large number of Latin American countries that adopted presidential constitutions in the nineteenth century.
3. Countries *retain* the institutions under which they consolidated their existence as a nation-state. Institutions are, in general, sticky, and major

---

[5] The transitions to pure parliamentarism took place in Ghana, Greece (twice), Lesotho, Myanmar, Pakistan, Sudan, Thailand (twice), and Turkey (twice). The transitions to mixed democracies took place in the Central African Republic, the Congo, Haiti, Madagascar, Mali, Niger (twice), Poland, and Portugal.

institutions such as the form of government are even "stickier" than less encompassing ones.

4. Military intervention took place in many countries, but it persisted (at least until the 1980s) in countries that had adopted presidential institutions. This persistence had little to do with the fact that these countries were presidential and a lot to do with the onset of the Cold War and the military's role in "fighting" it.

The instability of presidential democracies is thus due to the fact that the countries that adopted and retained presidential institutions are those where the military endured after WWII, during the Cold War. Had the military also endured in countries with parliamentary institutions, the same instability that characterizes presidential democracies would also have characterized parliamentary ones. According to this argument, then, the intrinsic features of presidentialism are not the reason why presidential democracies tend to break down more frequently than parliamentary ones. The problem of presidential democracies is not that they are "institutionally flawed." Rather, the problem is that they tend to exist in societies where democracies of any type are likely to be unstable. Therefore, the problem of survival of presidential democracies is actually the problem of survival of democracies in general, regardless of their form of government.

In the remainder of this chapter I shall develop each of these points.

Military Intervention in Politics

Countries, as we know, are not equally likely to suffer from a dictatorship; moreover, among those that experience one, countries are not equally likely to experience a dictatorship led by the military. The reasons are many and probably not systematically known. There is a large but inconclusive early literature on the causes of military intervention in politics. One story points to the degree of social and economic inequality, which generates demands that cannot be accommodated without threatening the existing order. The military intervenes to repress these demands and guarantee the survival of the status quo. This line of argument can be traced to "sociological" explanations for the intervention of the military in politics. It can also be associated with more recent (and, for that matter, more sophisticated and less functionalist) arguments such as that developed by Engerman and Sokoloff (1997), who account for the difficulties of Latin American democracies in terms of the repressive nature of the institutions that were set up to organize colonial production (see Acemoglu, Johnson, and Robinson 2001, 2002). It is argued that these institutions generate high levels of

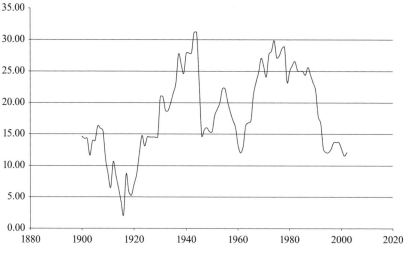

Figure 6.1   Proportion of Dictatorships Led by the Military, 1900–2002.

inequality, which in turn generate the need for repression to organize economic production, thus perpetuating themselves. Other accounts have added a "supply" factor by considering the military's corporate interests and the emergence of ideologies that promote and justify military control over the political system (Stepan 1971, 1988; O'Donnell 1973).

An alternative view is that military intervention in politics happened at a certain historical conjuncture – but that once it happened it triggered other military interventions. Londregan and Poole (1990) were probably the first to establish that coups breed other coups, trapping countries in a cycle of instability and poverty. Along these lines, Przeworski (2004), building on findings reported in Przeworski et al. (2000), shows that all countries that have experienced more than one breakdown of democracy did so at the hands of the military; this suggests that one intervention by the military is likely to lead to subsequent interventions. As for the juncture at which the military became "activated," Figure 6.1 suggests that the interwar period – beginning in 1918 but with an inflection in 1930 – is a good candidate: the proportion of authoritarian regimes led by the military increased from 6% in 1918 to 14% in 1920, to 21% in 1930, and to 31% in 1944. No other period in the twentieth century saw such a dramatic increase in the number of regimes led by the military.

The political activation of the military was not a specifically Latin American phenomenon. In 1917, only 25% of the dictatorships led by the military were located in Latin America. This number increased to 60% in 1921, but by 1926 it was down again to 33%; it increased again in 1930 to about 50%, where it remained until the end of WWII. The military dictatorships that emerged in Latin America in the first two decades of the twentieth century should not be seen as a mere continuation of the pattern of instability that characterized the region since independence. Przeworski and Curvale (2006) have shown that, by the third quarter of the nineteenth century, most Latin American countries had already put an end to the period of turmoil that followed independence. This means they were operating under a system of previously specified rules; in other words, they had stable political institutions.

Adoption of Initial Institutions

From the beginning of the nineteenth century to the breakup of the Soviet Union there have been five "waves" of independence in the world. The first, in Latin America, started in 1804 with Haiti's independence from France and lasted through the early 1820s; the second was due to the breakup of the Austro-Hungarian and Ottoman empires in the first two decades of the twentieth century; and the third came about with Africa's decolonization, which peaked in 1960 when seventeen new countries were created. The fourth wave occurred in the 1970s with the independence of small Caribbean countries; the last occurred with the breakup of the Soviet Union and Yugoslavia, leading to the emergence of nineteen new countries in Eastern and Central Europe and Central Asia.

There is probably no one set of factors that can account for the kind of constitutional framework that countries in each of these waves adopted. In nineteenth-century Latin America, after a considerable period of constitutional experimentation (Negretto and Aguilar-Rivera 2000; Gargarella 2004, 2005), all countries stabilized under presidential constitutions. European countries emerging out of the Austro-Hungarian and Ottoman empires adopted a variety of constitutions, but the majority had strong parliamentary elements. In Africa, some studies have suggested that the identity of the colonizer was central for shaping the constitution with which the new country started its life (Bernhard, Reenock, and Nordstrom 2004).

There might be factors that help explain why, given the availability of the choice, countries choose a presidential or a parliamentary constitution. Thus, it may be that the absence of a viable head of state (due to the occurrence of a revolution or an independence war) is associated with adoption of a presidential constitution, which provides for just such a head at the same time it constitutes the government. Likewise, it may be that the existence of a functioning legislature prior to independence, such as those that existed in India and in many

African and Caribbean countries under British rule, is associated with adoption of a parliamentary system in which the government is accountable to the assembly. But the point is that countries adopt constitutions at the moment they come into being; and they do so for reasons that are, if not idiosyncratic, at least related to the specific historical moments in which they emerge.

Some may object to the idea that institutions are adopted for reasons independent of the propensity toward militarism. For instance, countries where inequality is high will experience conflict and instability, which may lead to both militarism (which helps contain the escalation of conflict) and presidentialism (which allegedly provides for relatively strong leadership). In this sense, the connection between presidentialism and militarism is not a historical accident but instead the consequence of a common cause: high levels of inequality.

In fact, this argument is often given to explain the adoption of presidentialism in the Latin American countries that became independent in the nineteenth century. The idea is that these countries were polarized and far from egalitarian, which led to the emergence of the military. At the same time, as institutions were being "designed," presidentialism appeared as the preferred choice because it provided "strong" government presumably capable of dealing with conflicts generated by the high level of inequality and high degree of instability inherent to those countries. Thus, presidentialism was adopted for the same reasons that militarism emerged – contrary to my claim that they were independent from one another.

Although plausible, this explanation is historically inaccurate and presumes the existence of a choice that was not available at the time Latin American countries were adopting their constitutional frameworks. When presidential constitutions were adopted in these countries in the nineteenth century, the choice was not between presidential and parliamentary forms of government – as it may be today and might have been, for instance, when African countries became independent in the 1960s. Rather, the choice was between monarchy (regimes in which the government is headed by a hereditary leader) and republic (regimes in which the government is headed by people who cannot make any claims of heredity). Parliamentarism – that is, a form of government in which the government is dependent on the confidence of a legislative majority – simply did not exist as an option at the time that the Americas, Latin and otherwise, were crafting their basic institutions. As Cox (1987) has shown in his book on the emergence of cabinet government in England, cabinet responsibility is something that did not emerge until the last decades of the nineteenth century.

At independence, Latin American countries were struggling with the same fundamental problem that leaders of the newly independent United States were struggling with after 1776: how to constitute authority in a context where the king is no longer ruler. As the early constitutional history of Latin American countries demonstrates, there was considerable experimentation before they all settled on a presidential constitutional form; all of the experiments involved some kind of monarchy, either elective or hereditary. It is telling that the one country (Brazil) in Latin America that did not depose the king kept a constitutional monarchy that might have evolved into a parliamentary democracy. It is also telling that, once the king was deposed (principally because of the monarchy's identification with slavery and the "republican agitation" that erupted in the 1870s; see Viotti da Costa 2000), the form of government adopted was presidential. Presidentialism, one can say, was the solution to a common problem faced by countries that emerged as such in the late eighteenth and nineteenth centuries: how to constitute national authority when the head of the government had been removed.

Institutional Inertia

Basic constitutional frameworks are difficult to change. The reasons are not hard to see: they structure the expectations of the actors operating under them and, in order to change the framework, actors must be willing to leap into the unknown. At the same time, constitutions serve as focal points: all of the transitions to democracy that took place in Argentina since the 1930s resulted in the re-adoption (without much discussion) of the 1853 constitution, which had ushered in probably the longest period of political stability in that country's history.

Indeed, democracies that have changed their form of government are rare. There are only three cases of such change in the world since 1946: Brazil in 1961 and 1963 and France in 1958. Changes are more frequent after an authoritarian interregnum but still are not common. Since the end of the nineteenth century there have been seventy cases of re-democratization in 49 countries; the constitutional framework of the new democracy was different in fifteen cases. Of these, eight involved changes to or from mixed democracies and a mere seven cases involved changes from a purely parliamentary to a presidential constitutional framework. No country that had a presidential constitution under democracy re-emerged under a parliamentary constitution.

In fact, basic constitutional frameworks tend to remain in place even as regimes change. The staying power of these institutions is simply overwhelming given the number of opportunities that have existed for them to be altered. Changes do occur, of course, but they are not very frequent. In the case of Latin America, where the first big wave of independence took place, all countries (with one exception) had presidential institutions by the time politics stabilized after independence; they kept these institutions in spite of the cycles of democracy and dictatorship that many experienced since then. Latin American dictators were usually called "presidents" and often governed with the "help" of independently elected legislatures. Brazil, which adopted presidentialism only with the first republican constitution in 1891, is the sole exception; but since then, presidentialism has survived six constitutions (1934, 1937, 1946, 1966, 1969, 1988) in spite of explicit and vigorous attempts by some actors to introduce parliamentary institutions.

The continuity in basic constitutional frameworks can also be seen in the continuity of titles adopted by rulers under democracy and dictatorship. It is striking that the countries with leaders who were ever called presidents and/or prime ministers continued to have leaders who were called presidents and/or prime ministers later in their histories. Presidents existed in 67.6% and prime ministers in 65.2% of the country-years between 1946 and 2002. Nearly 37% of these years featured both a prime minister and a president. All but three countries that were first observed with a president in 1946 (or at independence) had a president in 2002. Prime ministers seem to be more ephemeral, but only in appearance. By 2002, fifteen of the forty countries that had a prime minister in 1946 or at independence did not have one in 2002; in eleven of these fifteen, the prime minister office had been abolished and reinstated at least once, and there is nothing to suggest that it may not come back to life again. In only four cases (Malawi in 1966, Nigeria in 1966, Seychelles in 1977, and Sudan in 1989) has the office of prime minister been abolished and the country gone on to live an extended period of time without such a figure. Thus even prime ministers, which under dictatorships seem to disappear more frequently than presidents, have staying power: once in place, they are likely to remain as part of the political landscape of a country.

Thus, "presidential" and "parliamentary" constitutions are resilient; once adopted, they provide the structure of offices and roles that actors will take for granted. When presidential democracies die, they most likely become dictatorships that are led by presidents. When parliamentary democracies die, prime ministers do not always disappear even if their powers do. The basic constitutional framework of countries tends to remain in place, regardless of whether or not government officials come to power through competitive elections.

Historical Coincidence

It is the coincidence of repeated military intervention in countries that had adopted presidential institutions that explains the pattern of unstable presidential democracies. The nexus between militarism and presidentialism is not the product of design or the outcome of a common cause. Rather, it simply reflects the fact that military dictatorships appeared, remained, and/or recurred – in other words, endured – in countries that had adopted presidential institutions.

Now refer back to Figure 6.1. The marked increase in the number of military dictatorships in the 1920s and 1930s is the result of democratic breakdowns in both Latin America and Europe. In 1938 the military ruled in dictatorships in Argentina, Bolivia, the Dominican Republic, El Salvador, Guatemala, Honduras, Nicaragua, Paraguay, Peru, and Venezuela. By this time, democracy had broken down in Austria, Bulgaria, Estonia, Finland, Germany, Greece, Italy, Latvia, Lithuania, Poland, Portugal (twice), Spain, and Yugoslavia. At the end of World War II, ten of nineteen Latin American countries were democratic. In the same year, most European countries that had not been formally or informally annexed by the Soviet Union in the course of the war were democratic (with the notable exceptions of Spain and Portugal). Not much changed with respect to political regimes in Europe until Portugal in 1975 and Spain in 1977 democratized. In Latin America, by 1970 all countries (with the exception of Colombia, Costa Rica, and Venezuela) were dictatorships, almost all of them led by the military.

Why, then, have postwar Austria, Germany, Italy, and Finland (and later Greece, Portugal, and Spain) become stable democracies, while not a single democracy that existed in 1946 survived in Latin America? Consider this assertion: Latin America continued to suffer from political instability because the dictatorships that were in place during World War II did not lose a war or, to put it in more general terms, were not discredited as a political force, as they were in Europe. There, the United States could not rely on authoritarian forces – discredited and defeated as they were during the war – to thwart the threat of communism. Hence the Cold War battles had to be waged through center-right democratic parties, such as the Christian Democrats in Germany and Italy. But in Latin America the right-wing military became the bulwark against the threat of communism, with the implication that it would step into the political arena whenever necessary. Obviously, the argument here is not that the military coups in Latin America were successful only, or even primarily, as instruments of U.S. intervention. I share what appears now to be the consensus view that military coups succeed only when they enjoy domestic civilian support. But if Latin American militaries had been discredited as the fascist forces in Europe were, these coups would not have been possible.

Thus, although parliamentary and presidential democracies are equally likely to die at the hands of the military, the military remained in a position to "kill" democratic regimes in an area of the world where, for reasons that should be traced to the constitutional experiments of the nineteenth century, presidential constitutions predominated. Where parliamentary institutions predominated, the military became discredited as a political force and its capacity to intervene in politics neutralized.[6] Dictators in Latin America found presidential institutions when they came to power, and this is what they left behind when they relinquished power. We can see, then, how a military–presidential nexus might have emerged from the coincidence of these historical processes.

The instability of presidential democracies is therefore a consequence of their following military dictatorships, which makes them inherently unstable. They follow military dictatorships, however, because of a set of historical circumstances that allowed the military to remain active and credible as a political force in a part of the world where presidential constitutions happened to be in place. Given the resilience of constitutional frameworks, presidential institutions in place when the military came into power would remain when the military relinquished power. If these institutions had been parliamentary then they would likewise have remained, and the puzzle with which this book started – that presidential democracies die more frequently than parliamentary ones – would not even have existed.

Observe that there is cause for optimism. There are economic and political reasons for us to believe that the spiral of instability has been broken in Latin America. In spite of the economic stagnation of Latin America in the past twenty years, many countries in the region (particularly those in the Southern Cone) now enjoy income levels at which threats to democracy are extremely rare. Even though they are relatively poor in comparison to Western Europe, right-wing Latin American elites have too much at risk economically to engage in yet another authoritarian adventure. But perhaps the more important reason is political. In Latin America, the military was disgraced both by its brutality and its indolence during the last wave of "bureaucratic-authoritarian" regimes. Given the absence of Cold War pressures, it seems that the prospects for a military return to power in the region are practically nonexistent.

Is the Military–Presidential Nexus About "Latin America"?

Much of the pattern we observe in connection with presidential democracies may stem from our historical tendency to observe presidentialism in Latin America,

---

[6] It is interesting to note in this respect that the two European countries that did not directly involve their military in WWII (and hence survived the conflict unscathed) were Spain and Portugal, where dictatorship survived into the 1970s. The other country that experienced military dictatorship – Greece – also had a military force that was not damaged by WWII.

where we also observe enduring military dictatorships. Although not all presidential democracies are located in Latin America (the United States and some countries in Africa and Asia account for 37% of them), nearly all democracies in the region are presidential (excepting only the sixteen months of mixed institutions adopted in August 1961 in Brazil). However, the eighteen countries of Latin America do account disproportionately for the number of dictatorships that are led by military leaders. Although "only" 22.8% of the military dictatorships observed between 1946 and 1999 were in Latin America, during this period 49.8% of all regimes and 63% of the democracies in the region were preceded by a military dictatorship. Is there anything about Latin America, as distinct from presidentialism or militarism, that might account for the pattern of instability of presidential democracies?

As we know, democracies that follow military dictatorships have shorter lives; and military dictatorships, in turn, have much shorter lives than civilian or monarchical ones. One should therefore expect that, once a country experiences a military dictatorship, a spiral of instability will characterize its subsequent history. Suppose a military regime overthrows a democracy; then, in view of the last two columns of Table 6.5 (which give first-order transition probabilities of the different regimes and their expected lives), we can expect this regime to last for fifteen years. Assume it is followed by presidentialism – which, given that it is preceded by a military dictatorship, is expected to last nineteen years (from Table 6.4) – and that when this presidential democracy is in turn overthrown the result is a military regime that again lasts fifteen years. One would then expect to witness three regime transitions in about fifty years, more or less the period (1946–2002) covered by our data set of observed political regimes.

This cycle, as one will readily recognize, is reminiscent of the history of many Latin American countries. Indeed, not only is regime transition more frequent in Latin America than in other regions, but the average number of transitions in this region is close to what one would expect given the cycle just described. As Table 6.6 shows, although Latin America comprises fewer than 10% of the world's countries, 37% of transitions to and from democracy have occurred there. Between 1946 and 2002, the average number of transitions in Latin America was 2.9 versus 0.5 outside this region. This instability could be the product of some unobserved characteristics of Latin American countries that have nothing to do with militarism and presidentialism. How important, then, is "Latin America" in accounting for the survival of democracies?

Examining column 5 of Table 6.3, we can see the impact of a dummy variable for Latin America (LA) on transitions to dictatorship while controlling for economic development level, presidentialism, and military legacy. As can be seen,

Table 6.6. *Regime Instability: Latin America and Elsewhere*

Number of regime transitions	Number of countries	Latin America	Rest of the world
0	127	0	127
1	37	5	32
2	15	5	10
3	7	2	5
4	4	1	3
5	6	2	4
6	1	1	0
7	0	0	0
8	1	1	0
9	1	1	0
TOTAL	199	18	181

neither presidentialism nor this LA has an impact on the survival of democracies. It is the military legacy of presidential democracies in Latin America, not their form of government or their location, that makes them more brittle.

Figure 6.2 allows us to compare the relative effects of presidentialism and militarism at different levels of economic development. As is apparent from the figure, the real divide in terms of democratic breakdown occurs between those democracies that were preceded by military dictatorships and those that were preceded by civilian dictatorships. At every level of income per capita (at least up to about PPP$6,000) for which democracies are still likely to break down, democracies preceded by military dictatorship are much more likely to become a dictatorship. The effect of presidentialism is simply nonexistent. An almost identical picture would emerge were we to keep the form of government constant and vary the region of the world and the authoritarian legacy of the current democratic regime.

This, however, is not all. Although no dictatorships left behind parliamentary democracies in Latin America, some presidential democracies followed civilian dictatorships. If what causes regime instability is the legacy of military dictatorships and not some "Latin American" factor, then it must be true that, within the region, presidential democracies that followed military dictatorships were more brittle than those that followed civilian dictatorships. And the same pattern must be true for both presidential and parliamentary democracies outside of Latin America.

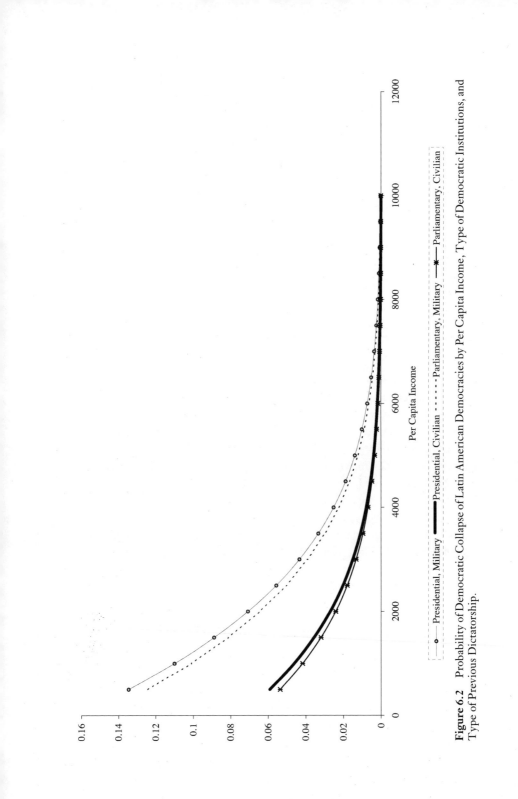

Figure 6.2 Probability of Democratic Collapse of Latin American Democracies by Per Capita Income, Type of Democratic Institutions, and Type of Previous Dictatorship.

We already know that this last statement is true. Because no parliamentary democracy ever existed in Latin America, the numbers reported in Table 6.4 indicate the probability that a non–Latin American parliamentary democracy will break down, conditioned on the type of dictatorship that preceded it. Recall that when the previous dictatorship was civilian, the expected life of the democracy was 89 years; and when the previous dictatorship was military, the expected life was only 20 years. A similar pattern, though not as dramatic, is true of presidential democracies outside of Latin America. Those that follow a civilian dictatorship tend to last for 37 years, whereas those that follow a military dictatorship tend to last for only 14 years. Finally, this is observed even among the presidential democracies within Latin America: those originating in civilian dictatorships are expected to live for 36 years, whereas those originating in military dictatorships are expected to live for 20 years. Clearly, the effect of military legacy seems to be weakened in Latin America, suggesting that there may exist other factors about the region that independently affect regime survival. Yet the effect of military legacy on the probability that a democracy will break down remains – regardless of whether the democracy is presidential or parliamentary and of whether it is in or outside of Latin America.

Thus, it is military intervention that mostly leads to instability in Latin America and, by extension, to instability of presidential democracies. We can therefore assert counterfactually that, had Latin America adopted parliamentary institutions in the aftermath of its independence, we would not be asking questions about the higher rates of regime instability of presidential democracies. The nexus between military dictatorships and presidential democracies is thus purely coincidental: military regimes are not more likely to overthrow presidential democracies than parliamentary ones, and military leaders are not more likely than other leaders to change the institutions they found. It just happened that military intervention occurred more frequently in the countries that adopted presidential institutions at independence, specifically in Latin America.

These systems were not established by "the military"; the very language is anachronistic. The military is a newcomer as an institution. As Rouquié (1994:236) observes, "there is no militarism in the strict sense of the term prior to the birth of standing armies and career officers," which did not happen in Latin America before the end of the nineteenth century, well after independence. It was only in the ten years following 1925, when the first military coups occurred in Ecuador and Chile, that the military stepped into politics as an organization. Argentina, Bolivia, Brazil, the Dominican Republic, Guyana, and Peru suffered military coups in 1930; the following year this was the fate of Ecuador and El Salvador, while Chile remained in the hands of ephemeral military juntas. From

159

then on, a spiral of instability dominated the history of most Latin American countries. As a matter of fact, the notion that Latin America has been perennially and inherently unstable from the outset needs to be revisited. Many countries in the region experienced relatively long periods of routine (though not democratic) politics, including regular transfers of power, before they became chronically unstable. Thus, instability in Latin America is probably a more recent phenomenon whose causes still need to be identified.

In summary, the higher instability of presidential democracies – a fact noted by many analysts since Linz, and one that I do not dispute – is not due to any inherent defect of systems based on the separation of executive and legislative powers. Neither does this instability have much to do with the exogenous conditions that are often invoked to account for it: level of economic development, size of the country, and geographic location. Although location does matter for regime instability, and Latin America is by far the least stable region of the world, I hope to have made explicit the mechanism that underlies this relationship: the nexus between the military and presidentialism, the product of a combination of historical circumstances that (as I pointed out earlier) are no longer in place.

We may therefore conclude that the problem of presidential democracies is not that they are "institutionally flawed." Rather, the problem is that they tend to exist in societies where democracies of any type are likely to be unstable. Hence, fears arising from the choice of many new democracies for presidential institutions are unfounded. From a strictly institutional point of view, presidentialism can be as stable as parliamentarism. Given that constitutional frameworks are difficult to change, striving to replace them may be wasteful from a political point of view. It would be a misguided use of resources to attempt to change an institutional structure on the grounds of democratic stability when the source of instability has nothing to do with that structure. Hence, that countries with presidential institutions are "stuck" with them does not mean that they will experience regime instability in the future. It also does not mean that there is no room for improvement or that institutional reforms are pointless. There are actions that can be taken to help democracy survive that do not require altering hard-to-change institutional structures.

Appendix 6.1: Coding "Military Legacy"

"Military Legacy" is a variable that distinguishes the type of dictatorship that existed prior to the current democracy. This variable takes the value of 1 when the current democracy followed a military dictatorship or 0 when it followed something else. "Something else" can be another kind of democracy (a rare event, though); a civilian dictatorship; a royal dictatorship; colonial status; or a regime that is unclassifiable because it has existed since time immemorial (e.g., the regime that preceded the current Swiss democracy or the current monarchy in Bhutan).

"Military Legacy" thus presupposes a classification of dictatorships into different types. Here I use the classification developed by Gandhi (2004), which distinguishes dictatorships according to the characteristics of their inner sanctums – that is, the place where real decisions are made and potential rivals are kept under close scrutiny. Monarchs rely on family and kin networks along with consultative councils in order to rule; military rulers confine key potential rivals from the armed forces within juntas; and civilian dictators usually create a smaller body within a regime party, a political bureau, to co-opt potential rivals. Because decision-making power lies within these small institutions, they generally indicate how power is organized within the regime, the forces to which dictators are responsible, and who may be likely to remove them. In this sense, a parallel can be traced between this way of distinguishing dictatorships and the distinction of democracies in terms of their form of government, which underscores precisely the institutions regulating the way governments are removed from power.

Dictatorships in which the executive comes to and maintains power on the basis of family and kin networks are classified as monarchies. Dictatorships in which the executive relies on the armed forces to assume and retain power are classified as military. All other dictatorships, many of which are characterized by the presence of a regime party, are civilian. Operationally, this classification relies on answers to the following questions:[7]

1. Who rules?
2. Does the head of government bear the title of "king" and have a hereditary successor and/or predecessor?
3. Is the head of government a current or past member of the armed forces?
4. Is the head neither monarchic nor military?

Who Rules? The first step in distinguishing dictatorships is to identify the effective ruler. In democracies this identification is easy: it is the president in presidential democracies and the prime minister in parliamentary and mixed democracies. In dictatorships, identification is frequently unproblematic: usually the

---

[7] The remainder of this appendix draws heavily on Cheibub and Gandhi (2006).

ruler is the president, the king, the prime minister, the head of the military junta, or the martial law administrator (the title adopted by dictators in Bangladesh in the 1970s). But sometimes the nominal ruler is not the effective head of the government. In most communist states the general secretary of the Communist Party is usually the effective head of government even though the chairman of the Council of State, or president, is the head of state. In other cases, such as in Somoza's Nicaragua, an *éminence grise* lurks behind the scenes as elections duly occur and presidents change according to constitutional rules. Operationally, the nominal ruler is assumed to be the effective ruler unless there is evidence (from the historical record) of such an *éminence grise*. Deng Xiaoping, for instance, never occupied any high-level formal position in the Chinese government; yet everyone recognizes that he ruled after Mao Zedong's death in the mid-1970s until his own death in 1997.

Does the Head of Government Bear the Title of "King" and Have a Hereditary Successor and/or Predecessor? The ruler is a monarch if he (i) bears the title of "king" or "emir" and (ii) takes power or is replaced by rules of hereditary succession. Most monarchs are identified by their title alone. The second rule applies in slightly more complicated cases in which the title of "king" has been taken more recently. In two instances during the postwar period, a member of the armed forces seized power and declared himself king. If he succeeded in passing power to a family member – as did Reza Khan to his son, Mohammad Reza Pahlavi, in Iran – then both members are considered to be monarchs. If he failed, he is not considered to be a monarch; he will be either a military or a civilian dictator. Thus, Jean-Bedel Bokassa, a colonel in the Central African Republic's army, seized power in 1966 and declared himself Emperor; but Bokassa was deposed in 1979, before he was able to have his son succeed him. For reasons that will become clear in what follows, his rule is classified as a case of military dictatorship.

This rule highlights an important point about modern-day monarchs. In considering whether a ruler is a "rightful successor," what matters is only whether the ruler belongs to the current family in power. In other words, whether that family or individual has historically well-founded claims to the throne is immaterial, since contemporary monarchs rule in countries that often were carved by colonial powers without reference to historical claims or social considerations.

Is the Head of Government a Current or Past Member of the Armed Forces? The effective head of government is a military ruler if he is (or was) a member of the institutionalized military prior to taking power. Even if he retired from service, shedding the uniform does not eliminate his military status. Attempts to appear more palatable to voters who are more accustomed to civilian rule do not erase these rulers' connections and access to the armed forces.

Not included as military dictators are those rulers who come to power as heads of guerilla movements. Successful insurgency leaders – such as Castro in Cuba, Ortega in Nicaragua, Musaveni in Uganda, and Kagame in Rwanda – are considered to be civilian rulers. One might object that heads of guerilla movements, often like military rulers, come to power using violence. In addition, once in power, these rulers often give themselves military titles or become heads of the armed forces themselves. Yet there are three good reasons for not considering those involved in guerilla movements to be military dictators. First, not all leaders who originated from guerilla movements were involved in fighting. Many of them were members of the civilian, political arm of the successful movement and have no more experience in warfare than the average civilian on the street. In addition, some guerilla leaders, once they take power, never assume a formal military role. Even though Castro wears fatigues, the leadership of the Cuban armed forces belongs to his brother Raúl. Finally, and most importantly, since they were never a member of the armed forces, these leaders do not answer to that institution. And since the constraints and support offered by the armed forces to one of their members in power are the main reasons for distinguishing military from nonmilitary leaders, guerilla leaders do not fall into this category.

Is the Head neither Monarchic nor Military?   As previously mentioned, civilian leaders often create a regime party through which they govern. Yet, unlike kin networks with monarchs and the armed forces with military rulers, the party does not define the civilian ruler. The diversity of modes of government is what characterizes civilian rulers, and for this reason it is best to leave them as a residual category. Thus, if dictators do not qualify as either monarchs or military rulers, they are civilian.

Dictatorships have existed in 139 countries between 1946 and 2002, for a total of 4,607 country-years; 51% of them were led by a civilian leader, 34% by a military leader, and 15% by a monarch. In order to code "Military Legacy," the type of dictatorship that preceded the democracies that existed in 1946 had to be assessed. There were 31 democracies in 1946: fifteen were parliamentary, three were mixed, and the remaining thirteen were presidential. Seven of the parliamentary democracies that existed in 1946 were preceded by authoritarian monarchies (Belgium, Denmark, Luxembourg, the Netherlands, Norway, Sweden, and the United Kingdom); five were preceded by colonial rule (Australia, Canada, Ireland, Lebanon, and New Zealand), two by military dictatorships (France and Greece), and one by a civilian dictatorship (Italy). One of the three mixed democracies that existed in 1946 was preceded by colonial rule (Iceland), and two were preceded by civilian dictatorships (Austria and Finland). Finally, seven of the presidential democracies that existed in 1946 were preceded by military dictatorships (Argentina, Chile, Costa Rica, Cuba, Guatemala, Peru, and Venezuela), three by civilian dictatorships (Brazil, Colombia, and Uruguay), two by colonial rule (the Philippines and the United States), and one was unclassified (Switzerland).

7

Conclusion

We need to put to rest the notion that presidential institutions are not conducive to democratic consolidation. I hope to have shown in the previous chapters that, sensible as it may appear, this notion finds no empirical support in the data. True, presidential democracies are more unstable than parliamentary ones; but this instability is not caused by the incentives generated by presidentialism itself. Presidential democracies die not because the institutions are such that they compel actors to seek extra-constitutional solutions to their conflicts. The conflicts themselves should take some of the blame, since they are probably hard to reconcile under any institutional framework. And given an "activated" military, it is certainly comprehensible why democracies – of any type – should break down into authoritarian systems.

If this is the case, then we are in a position to shift the emphasis of current thinking about political reforms in presidential democracies. As we have seen, much of the literature about democratic forms of government has focused on the relationship between the government and the legislature and the alleged implications of the ways in which this relationship is organized: conflict under presidentialism and cooperation under parliamentarism. This book should make it apparent that these consequences have been at least exaggerated and that differences in interbranch relationships across the two systems are more of degree than of quality.

Thus, the general tone of the literature on presidentialism has been to emphasize the role of specific institutional arrangements in helping to circumvent the presidential system's propensity for conflict and paralysis. For example, strong presidential powers would be undesirable because they may lead to conflicts with the legislature and eventual governability crises. Concurrent and/or two-round presidential elections, in turn, would be a positive feature of presidential systems given that they tend to reduce the number of political parties and thereby increase the survival chances of presidential democracies; in contrast, legislative elections organized on the basis of proportional representation would lead to a relatively high number of political parties and thus would be bad for the survival of democracy. Finally, presidential term limits would be necessary to curb the powers of the president, which – if left unchecked – might have a detrimental effect on democracy.

Here I suggest that we look at these same institutions from a different perspective. Given that presidential institutions per se do not kill democracy and given that countries that are now presidential are likely to remain so, it follows that institutions such as presidential powers, electoral systems, and presidential term limits can be seen as ways to enhance goals other than governability, such as representation and accountability. No longer must we allow preoccupation with governability and the survival of democracy to be the overriding concern of reforms; other goals can, and should, be taken into consideration when thinking of ways to improve existing presidential systems. Let me elaborate on this.

Constitutional Limits on Presidential Re-election

Most presidential constitutions set a limit to the number of times that a president can be re-elected. Cheibub (1998) reports that, between 1946 and 1996, only 18% of the presidents in pure presidential regimes were in systems where no restrictions on re-election existed (these included the Philippines prior to 1971 and the Dominican Republic between the mid-1960s and early 1990s); another 18% were in systems, such as the United States, where presidents could be re-elected once. If we exclude from this group the presidents who were already serving their second term and hence could not run again, we find that, during the 1946–1996 period, the proportion of presidents that could be re-elected was only 28.3%. Until the early 1990s, the most common constitutional limit on presidential re-election was the "one term out" rule, according to which a president had to wait for a full term out of office before standing for election again. Since then, countries such as Argentina and Brazil have changed their constitutions and adopted the two-terms limit that has existed in the United States since the 1940s.

Presidential term limits are important because they affect the link between the president and voters. Elections are normally considered to be one of the most important instruments for inducing governments to act in the interest of voters. This is how it is supposed to work: anticipating voters' future judgment of their past performance, politicians are induced to pursue the interests of voters in order to be re-elected (Manin 1997). Whether elections are actually sufficient to induce this kind of behavior on the part of politicians is a controversial matter (see Cheibub and Przworski 1999). It is clear, however, that if elections are to affect the behavior of politicians at all then voters must be able (a) to punish incumbents who perform badly by throwing them out of office and (b) to reward incumbents who perform well by giving them another term in office. Both are necessary if elections are to induce governments to act in the interest of voters. But constitutional term limits break this link by preventing voters from rewarding good incumbents.

The rationale for instituting term limits for presidents in the first place is reasonable, for such limits are meant to prevent incumbents from taking advantage of their position in order to remain in power. Indeed, the little evidence that is available suggests that presidents do indeed have a large advantage when they are legally permitted to run for re-election. As Cheibub and Przeworski (1999) report, among 22 presidents who faced re-election without impending term limits between 1950 and 1990, only six were actually defeated (although eight others chose, for one reason or another, not to stand for re-election). Given that incumbents won in eight and lost in six elections, their odds of being re-elected were 1.3 to 1; the odds for prime ministers in parliamentary systems were 0.66 to 1.

Thus, although incumbent presidents seem to have a clear advantage when they are legally permitted to run for re-election, most presidential systems prevent incumbents from exploiting this advantage by requiring them to leave office whether or not voters want them to stay. In this way, "excessively" strong presidents are prevented from emerging, and the risks to presidential democracies are allegedly reduced.

However, what constitutes an excessively strong president (i.e., one who abuses the power of incumbency) is unclear, and I submit that the bar is set at a relatively low point given the model that has dominated research on presidential democracies: that presidents are bound to clash with the legislature, inducing unresolvable stalemates. But if such a conflict is not presupposed, the notion of strong presidents becomes less alarming and the bar beyond which their strength becomes excessive is set at a higher point.

Even if we agree that the incumbency advantage of presidents needs to be tamed, constitutional term limits for presidents may be too blunt an instrument because it fundamentally interferes with the relationship between voters and presidents and preempts the possibility that elections may operate as mechanisms of accountability. There may be other institutions that achieve the same goal without exacting such a high price. Some of them include strict regulation of campaign finance and procedures, equal distribution of public political campaign funds in order to reduce barriers to entry into political competition, free access to media, and the strengthening of agencies that oversee campaigns. These are devices that will limit the ability of presidents to use their office for undue electoral advantage without removing their incentives to perform well with an eye toward being re-elected.

Legislative and Presidential Electoral Systems

Presidentialism may be affected by the way both congress and the president are elected.

Current thinking about presidentialism, as we have seen, is that it must avoid high levels of partisan fragmentation in the assembly. The easiest (it is believed) and simplest way of limiting the number of political parties is to design a restrictive electoral system – one that adopts, for instance, single-member districts, relatively high thresholds for legislative representation, strong legal requirements for the establishment of political parties, or a combination of these features. The result is a party system with a small number of parties and thus, it is believed, a more stable government – in other words, a government supported by a majority (consisting of one or a few parties) that is capable of approving its legislation in the assembly.

But as Chapter 4 demonstrated, the facts that underlie this reasoning are questionable. The relationship between risk of democratic breakdown and legislative fragmentation is not linear for presidential democracies, so reducing the number of parties will not necessarily reduce the risk of democratic breakdown. Similarly, there is no empirical support for the notions that it is harder for presidents to form coalitions when party fragmentation is high, that a presidential democracy is more fragile when no coalitions are formed, or that single-party minority presidential governments are less legislatively effective than coalition governments. It thus seems that presidential democracies adopting "permissive" electoral systems, such as those based on proportional representation, do not really pay a price in terms of the government's ability to govern. They can keep electoral rules that allow for a high degree of representativeness without increasing the probability of democratic breakdown.

As for the way presidents are elected, there are two aspects I would like to emphasize here. The first concerns the rules for the election of presidents; the second concerns the timing of presidential elections relative to legislative elections.

One of the advantages of presidentialism is that it provides for one office with a national constituency. This may become especially important in situations of high political volatility and heterogeneity, since the presidency may operate as a force toward unity and integration. Yet in order for this to occur, the rules for electing the president must be carefully crafted so that they provide an incentive for integration rather than a reinforcement of existing political, ethnic, geographic, or religious cleavages. There is no one formula that may be generally applied in designing a presidential electoral system in a context of heterogeneity. This is so because, as Horowitz (2000) has shown, the best system depends on the specific distribution of cleavages across the national territory. One mechanism, for instance, requires that contestants seek votes outside of their narrowly defined constituencies in order to be successful. Horowitz (2000) discusses the system used in Nigeria under its 1979 constitution, where the winner of the presidential election must obtain a plurality of the national vote and at least one fourth of the vote in at least two thirds of the states. Another mechanism, also discussed by Horowitz, is the so-called alternative vote used in Sri Lanka's presidential elections, where voters are asked to rank all contestants except one. If no candidate wins an outright majority of the votes then all but the top two candidates are eliminated, and the second and subsequent preferences on the ballots are counted until one candidate garners more than 50% of the vote. Thus, to the extent that no candidate can expect to obtain a majority in the initial balloting, all candidates will have an incentive to reach beyond their own constituencies in order to be ranked relatively high in other groups' preferences. A functionally similar procedure – the two-round presidential election – has been adopted in most Latin American countries. Here elections are held and, if no candidate obtains more than half of the votes, a second round takes place with the participation of the two candidates with the highest number of votes. This differs from the alternative vote in that voters rank only up to their second choice and the ranking occurs at a later stage. These are just some examples of a menu of possibilities that may, in fact, be quite large. What they have in common is using the presidential election to mitigate some potentially problematic cleavages and serve as a force that generates incentives for integration.

Presidential and legislative elections can occur always at the same time (as in Costa Rica) or always at different times (as in Brazil during the 1946–1964 democratic period), or they may alternate (as in the United States, where a legislative term of two years and a presidential term of four years means that elections coincide every four years). There is some evidence that simultaneous elections tend to reduce the number of political parties (Shugart 1995; Golder 2006). Presidents generate large coattail effects, thus aiding the election of legislators of their own parties. This provides a strong incentive for individual legislators to join parties with a real chance of generating a viable presidential candidate, and it may ultimately help produce presidents from parties controlling a relatively large share of seats in the legislature. Thus, if fragmentation of the party system is a concern, then the stipulation of concurrent presidential and legislative elections may help reduce the number of political parties in competition without the need to implement a restrictive electoral system for legislative elections. The price, however, is that a system of concurrent presidential and legislative elections deprives voters of the opportunity to signal their approval or disapproval of government performance in the middle of the presidential term.

Legislative and Agenda Powers of the Presidency

As we saw in Chapter 4, almost all presidential constitutions give some legislative powers to the presidency. The most important powers include veto, decree, and urgency powers, as well as the government's exclusive power to introduce legislation in some specified areas.

Veto power stems from the provisions that legislative acts must be signed by the president in order for them to become law and that the president may refuse to sign them. When the president can refuse the bill only in its entirety, the president has only *complete* or *total* veto power; when the president may object to portions of the bill, the president has *partial* veto power. But the terminology here is misleading: since presidents with partial veto power are not presented with an all-or-nothing choice, they have more ways to influence legislation and hence are more powerful. When the president vetoes a bill (either partially or completely), it is often sent back to the legislature, which is then given the opportunity to reaffirm its will and override the presidential veto. The legislative majority required for veto override is usually larger than the majority required for the approval of the bill in the first place. Most presidential constitutions (including the U.S. Constitution and the majority of the Latin American presidential constitutions) require a two-thirds majority of the legislature in order to override a presidential veto. If such a majority exists, the president is required to sign the bill and it then becomes law.

Decree power refers to the executive's ability to issue new laws, a power that exists in many constitutions, both presidential and parliamentary. Decree power varies widely (Carey and Shugart 1998). First, it varies with respect to the areas where decrees may be issued. Some constitutions allow only for presidential "executive orders" – that is, purely administrative proclamations pertaining to the implementation of laws already approved by the legislature. Others allow for presidential decrees under special circumstances, which are often sufficiently vague that presidential action is possible in virtually any area (e.g., "relevance," "urgency," "economic or financial matters when so required by the national interest").[1] Second, presidential decree power varies with respect to its time frame. Presidential decrees typically enter into effect as soon as they are issued. In a few cases, their effect is delayed for a specified time during which the legislature is given the opportunity to reject them. Finally, executive decrees in some cases become permanent laws, whereas in other cases they expire if not approved by the legislature within some time frame.

In many presidential constitutions, presidents are allowed to declare a bill "urgent." When this is done, the assembly is required to vote on the bill within a relatively short time period (e.g., 30 or 45 days), and legislative work is paralyzed until such a vote takes place. The president is thus empowered to directly affect the order of business of the legislative body.

Finally, as also discussed Chapter 4, many constitutions grant the government exclusive power to introduce certain legislation. Presidentialism in the United States is virtually unique among presidential democracies in requiring all legislation to be initiated from within the congress. In most other presidential democracies, the role of the assembly in initiating legislation is limited in some areas, such as setting the size of the armed forces, creating jobs, structuring public administration, and (most importantly) establishing the budget. These bills can normally be amended by the assembly even if constrained by provisions stipulating, for example, that it can only propose amendments that do not increase the deficit or the overall level of spending. Yet even when granted the power to freely amend, the assembly is dealing with an agenda that is set by the president and not by itself.

All these features of presidential agenda powers are rather consequential, and they combine to yield institutionally weaker or stronger presidencies. Although there are many who believe that strong presidents create problems by clashing with congress and eventually generating government or even regime crises, the results presented in previous chapters join others (Figueiredo and Limongi 2000a,b; Siavelis 2000; Amorim Neto, Cox, and McCubbins 2003; Jones and Hwang 2005) in pointing out that strong presidencies are not necessarily bad for the operation of presidential constitutions. For instance, the strong presidential agenda powers established by the post-authoritarian constitutions of Brazil and Chile are largely responsible for the high level of legislative success of their governments. The case of Brazil seems to be most relevant here given the large number of centrifugal elements built into the system, which in combination with presidentialism might suggest a highly volatile and ungovernable

---

[1] Decree power under "special" circumstances should not be confused with constitutional emergency powers, which allow for the temporary suspension of some constitutional provisions in specified circumstances.

country: a federally structured country with economically diverse regions, weak political parties, and an electoral system for the assembly (open-list proportional representation) with low barriers to entry and features that make state governors influential over party decisions. Nonetheless, legislative behavior in the Brazilian congress has exhibited remarkably high levels of partisanship, with presidents capable of relying on a stable coalition that supports them on most of their legislative agenda (Figueiredo and Limongi 1999). This unexpected pattern is, in fact, a function of the president's legislative powers granted by the 1988 constitution, which include all of the powers discussed previously: partial veto, decree power, the power to request urgency in the consideration of specific legislation, and the sole power to initiate budget legislation.[2]

In their various papers, Figueiredo and Limongi have uncovered the mechanism whereby the powers of the presidency positively affect the capacity of presidential governments to act in the face of many adverse institutional conditions. The concentration of legislative powers in the executive (coupled with a highly centralized decision-making structure in the legislature) renders the individual and independent action of legislators futile. For them, the rational course of legislative behavior is to follow their parties' directives in congress, since this is the only way they will be able to influence public policies and to obtain the resources needed in seeking from the electorate a renewal of their mandates. It is this centralization of the decision-making process, these authors argue, that explains the high degree of legislative success of Brazilian presidents, a success not unlike those obtained in parliamentary democracies.

Thus, institutionally strong presidents are not necessarily detrimental to the functioning of presidential democracies. Attempts to weaken presidents on the ground that they usurp the assembly's rightful power (see Croissant 2003) should be considered in light of the benefits they bring about in terms of government performance.

The superior survival record of parliamentary democracies over presidential democracies has long been explained in terms of the fundamental difference between these two systems: the separation of executive and legislative authorities

---

[2] The legislative success of the government is also aided by the highly centralized organization of congress, with party leaders wielding enough power to bypass (when necessary) the work of permanent committees and set the agenda for the floor. This organization, of course, is not a constitutional feature and resulted from a decision of the assembly itself. However, it is essential for allowing the president to form stable legislative coalitions with a relatively small number of political parties, despite all the forces that conspire against such stability. See Figueiredo and Limongi (2000a,b), Amorim Neto (2002), and Armijo, Faucher, and Dembinska (2004).

in presidentialism and their fusion in parliamentarism. A number of consequences are supposed to follow from this difference, leading (in one way or another) to conflict between government and assembly in presidentialism or to their cooperation in parliamentarism. A "majoritarian imperative" that supposedly characterizes parliamentary regimes is thought to provide adequate legislative support for the government. This same imperative provides ineluctable incentives for political parties to cooperate with the government and for individual members of parliament to comply with party directives. As a consequence, highly disciplined parties tend to cooperate with each other in forming legislative coalitions that governments will emerge from and then rely upon for their existence. Crises do occur, but they can be resolved by the formation of a new government or the emergence of a new majority.

Since these are consequences of the fusion of powers characteristic of parliamentarism, they should be absent in presidentialism. And in fact, nothing in presidential regimes guarantees that the government will be able to count on an adequate basis of support in congress. As a result, incentives to cooperate are supposed to be few: political parties, it is thought, have no reason to bear the cost of incumbency at election and hence will try to distance themselves from the government; and individual members of congress face no risk of losing their jobs regardless of how they vote. Unless elections return a majority for the president, presidential democracies are destined to experience stalemate and will ultimately break down.

Although I do not deny that parliamentary regimes live longer than presidential regimes, this book has taken issue with the idea that this difference is due to the separation or fusion of executive and legislative authorities. It has shown that many of the results that are viewed as following from this principle should not be expected as a matter of either logic or empirics. More importantly, I showed that the conditions that should be conducive to the death of presidential democracies – were the conventional view of presidentialism correct – actually have no impact on the survival of these regimes. The higher instability of presidential democracies can be entirely attributed to their authoritarian legacy; it has nothing to do with their constitutional structure.

We therefore have no reason to be concerned with the fact that many recent democracies have chosen presidential systems. Such concern stems from the fear that new democracies face the daunting task of restructuring their economies, which can generate profound strains on the system. These difficulties are thought to be compounded to the point of paralysis, or worse, when executives must navigate the complications of a divided control of government and the explosive potential for deadlocks.

The analysis in this book shows that these fears are unfounded. With the possible exceptions of Peru under Fujimori (Kenney 2004) and Ecuador in 2000, none of the democratic regimes that emerged in the past ten or fifteen years have succumbed to the strains of what we could call a crisis of governability. At the same time, most have made significant strides in restructuring their economies. Perhaps the pace of change has not been to the satisfaction of some, thus generating frustration and a sense that not enough is being done. But the fact remains that recent presidential democracies have accomplished quite a bit under a range of political conditions. There is no reason – at least no reason intrinsic to the nature of the form of government – why they should not continue to accomplish as much.

Appendix: Definition and Sources of Variables

This appendix contains the definition and sources of each variable contained in the data set compiled for this book. The first section lists each variable alphabetically. Each variable is marked as belonging to one of four groups: regime variables [R]; government and partisan variables [G]; constitutional variables [C]; and other variables [O]. The second section lists the sources for the variables in each of the first three groups. Sources for the variables marked [O] are given at the end of their definition in the first section.

Definitions

AGE   Age of democracy. Count variable indicating the age of the regime (as coded by HINST), with the first year of the regime coded 1. [R]

AMEND1   Restrictions of legislature's amendment capacity. Dummy variable coded 1 if the constitution restricts the legislature's power to amend the budget bill, 0 otherwise. Narrow measure. AMEND1 = 1 if LEGAMEN = 1 and RESTAMEN = 1 and INCAMEN = 0. [C]

AMEND2   Restrictions of legislature's amendment capacity. Dummy variable coded 1 if the constitution restricts the legislature's power to amend the budget bill, 0 otherwise. Broader measure. AMEND2 = 1 if AMEND1 = 1, or if LEGAMEN = 1 and RESTAMEN = 1 and INCAMEN = 1, or if LEGAMEN = 1 and RESTAMEN = 0 and INCAMEN = 0. [C]

BICAM   Bicameralism. Dummy variable coded 1 if there are two or more chambers, 0 otherwise. [C]

CIVILIAN   Dummy variable coded 1 if the regime that preceded the current regime was a dictatorship headed by a civilian (as coded by PREVINST), 0 otherwise. [R]

COALAGE   Coalition age. Count variable indicating the age of a coalition in years, as defined by COALFLAG. There is no "left censoring," as the value for 1946 corresponds to the age of the coalition that was in place then. [G]

COALFLAG   Coalition flag. Dummy variable coded 1 when a new coalition is formed. A new coalition is formed when one of the following conditions is met: (1) the share of seats held by the government (GOVSH) changes; (2) the share of seats held by the first government party (GOVP1SH) changes; (3) the share of seats of the party of the head of government (HSH) changes; or (4) the number of parties in the government (NGOVP) changes. [G]

COALGOV   Coalition government. Dummy variable coded 1 if at least two parties hold cabinet positions in a government (NGOVP > 1), 0 otherwise. [G]

COALMAJ   Coalition majority government. Dummy variable coded 1 for governments composed of at least two parties who together hold *more* than 50% of the seats in the lower (or only) legislative house when no party alone holds more than 50% of the seats in that house, 0 otherwise. COALMAJ = 1 if MINSIT = 1 and COALGOV = 1 and MAJGOV = 1. [G]

COALMIN   Coalition minority government. Dummy variable coded 1 for governments composed of at least two parties who together hold *less* than 50% of the seats in the lower (or only) legislative house when no party alone holds more than 50% of the seats in that house, 0 otherwise. COALMIN = 1 if MINSIT = 1 and COALGOV = 1 and MAJGOV = 0. [G]

COALSPL   Coalition spell. Number of successive spells of coalition government, as defined by COALFLAG. [G]

DIVIDED   Divided government. Dummy variable coded 1 for governments that hold less than 50% of the seats in the lower (or only) legislative house when one party alone holds more than 50% of the seats in that house. DIVIDED = 1 if MINSIT = 0 and MINGOV = 1. [G]

DOM1   Dominant president, version 1. Dummy variable coded 1 when the president dominates the budget process, 0 otherwise. DOM1 = 1 if INITIATE = 1 and AMEND2 = 1 and REVERSAL = 1. [C]

176

Appendix: Definition and Sources of Variables

DOM2 Dominant president, version 2. Dummy variable coded 1 when the president dominates the budget process, 0 otherwise. DOM2 = 1 if INITIATE = 1 and AMEND2 = 1 and REVERSAL = 0. [C]

DOM3 Dominant president, version 3. Dummy variable coded 1 when the president dominates the budget process, 0 otherwise. DOM3 = 1 if INITIATE = 0 and AMEND2 = 1 and REVERSAL = 1. [C]

EFFVETO Effective veto. Dummy variable coded 1 when the president has effective veto powers, 0 otherwise. The president has effective veto powers when the constitution grants such powers and the distribution of seats in the legislature is such that the president is able to exercise them; see Chapter 4 for details. [C]

ENDCOAL End of coalition government. Dummy variable coded 1 for the last year of a coalition government, as defined in COALFLAG. [G]

EP Effective number of parties. Defined as $1/(1 - F)$, where F = party fractionalization index. [G]

FHINST Flag new regime. Dummy variable coded 1 in the first year a new regime (as coded by HINST) is observed, 0 otherwise. [R]

FLAGC Flag country. Dummy variable coded 1 in the first year a country appears in the data set, 0 otherwise. [O]

GOVSH Government share. Share of seats held by all government parties in the lower (or only) legislative house. [G]

HINDEP Head independent. Dummy variable coded 1 if the head of the government is an independent or nonpartisan individual or a collective body (such as in Uruguay 1952–1967 and Switzerland) or of indeterminate party affiliation, 0 otherwise. [G]

HINST Head institutions. Regime classification based on the effective head of government. Coded 0 for parliamentary democracies; 1 for mixed democracies; 2 for presidential democracies; 3 for civilian dictatorships; 4 for military dictatorships; and 5 for royal dictatorships. [R]

HINSTLAG HINST lagged by one year. [R]

HLGSTP Head's largest party. Dummy variable coded 1 if the party of the effective head of government is the largest in the lower (or only) legislative house, 0 otherwise. [G]

HSH   Head's party share. Share of seats held by the party of the effective head of the government (the prime minister when HINST $= 0$ or 1; the president when HINST $= 2$). [G]

INDEPSH   Independents' share. Share of seats in the lower (or only) legislative house held by independents. [G]

INITIATE   Dummy variable coded 1 if the constitution grants the executive exclusive power to initiate the budget bill, 0 otherwise. [C]

LEGEFF   Legislative effectiveness. Proportion of legislative initiatives of the executive that are approved by the lower house of the national legislature. Measured by the number of executive proposals approved in the lower house of the national legislature divided by the total number of proposals introduced by the executive in a given period (Saiegh 2004; Cheibub et al. 2004). [O]

LEGELEC   Legislative elections. Dummy variable coded 1 if there was a legislative election in the current year, 0 otherwise. [G]

LGST1SH   Largest party's share. Proportion of seats held by the largest party in the lower (or only) legislative house. [G]

LGST2SH   Second-largest party's share. Proportion of seats held by the second-largest party in the lower (or only) legislative house. [G]

LGST3SH   Third-largest party's share. Proportion of seats held by the third-largest party in the lower (or only) legislative house. [G]

LGST4SH   Fourth-largest and smaller party's share. Proportion of seats held by the fourth-largest and smaller parties in the lower (or only) legislative house. [G]

LGSTP1   Dummy variable coded 1 if the party of the effective head of government is the largest in the lower (or only) legislative house, 0 otherwise. [G]

LGSTP2   Dummy variable coded 1 if the party of the effective head of government is the second-largest in the lower (or only) legislative house, 0 otherwise. [G]

LGSTP3   Dummy variable coded 1 if the party of the effective head of government is the third-largest in the lower (or only) legislative house, 0 otherwise. [G]

MAJGOV   Majority government. Dummy variable coded 1 if the parties in the government together hold more than 50% of the seats in the lower (or only) legislative house, 0 otherwise. MAJGOV $= 1$ if GOVSH > 0.50. [G]

MAJSIT   Majority situation. Dummy variable coded 1 when one party alone holds more than 50% of the seats in the lower (or only) legislative house, 0 otherwise. MAJSIT = 1 if LGST1SH > 0.50. [G]

MILITARY   Dummy variable coded 1 if the regime that preceded the current regime was a dictatorship headed by the military (as coded by PREVINST), 0 otherwise. [R]

MINGOV   Minority government. Dummy variable coded 1 if the parties in the government together hold less than 50% of the seats in the lower (or only) legislative house, 0 otherwise. MINGOV = 1 if GOVSH ≤ 0.50. [G]

MINSIT   Minority situation. Dummy variable coded 1 when no party alone holds more than 50% of the seats in the lower (or only) legislative house, 0 otherwise. MINSIT = 1 if LGST1SH < 0.50. [G]

NG   Annual rate of growth of per capita income, computed on the basis of NLEVEL. [O]

NGOVP   Number of government parties. Number of parties with legislative seats holding portfolios in the government. [G]

NLEVEL   Income level. Real gross domestic product per capita at 1985 international prices, Chain index (Heston, Summers, and Aten 2002; World Bank 2004). [O]

NOPPP   Number of opposition parties. Number of parties with legislative seats not holding portfolios in the government. [G]

NTOTP   Total number of parties. NTOTP = NGOVP + NOPPP. [G]

OPPSH   Opposition's share. Share of seats in the lower (or only) legislative house held by parties not participating in the government. [G]

OTHSH   Others' share. Share of seats in the lower or only legislative house held by "other" parties. [G]

OVERRIDE   Veto override. Dummy variable coded 1 if constitution grants assembly the right to override a presidential veto, 0 otherwise. [C]

POP   Population in thousands (World Bank 2004). [O]

POPL1M80   Population less than one million. Dummy variable coded 1 for countries with population of less than one million in 1980, 0 otherwise. [O]

PRESDOM   Presidential dominance. Dummy variable coded 1 if the president dominates the budget process, 0 otherwise. PRESDOM = DOM1 + DOM2 + DOM3. [C]

PRESELEC   Presidential elections. Dummy variable coded 1 if there was a presidential election in the current year, 0 otherwise. [G]

PREVINST   Previous regime. Type of regime that existed prior to the current regime. Coded −2 when it is impossible to determine the previous regime because the country has existed since time immemorial; −1 when the current regime is the first since the country became independent; 0 when the previous regime was a parliamentary democracy; 1 if it was a mixed democracy; 2 if it was a presidential democracy; 3 if it was a civilian dictatorship; 4 if it was a military dictatorship; 5 if it was a royal dictatorship. [R]

PROCED   Procedure for legislative vote to override presidential veto. Coded 0 if there is no veto; 1 if unicameral legislature; 2 if bicameral and veto override is by a vote in a joint session of both houses; 3 if bicameral and veto override is by a separate vote in each house; 4 if bicameral and veto override is by a vote in the lower house only; 5 if bicameral and veto override is by a decision of a third party (court or referendum). [C]

PVMAJ   Partial veto majority. Type of majority necessary to override a partial presidential veto. Coded 1 if 20% of the members present at the time of voting; 2 if 20% of the members of the legislative body; 3 if 25% of the members present at the time of voting; 4 if 25% of the members of the legislative body; 5 if 33.3% of the members present at the time of voting; 6 if 33.3% of the members of the legislative body; 7 if 50% of the members present at the time of voting; 8 if 50% of the members of the legislative body; 9 if 60% of the members present at the time of voting; 10 if 60% of the members of the legislative body; 11 if 66.6% of the members present at the time of voting; 12 if 66.6% of the members of the legislative body; 13 if 75% of the members present at the time of voting; 14 if 75% of the members of the legislative body. [C]

REGION   Region of the world. Coded 1 for Sub-Saharan Africa; 2 for South Asia; 3 for East Asia; 4 for South East Asia; 5 for Pacific Islands/Oceania; 6 for Middle East/North Africa; 7 for Latin America; 8 for Caribbean or non-Iberic America; 9 for Eastern Europe/Soviet Union; 10 for industrial countries; 11 for oil countries. [O]

REVERSAL   Dummy variable coded 1 if the constitutional provisions that specify what should happen if the budget law is not approved favor the president,

0 otherwise. REVERSAL = 1 if RP = 1 and RPTYPE = 2, or if RPTYPE = 1 and INITIATE = 1 and AMEND2 = 1. [C]

RP   Reversal point. Dummy variable coded 1 if the constitution specifies what should happen if the budget law is not approved, 0 otherwise. [C]

RPTYPE   Reversal point type. Constitutional provisions that specify what should happen if the budget law is not approved. Coded 0 if the congress' budget is to be adopted; 1 if the previous year's budget is to be adopted; 2 if the executive's budget is to be adopted; 3 if the bill under discussion is to be adopted and neither the executive nor the legislative has the exclusive legislative initiative (e.g., Niger's 1999 constitution). [C]

SINGMAJ   Single-party majority government. Dummy variable coded 1 for governments composed of a single party that holds more than 50% of the seats in the lower (or only) legislative house, 0 otherwise. SINGMAJ = 1 if MINSIT = 0 and COALGOV = 0 and MAJGOV = 1. [G]

SITFLAG   Situation flag. Dummy variable coded 1 for every time the distribution of seats in the lower house changes or there is an election (even if the distribution of seats remains the same), 0 otherwise. [G]

SITSPELL   Situation spell. Number of successive spells of situations, as defined by SITFLAG. [G]

STRA   Sum of past transitions to authoritarianism. If a country experienced more than one transition to authoritarianism before 1946, STRA is coded 1 in 1946 (Przeworski et al. 2000). [O]

SUPMAJ   "Super majority" government. Dummy variable coded 1 for governments composed of at least two parties when one of them holds more than 50% of the seats in the lower (or only) legislative house, 0 otherwise. SINGMAJ = 1 if MINSIT = 0 and COALGOV = 1 and MAJGOV = 1. [G]

t0   Count variable indicating age of regime (as coded by HINST), with the first year of the regime coded 0. [R]

TJK   Regime transition. Dummy variable coded 1 if a transition occurred from any type of democracy to any type of dictatorship (as coded by HINST) or vice versa, 0 otherwise. The following countries experienced regime transition in 1946: Argentina, Brazil, Czechoslovakia, Greece, Italy, and Lebanon. Cyprus experienced a regime transition in 1983, the first year Greek Cyprus

(COUNTRY = 188) is observed. There are 158 transitions to and from democracy in the data set. [R]

TJKLED   TJK led by one year. [R]

TVMAJ   Total veto majority. Type of majority necessary to override a total presidential veto. Coded 1 if 20% of members present at the time of voting; 2 if 20% of the members of the legislative body; 3 if 25% of the members present at the time of voting; 4 if 25% of the members of the legislative body; 5 if 33.3% of the members present at the time of voting; 6 if 33.3% of the members of the legislative body; 7 if 50% of the members present at the time of voting; 8 if 50% of the members of the legislative body; 9 if 60% of the members present at the time of voting; 10 if 60% of the members of the legislative body; 11 if 66.6% of the members present at the time of voting; 12 if 66.6% of the members of the legislative body; 13 if 75% of the members present at the time of voting; 14 if 75% of the members of the legislative body. [C]

VETO   Variable that codes whether the constitution grants the president veto power. Coded 0 if there is no veto power (or the constitution is silent about it); 1 if the constitution grants unconditional veto power; 2 if the constitution grants conditional veto power. [C]

VETOTYPE   Type of presidential veto. Coded 1 if total; 2 if partial; 3 if both. [C]

Sources

Regime Variables [R]

Author's own classification. Countries were first classified as democracies and dictatorships for each year between 1946 and 2002 according to the rules discussed in Chapter 2, which update the procedure developed in Przeworski et al. (2000). The classification of democracies into parliamentary, mixed, or presidential was performed according to the rules discussed in Chapter 2. The classification of dictatorships into civilian, military, or royal is taken from Gandhi (2004).

Government and Party Variables [G]

Information on the partisan composition of the government and distribution of legislative seats was taken from the following sources.

Appendix: Definition and Sources of Variables

General   Banks (various years); Banks, Day, and Muller (1997); Cheibub and Kalandrakis (2004); Inter-Parliamentary Union (Parline Database, ⟨http://www.ipu.org/parline-e/parlinesearch.asp⟩); Keesing's Contemporary Archives (various years) and ⟨http://www.keesings.com/⟩; Library of Congress Country Studies, ⟨http://lcweb2.loc.gov/frd/csquery.html⟩; Library of Congress Portals to the World, ⟨http://www.loc.gov/rr/international/portals.html⟩; *Regional Surveys of the World* (various years); U.S. Department of State, Country Reports on Human Rights Practices for 1999, ⟨http://www.usis.usemb.se/human/human1999/toc.html⟩.

Europe and OECD   Lane et al. (1997); Parties and Elections in Europe, ⟨http://www.parties-and-elections.de/indexe.html⟩; Woldendorp et al. (1993); Zarate's Political Collections – European Governments, ⟨http://www.terra.es/personal2/monolith/00europa.htm⟩.

Africa   Bratton and van de Walle (1996); Doro (various years); Mozaffar (2004); Nohlen, Krennerich, and Thibaut (1999).

Asia and the Pacific   Banlaoi and Carlos (1996a,b); Yonhyok (1997); Nohlen, Grotz, and Hartman (2001).

Latin America   Deheza (1997); Nohlen (1993); Political Database of the Americas, ⟨http://www.georgetown.edu/pdba/english.html⟩; Valenzuela (1994).

Constitutional Variables [C]

Constituciones Hispanoamericanas, ⟨http://www.cervantesvirtual.com/portal/Constituciones/⟩; Constitution Finder, University of Richmond, ⟨http://confinder.richmond.edu/⟩; Blaustein and Flanz (various years) and ⟨http://www.oceanalaw.com/⟩; Political Database of the Americas, ⟨http://www.georgetown.edu/pdba/english.html⟩.

References

Acemoglu, Daron, Simon Johnson, and James A. Robinson. "The Colonial Origins of Comparative Development: An Empirical Investigation." *American Economic Review* 91, no. 5 (2001): 1369–1401.

"Reversal of Fortune: Geography and Institutions in the Making of the Modern World Income Distribution." *Quarterly Journal of Economics* 117, November (2002): 1231–94.

Ackerman, Bruce. "The New Separation of Powers." *Harvard Law Review* 113, no. 3 (2000): 642–727.

Ahmad, Zakaria Haji. "Malaysia: Quasi Democracy in a Divided Society." In Larry Diamond, Juan J. Linz, and Seymour M. Lipset (Eds.), *Democracy in Developing Countries: Asia*. Boulder, CO: Lyne Rienner, 1988.

Altman, David. "The Politics of Coalition Formation and Survival in Multiparty Presidential Democracies: The Case of Uruguay, 1989–1999." *Party Politics* 6, no. 3 (2000): 259–83.

Alvarez, Michael. "Presidentialism and Parliamentarism: Which Works? Which Lasts?" Ph.D. dissertation, Department of Political Science, University of Chicago, 1997.

Alvarez, Michael E., José Antonio Cheibub, Fernando Limongi, and Adam Przeworski. "Classifying Political Regimes." *Studies in Comparative International Development* 31, no. 2 (1996): 3–36.

Ames, Barry. *The Deadlock of Democracy in Brazil*. Ann Arbor: University of Michigan Press, 2001.

Amorim Neto, Octavio. "Of Presidents, Parties, and Ministers: Cabinet Formation and Legislative Decision-Making under Separation of Powers." Ph.D. dissertation, University of California, San Diego, 1998.

"The Puzzle of Party Discipline in Brazil." *Latin American Politics and Society* 44, no. 1 (2002): 127–44.

"Lula Sob a Luz da História." *O Globo,* June 7 (2005).

Amorim Neto, Octavio, Gary Cox, and Matthew D. McCubbins. "Agenda Power in Brazil's Camara Dos Deputados, 1989–98." *World Politics* 55, no. 4 (2003): 550–78.

Andrews, William G. "The Constitutional Prescription of Parliamentary Procedures in Gaullist France." *Legislative Studies Quarterly* 3, no. 3 (1978): 465–506.

Armijo, Leslie Elliott, Philippe Faucher, and Magdalena Dembinska. "Compared to What? Assessing Brazilian Political Institutions." Paper presented at the Annual Meeting of the International Studies Association, Montreal, 2004.

Austen-Smith, David, and Jeffrey Banks. "Elections, Coalitions, and Legislative Outcomes." *American Political Science Review* 82, no. 2 (1988): 405–22.

Banks, Arthur S. *Political Handbook of the World*. New York: McGraw-Hill (various years).

Banks, Arthur S., Alan J. Day, and Thomas C. Muller. *Political Handbook of the World 1997*. New York: McGraw-Hill, 1997.

Banlaoi, Rommel C., and Clarita R. Carlos. *Political Parties in the Philippines: From 1900 to the Present*. Makati City, Philippines: Konrad Adenauer Foundation, 1996a.

　Elections in the Philippines: From Pre-Colonial Period to the Present. Makati City, Philippines: Konrad Adenauer Foundation, 1996b.

Baron, David P. "Comparative Dynamics of Parliamentary Government." *American Political Science Review* 92 (1998): 593–610.

Bernhard, Michael, Timothy Nordstrom, and Christopher Reenock. "Economic Performance, Institutional Intermediation, and Democratic Survival." *Journal of Politics* 63, no. 3 (2001): 775–803.

Bernhard, Michael, Christopher Reenock, and Timothy Nordstrom. "The Legacy of Western Overseas Colonialism on Democratic Survival." *International Studies Quarterly* 48, no. 1 (2004): 225–50.

Binder, Sarah A. "The Dynamics of Legislative Gridlock, 1947–96." *American Political Science Review* 93 (1999): 519–34.

Blaustein, A. P., and G. H. Flanz (Eds.). *Constitutions of the Countries of the World*. Dobbs Ferry, NY: Oceana (various years).

Boothroyd, David. *Government Defeats on the Floor of the House of Commons 2001* [cited 14 September 2005], ⟨http://www.election.demon.co.uk/defeats.html⟩.

Bowler, Shaun, David M. Farrell, and Richard S. Katz. "Party Cohesion, Party Discipline, and Parliaments." In Shaun Bowler, David M. Farrell, and Richard S. Katz (Eds.), *Party Discipline and Parliamentary Government*, pp. 3–22. Columbus: Ohio State University Press, 1999.

Bratton, Michael, and Nicolas van de Walle. *Political Regimes and Regime Transitions in Africa: A Comparative Handbook*. East Lansing: Department of Political Science, Michigan State University, 1996.

　Democratic Experiments in Africa: Regime Transitions in Comparative Perspective. Cambridge University Press, 1997.

Cameron, Charles M. *Veto Bargaining: Presidents and the Politics of Negative Power*. Cambridge University Press, 2000.

Carey, John M. "Institutional Design and Party Systems." In Larry Diamond, Marc F. Plattner, Yun-han Chu, and Hung-mao Tien (Eds.), *Consolidating the Third Wave Democracies: Themes and Perspectives*, pp. 67–92. Baltimore: Johns Hopkins University Press, 1997.

　"Political Institutions, Competing Principals, and Party Unity in Legislative Voting." Unpublished manuscript, Department of Government, Dartmouth College, Hanover, NH, 2004.

Carey, John M., and Matthew Soberg Shugart. "Incentives to Cultivate a Personal Vote: A Rank Ordering of Electoral Formulas." *Electoral Studies* 14, no. 4 (1994): 417–39.

References

"Calling Out the Tanks or Filling Out the Forms?" In John M. Carey and Matthew Soberg Shugart (Eds.), *Executive Decree Authority*, pp. 1–32. Cambridge University Press, 1998.

Carlson, Rolf Eric. "Presidentialism in Africa: Explaining Institutional Choice." Ph.D. dissertation, Department of Political Science, University of Chicago, 1998.

Cheibub, José Antonio. "Elections and Alternation in Power in Democratic Regimes." Paper presented at the Annual Meeting of the American Political Science Association, Boston, 1998.

"Minority Governments, Deadlock Situations, and the Survival of Presidential Democracies." *Comparative Political Studies* 35, no. 3 (2002): 284–312.

Cheibub, José Antonio, and Jennifer Gandhi. "Classifying Political Regimes: A Six-Fold Classification of Democracies and Dictatorships." Unpublished manuscript, Department of Political Science, Yale University, New Haven, CT, 2006.

Cheibub, José Antonio, and Anastassios Kalandrakis. "Global Database of Political Institutions and Economic Performance." Globalization and Self-Determination Project, Yale Center for International and Area Studies, Yale University, New Haven, CT, 2004.

Cheibub, José Antonio, and Adam Przeworski. "Democracy, Elections, and Accountability for Economic Outcomes." In Adam Przeworski, Susan C. Stokes, and Bernard Manin (Eds.), *Democracy and Accountability*, pp. 222–50. Cambridge University Press, 1999.

Cheibub, José Antonio, Adam Przeworski, and Sebastian Saiegh. "Government Coalitions and Legislative Success under Parliamentarism and Presidentialism." *British Journal of Political Science* 34, no. 4 (2004): 565–87.

Coleman, John J. "Unified Government, Divided Government, and Party Responsiveness." *American Political Science Review* 93 (1999): 821–36.

Collier, David, and Robert Adcock. "Democracy and Dichotomies: A Pragmatic Approach to Choices about Concepts." *Annual Review of Political Science* 2 (1999): 537–65.

Cotta, Maurizio. "The Centrality of Parliament in a Protracted Democratic Consolidation." In Ulrike Liebert and Maurizio Cotta (Eds.), *Parliament and Democratic Consolidation in Southern Europe*, pp. 55–91. London: Pintere, 1990.

Cox, Gary. *The Efficient Secret: The Cabinet and the Development of Political Parties in Victorian England*. Cambridge University Press, 1987.

Cox, Gary, and Matthew D. McCubbins. *Legislative Leviathan: Party Government in the House*. Berkeley: University of California Press, 1993.

Croissant, Aurel. "Legislative Powers, Veto Players, and the Emergence of Delegative Democracy: A Comparison of Presidentialism in the Philippines and South Korea." *Democratization* 10, no. 3 (2003): 68–98.

Damgaard, Erik. "Denmark: Experiments in Parliamentary Government." In Erik Damgaard (Ed.), *Parliamentary Change in Nordic Countries*. Oslo: Scandinavian University Press, 1992.

Davidson-Schmich, Louise K. "The Development of Party Discipline in New Parliaments: Eastern German State Legislatures 1990–2000." *Journal of Legislative Studies* 9, no. 4 (2003): 88–101.

Deheza, Grace Ivana. "Gobiernos de Coalición en el Sistema Presidencial: América del Sur." Ph.D. dissertation, European University Institute, Florence, 1997.

Deininger, Klaus, and Lyn Squire. "A New Data Set Measuring Income Inequality." *World Bank Economic Review* 10, no. 3 (1996): 565–91.

Depauw, Sam. "Government Party Discipline in Parliamentary Democracies: The Cases of Belgium, France and the United Kingdom in the 1990s." *Journal of Legislative Studies* 9, no. 4 (2003): 130–46.

Desposato, Scott. "Parties for Rent? Careerism, Ideology, and Party Switching in Brazil's Chamber of Deputies." Unpublished manuscript, Department of Political Science, University of California, San Diego, 2005.

Desposato, Scott, and David Samuels. "The Search for Party Discipline in the Brazilian Legislature and Implications for Comparative Institutional Research." Paper presented at the Latin American Studies Association Meeting, Dallas, 2003.

Di Palma, Giuseppe. "Institutional Rules and Legislative Outcomes in the Italian Parliament." *Legislative Studies Quarterly* 1 (1976): 147–79.

Diermeier, Daniel, and Timothy Feddersen. "Cohesion in Legislatures and the Vote of Confidence Procedure." *American Political Science Review* 92 (1998): 611–22.

Diermeier, Daniel, and Keith Krehbiel. "Institutionalism as a Methodology." *Journal of Theoretical Politics* 15, no. 2 (2003): 123–44.

Diermeier, Daniel, and Antonio Merlo. "Government Turnover in Parliamentary Democracies." *Journal of Economic Theory* 94, no. 1 (2000): 46–79.

Doro, Marion (Ed.). *Africa Contemporary Record: Annual Survey and Documents*. New York: Africana (various years).

Duverger, Maurice. "A New Political System Model: Semi-Presidential Government." *European Journal of Political Research* 8, no. 2 (1980): 166–87.

Elgie, Robert. "Models of Executive Politics: A Framework for the Study of Executive Power Relations in Parliamentary and Semi-Presidential Regimes." *Political Studies* 45 (1997): 217–31.

"Semi-Presidentialism: Concepts, Consequences, and Contested Explanations." *Political Studies Review* 2 (2004): 313–30.

"A Fresh Look at Semipresidentialism: Variations on a Theme." *Journal of Democracy* 16, no. 3 (2005): 98–112.

Elkins, Zachary. "Designed by Diffusion: International Networks and the Spread of Democracy." Ph.D. dissertation, Department of Political Science, University of California, Berkeley, 2003.

Engerman, Stanley L., and Kenneth L. Sokoloff. "Factor Endowments, Institutions, and Differential Paths of Growth among New World Economies: A View from Economic Historians of the United States." In Stephen Haber (Ed.), *How Latin America Fell Behind*, pp. 260–304. Palo Alto, CA: Stanford University Press, 1997.

Figueiredo, Argelina. "O Executivo nos Sistemas de Governo Democráticos." *Revista Brasileira de Informação Bibliográfica em Ciências Sociais, BIB* 58 (2005), pp. 7–28.

Figueiredo, Argelina, and Fernando Limongi. *Executivo e Legislativo Na Nova Ordem Constitucional*. Rio de Janeiro: Editora FGV, 1999.

"Presidential Power, Legislative Organization and Party Behavior in the Legislature." *Comparative Politics* 32, no. 2 (2000a): 151–70.

"Constitutional Change, Legislative Performance and Institutional Consolidation." *Brazilian Review of Social Sciences* 1, Special Issue (2000b): 73–94.

References

"Agenda Power in the Brazilian Democracy: Government Performance in a Multiparty Presidential System." CEBRAP, São Paulo, 2005.

Fiorina, Morris. *Divided Government*, 2nd ed. Boston: Allyn & Bacon, 1996.

Fish, M. Steven. "The Dynamics of Democratic Erosion." In Richard D. Anderson, Jr., M. Steven Fish, Stephen E. Hanson, and Philip G. Roeder (Eds.), *Postcommunism and the Theory of Democracy*. Princeton, NJ: Princeton University Press, 2001.

Foweraker, Joe, and Todd Landman. "Constitutional Design and Democratic Performance." *Democratization* 9, no. 2 (2002): 43–66.

Freedom House. *Freedom in the World*. New York: Freedom House, 1992.

Freedom in the World 2005. New York: Freedom House, 2005.

Frye, Timothy. "A Politics of Institutional Choice: Post-Communist Presidencies." *Comparative Political Studies* 30, no. 5 (1997): 523–53.

Gandhi, Jennifer. "Political Institutions under Dictatorship." Ph.D. dissertation, Department of Politics, New York University, 2004.

Gargarella, Roberto. "Towards a Typology of Latin American Constitutionalism, 1810–60." *Latin American Research Review* 39, no. 2 (2004): 141–53.

"The Constitution of Inequality: Constitutionalism in the Americas, 1776–1860." *International Journal of Constitutional Law* 3, no. 1 (2005): 1–23.

Golder, Matt. "Presidential Coattails and Legislative Fragmentation." *American Journal of Political Science* 50, no. 1 (2006): 34–48.

González, Luis Eduardo, and Charles Guy Gillespie. "Presidentialism and Democratic Stability in Uruguay." In Juan J. Linz and Arturo Valenzuela (Eds.), *The Failure of Presidential Democracy: The Case of Latin America*, pp. 151–78. Baltimore: Johns Hopkins University Press, 1994.

Hartlyn, Jonathan. "Presidentialism and Colombian Politics." In Juan J. Linz and Arturo Valenzuela (Eds.), *The Failure of Presidential Democracy: The Case of Latin America*, pp. 220–53. Baltimore: Johns Hopkins University Press, 1994.

Hazan, Reuven Y. "Does Cohesion Equal Discipline? Towards a Conceptual Delineation." *Journal of Legislative Studies* 9, no. 4 (2003): 1–11.

Heller, William B., and Carol Mershon. "Party Switching in the Italian Chamber of Deputies, 1996–2001." *Journal of Politics* 67, no. 2 (2005): 536–59.

Heston, Alan, Robert Summers, and Bettina Aten. "Penn World Table Version 5.6." Center for International Comparisons at the University of Pennsylvania, Philadelphia, 2002.

Horowitz, Donald L. *Ethnic Groups in Conflict*, 2nd ed. Berkeley: University of California Press, 2000.

Huang, The-fu. "Party Systems in Taiwan and South Korea." In Larry Diamond, Marc F. Plattner, Yun-han Chu, and Hung-mao Tien (Eds.), *Consolidating the Third Wave Democracies: Themes and Perspectives*, pp. 135–59. Baltimore: Johns Hopkins University Press, 1997.

Huber, John D. "The Vote of Confidence in Parliamentary Democracies." *American Political Science Review* 90 (1996): 269–82.

Johannsen, Lars, and Ole Nørgaard. "IPA: The Index of Presidential Authority: Explorations into the Measurement of the Impact of a Political Institution." Unpublished manuscript, Department of Political Science, University of Aarhus, 2003.

Jones, Mark P. *Electoral Laws and the Survival of Presidential Democracies.* Notre Dame, IN: Notre Dame University Press, 1995.

Jones, Mark P., and Wonjae Hwang. "Party Government in Presidential Democracies: Extending Cartel Theory beyond the U.S. Congress." *American Journal of Political Science* 49, no. 2 (2005): 267–82.

Kalandrakis, Anastassios. "General Equilibrium Parliamentary Government." Ph.D. dissertation, Department of Political Science, University of California, Los Angeles, 2000.

Kalandrakis, Tasos. "General Political Equilibrium in Parliamentary Democracies." Paper presented at the Annual Meeting of the American Political Science Association, Atlanta, 1999.

Keefer, Philip. "DPI2000 – Database of Political Institutions: Changes and Variable Definitions." Development Research Group, World Bank, Washington, DC, 2002.

Keesing's Contemporary Archives. *Keesing's Record of World Events.* London: Keesing's Worldwide (various years).

Kenney, Charles. *Fujimori's Coup and the Breakdown of Democracy in Latin America.* Notre Dame, IN: University of Notre Dame Press, 2004.

Kim, HeeMin. "Rational Choice Theory and Third World Politics: The 1990 Party Merger in Korea." *Comparative Politics* 30, no. 1 (1997): 83–100.

Kitschelt, Herbert. "Linkages between Citizens and Politicians in Democratic Polities." *Comparative Political Studies* 33, no. 6/7 (2000): 845–79.

Krehbiel, Keith. "Constituency Characteristics and Legislative Preferences." *Public Choice* 76 (1992): 21–37.

Kristinsson, Gunnar Helgi. "Iceland." In Robert Elgie (Ed.), *Semi-Presidentialism in Europe,* pp. 86–103. Oxford University Press, 1999.

Krouwel, André. "Measuring Presidentialism of Central and East European Countries." Working Paper no. 02/2003, Department of Political Science, Vrije Universiteit, Amsterdam, 2003.

Lane, Jan-Erik, David McKay, and Kenneth Newton. *Political Data Handbook: OECD Countries,* 2nd ed. Oxford University Press, 1997.

Laver, Michael, and Norman Schofield. *Multiparty Government: The Politics of Coalition in Europe.* Ann Arbor: University of Michigan Press, 1998.

Laver, Michael, and Kenneth A. Shepsle. *Making and Breaking Governments: Cabinets and Legislatures in Parliamentary Democracies.* Cambridge University Press, 1996.

Lawrence, Chris, and Jennifer Hayes. "Regime Stability and Presidential Government: A Preliminary Analysis." Paper presented at the Southern Political Science Association, Atlanta, 2000.

Lijphart, Arend. *Patterns of Democracy: Government Forms and Performance in Thirty-six Countries.* New Haven, CT: Yale University Press, 1999.

"Democracy in the Twenty-first Century: Can We Be Optimistic?" *The Eighteenth Uhlenbeck Lecture.* Wassenaar: Netherlands Institute for Advanced Study in the Humanities and Social Sciences, Institute of the Royal Netherlands Academy of Arts and Sciences, 2000.

"Constitutional Design for Divided Societies." *Journal of Democracy* 15, no. 2 (2004): 96–109.

References

Limongi, Fernando, and Argelina Figueiredo. "As Bases Institucionais do Presidencialismo de Coalizão." *Lua Nova* 44 (1998): 81–106.

Linz, Juan J. *The Breakdown of Democratic Regimes: Crisis, Breakdown, and Reequilibration.* Baltimore: Johns Hopkins University Press, 1978.

"The Perils of Presidentialism." *Journal of Democracy* 1, no. 1 (1990a): 51–69.

"The Virtues of Parliamentarism." *Journal of Democracy* 1, no. 4 (1990b): 84–91.

"Presidential or Parliamentary Democracy: Does It Make a Difference?" In Juan J. Linz and Arturo Valenzuela (Eds.), *The Failure of Presidential Democracy: The Case of Latin America,* pp. 3–90. Baltimore: Johns Hopkins University Press, 1994.

Linz, Juan J., and Alfred Stepan. *Problems of Democratic Transition and Consolidation: Southern Europe, South America, and Post-Communist Europe.* Baltimore: Johns Hopkins University Press, 1996.

Loewenberg, Gerhard, and Samuel C. Patterson. *Comparing Legislatures.* Boston: Little, Brown, 1979.

Londregan, John B., and Keith T. Poole. "Poverty, the Coup Trap, and the Seizure of Executive Power." *World Politics* 42 (1990): 151–83.

Mainwaring, Scott. "Presidentialism in Latin America." *Latin American Research Review* 25, no. 1 (1990): 157–79.

"Politicians, Parties, and Electoral Systems: Brazil in Comparative Perspective." *Comparative Politics* 24 (1991): 21–43.

"Presidentialism, Multipartism, and Democracy: The Difficult Combination." *Comparative Political Studies* 26, no. 2 (1993): 198–228.

Rethinking Party Systems in the Third Wave of Democratization: The Case of Brazil. Stanford, CA: Stanford University Press, 1999.

Mainwaring, Scott, and Timothy R. Scully. "Introduction: Party Systems in Latin America." In Scott Mainwaring and Timothy R. Scully (Eds.), *Building Democratic Institutions: Party Systems in Latin America,* pp. 1–34. Stanford, CA: Stanford University Press, 1995.

Mainwaring, Scott, and Matthew Soberg Shugart. "Conclusion: Presidentialism and the Party System." In Scott Mainwaring and Matthew Soberg Shugart (Eds.), *Presidentialism and Democracy in Latin America,* pp. 394–439. Cambridge University Press, 1997.

Manin, Bernard. *The Principles of Representative Government.* Cambridge University Press, 1997.

Mayer, Kenneth. *With the Stroke of a Pen: Executive Orders and Presidential Power.* Princeton, NJ: Princeton University Press, 2001.

Mayhew, David R. *Congress: The Electoral Connection.* New Haven, CT: Yale University Press, 1974.

Divided We Govern: Party Control, Lawmaking, and Investigations, 1946–1990. New Haven, CT: Yale University Press, 1991.

Medina, Luis F. "Legislatures vs. Political Parties: Endogenous Policy with Strategic Voters." Unpublished manuscript, Department of Political Science, University of Chicago, 2001.

Mershon, Carol. "The Costs of Coalition: Coalition Theories and Italian Governments." *American Political Science Review* 90, no. 3 (1996): 534–54.

"The Costs of Coalition: A Five-Nation Comparison." In Shaun Bowler, David M. Farrell, and Richard S. Katz (Eds.), *Party Discipline and Parliamentary Government*, pp. 227–68. Columbus: Ohio State University Press, 1999.

Metcalf, Lee Kendall. "Measuring Presidential Power." *Comparative Political Studies* 33, no. 5 (2000): 660–85.

Moestrup, Anna Sophia Nyholm. "Semipresidentialism in Comparative Perspective: Its Effects on Democratic Survival." Ph.D. dissertation, Department of Political Science, George Washington University, Washington, DC, 2004.

Mozaffar, Shaheen. "Africa: Electoral Systems in Emerging Democracies." In Josep Colomer (Ed.), *The Handbook of Electoral System Choice*. New York: Palgrave Macmillan, 2004.

Negretto, Gabriel L., and Jose Antonio Aguilar-Rivera. "Rethinking the Legacy of the Liberal State in Latin America: The Cases of Argentina (1853–1916) and Mexico (1857–1910)." *Journal of Latin American Studies* 32 (2000): 361–97.

Niño, Carlos Santiago. "Hyperpresidentialism and Constitutional Reform in Argentina." In Arend Lijphart and Carlos H. Waisman (Eds.), *Institutional Design in New Democracies: Eastern Europe and Latin America*, pp. 161–74. Boulder, CO: Westview, 1996.

Nohlen, Dieter. *Enciclopedia Electoral Latinoamericana y Del Caribe*. San Jose, Costa Rica: Instituto Interamericano de Derechos Humanos, 1993.

Nohlen, Dieter, Florian Grotz, and Christof Hartman (Eds.). *Elections in Asia and the Pacific: A Data Handbook*. Oxford University Press, 2001.

Nohlen, Dieter, Michael Krennerich, and Bernhard Thibaut (Eds.). *Elections in Africa: A Data Handbook*. Oxford University Press, 1999.

O'Donnell, Guillermo. *Modernization and Bureacratic-Authoritarianism: Studies in South American Politics*. Berkeley: Institute of International Studies, University of California, 1973.

"Delegative Democracy." *Journal of Democracy* 5 (1994): 55–69.

Ozbudun, Ergun. *Party Cohesion in Western Democracies: A Causal Analysis*. Beverly Hills, CA: Sage, 1970.

Paz-Soldan, José Pareja. *Historia de las Constituciones Nacionales*. Lima: ZENIT, 1943.

Pereira, Carlos, and Bernardo Mueller. "The Cost of Governing: Strategic Behavior of the President and Legislators in Brazil's Budgetary Process." *Comparative Political Studies* 37, no. 7 (2004): 781–815.

Pereira, Carlos, Timothy J. Power, and Lucio Rennó. "Under What Conditions Do Presidents Resort to Decree Power? Theory and Evidence from the Brazilian Case." *Journal of Politics* 67, no. 1 (2005): 178–200.

Pérez-Liñán, Aníbal S. "The Political and Economic Consequences of Executive–Legislative Crises." Paper presented at the Latin American Studies Association Annual Meeting, Dallas, 2003.

Power, Timothy J., and Mark Gasiorowski. "Institutional Design and Democratic Consolidation in the Third World." *Comparative Political Studies* 30, no. 2 (1997): 123–56.

Przeworski, Adam. *Democracy and the Market: Political and Economic Reforms in Eastern Europe and Latin America*. Cambridge University Press, 1991.

"Economic Development and Transitions to Democracy." Unpublished manuscript, Department of Politics, New York University, 2004.

References

Przeworski, Adam, Michael E. Alvarez, José Antonio Cheibub, and Fernando Limongi. *Democracy and Development: Political Institutions and Well-Being in the World, 1950–1990.* Cambridge University Press, 2000.

Przeworksi, Adam, and Carolina Curvale. "Political Institutions and Economic Development in the Americas: The Long Run." Unpublished manuscript, Department of Politics, New York University, 2006.

Regional Surveys of the World. London: Europa Publications (various years).

Riggs, Fred W. "The Survival of Presidentialism in America: Para-Constitutional Practices." *International Political Science Review* 9, no. 4 (1988): 247–78.

Roper, Steven D. "Are All Semipresidential Regimes the Same? A Comparison of Premier-Presidential Regimes." *Comparative Politics* 34, no. 3 (2002): 253–72.

Rouquié, Alain. "The Military in Latin American Politics Since 1930." In Leslie Bethell (Ed.), *Latin America Since 1930* (Cambridge History of Latin America, vol. 6). Cambridge University Press, 1994.

Rose, Richard. "British MPs: More Bark Than Bite?" In Ezra N. Suleiman (Ed.), *Parliaments and Parliamentarians in Democratic Politics.* New York: Holmes & Meier, 1986.

Saiegh, Sebastian M. "Government Defeat: Coalitions, Responsiveness, and Legislative Success." Ph.D. dissertation, Department of Politics, New York University, 2004.

Samuels, David. *Ambition, Federalism, and Legislative Politics in Brazil.* Cambridge University Press, 2003.

Samuels, David, and Kent Eaton. "Presidentialism and, or, and versus Parliamentarism: The State of the Literature and an Agenda for Future Research." Paper presented at the Conference on the Consequences of Political Institutions in Democracy, Duke University, Durham, NC, 2002.

Sartori, Giovanni. *Parties and Party Systems: A Framework for Analysis.* Cambridge University Press, 1976.

"Neither Presidentialism nor Parlimentarism." In Juan J. Linz and Arturo Valenzuela (Eds.), *The Failure of Presidential Democracy: The Case of Latin America,* pp. 106–18. Baltimore: Johns Hopkins University Press, 1994.

Schleiter, Petra. "Mixed Constitutions and Political Instability." *Democratization* 10, no. 1 (2003): 1–26.

Schleiter, Petra, and Edward Morgan-Jones. "Semi-Presidential Regimes: Providing Flexibility or Generating Representation and Governance Problems?" Paper presented at the Annual Meeting of the American Political Science Association, Washington, DC, 2005.

Shugart, Matthew Soberg. "The Electoral Cycle and Institutional Sources of Divided Presidential Government." *American Political Science Review* 89, no. 2 (1995): 327–43.

Shugart, Matthew Soberg, and John M. Carey. *Presidents and Assemblies: Constitutional Design and Electoral Dynamics.* Cambridge University Press, 1992.

Shugart, Matthew Soberg, and Stephan Haggard. "Institutions and Public Policy in Presidential Systems." In Stephan Haggard and Matthew McCubbins (Eds.), *Presidents, Parliaments, and Policy.* Cambridge University Press, 2001.

Shugart, Matthew Soberg, and Scott Mainwaring. "Presidentialism and Democracy in Latin America: Rethinking the Terms of the Debate." In Scott Mainwaring and Matthew Soberg Shugart (Eds.), *Presidentialism and Democracy in Latin America,* pp. 12–54. Cambridge University Press, 1997.

Siavelis, Peter. *The President and Congress in Post-Authoritarian Chile: Institutional Constraints to Democratic Consolidation.* University Park: Pennsylvania State University Press, 2000.

Stanton, Kimberly Ann. "Transforming a Political Regime: The Chilean Constitution of 1925." Ph.D. dissertation, Department of Political Science, University of Chicago, 1997.

Stepan, Alfred. *Military in Politics: Changing Patterns in Brazil.* Princeton, NJ: Princeton University Press, 1971.

   Rethinking Military Politics: Brazil and the Southern Cone. Princeton, NJ: Princeton University Press, 1988.

Stepan, Alfred, and Cindy Skach. "Constitutional Frameworks and Democratic Consolidation." *World Politics* 46, no. 1 (1993): 1–22.

Strøm, Kaare. *Minority Government and Majority Rule.* Cambridge University Press, 1990.

   "Delegation and Accountability in Parliamentary Democracies." *European Journal of Political Research* 37, no. 3 (2000): 261–89.

Strøm, Kaare, and Wolfgang C. Müller. "The Keys to Togetherness: Coalition Agreements in Parliamentary Democracies." *Journal of Legislative Studies* 5, no. 3/4 (1999): 255–82.

Suberu, Rotimi T., and Larry Diamond. "Institutional Design, Ethnic Conflict-Management and Democracy in Nigeria." In Andrew Reynolds (Ed.), *The Architecture of Democracy: Constitutional Design, Conflict Management, and Democracy,* pp. 400–28. Oxford University Press, 2002.

Than, Tin Maung Maung. "The Essential Tension: Democratization and the Unitary State in Myanmar (Burma)." *South East Asia Research* 12, no. 2 (2004): 187–212.

Tsebelis, George. "Decision Making in Political Systems: Veto Players in Presidentialism, Parliamentarism, Multicameralism and Multipartyism." *British Journal of Political Science* 25 (1995): 289–325.

   Veto Players: How Political Institutions Work. Princeton, NJ: Princeton University Press, 2002.

Turan, Ilter. "Changing Horses in Midstream: Party Changers in the Turkish National Assembly." *Legislative Studies Quarterly* 10, no. 1 (1985): 21–34.

Valenzuela, Arturo. "Party Politics and the Crisis of Presidentialism in Chile: A Proposal for a Parliamentary Form of Government." In Juan J. Linz and Arturo Valenzuela (Eds.), *The Failure of Presidential Democracy: The Case of Latin America,* pp. 91–150. Baltimore: Johns Hopkins University Press, 1994.

   "The Crisis of Presidentialism in Latin America." In Scott Mainwaring and Arturo Valenzuela (Eds.), *Politics, Society, and Democracy: Latin America,* pp. 121–39. Boulder, CO: Westview, 1998.

   "Latin American Presidencies Interrupted." *Journal of Democracy* 15, no. 4 (2004): 5–19.

van de Walle, Nicolas. "Presidentialism and Clientelism in Africa's Emerging Party Systems." *Journal of Modern African Studies* 41, no. 2 (2003): 297–321.

Verney, Douglas. "The Analysis of Political Systems." In Arend Lijphart (Ed.), *Parliamentary versus Presidential Government.* Oxford University Press, 1992 [1979].

Viotti da Costa, Emilia. *The Brazilian Empire: Myths and Histories.* Chapel Hill: University of North Carolina Press, 2000.

References

Wallack, Jessica Seddon, Alejandro Gaviria, Ugo Panizza, and Ernesto Stein. "Political Particularism Around the World." *World Bank Economic Review* 17, no. 1 (2003): 133–43.

Warwick, Paul V. *Government Survival in Parliamentary Democracies.* Cambridge University Press, 1994.

Woldendorp, Jaap, Hans Keman, and Ian Budge. *Handbook of Democratic Government: Party Government in 20 Democracies (1945–1990).* Dordrecht: Kluwer, 1993.

World Bank. *World Development Indicators* (CD-ROM). Washington, DC: World Bank, 2004.

Yonhyok, Choe. *How to Manage Free and Fair Elections: A Comparison of Korea, Sweden and the United Kingdom.* Göteborg, Sweden: Göteborg University Press, 1997.

Zelaznik, Javier. "The Building of Coalitions in the Presidential Systems of Latin America: An Inquiry into the Political Conditions of Governability." Ph.D. dissertation, University of Essex, 2001.

Index

Ackerman, B., 14
Africa, 4
Ahmad, Z. H., 29
Albania, 54n7, 76
alternation in power rule, 30–3
Alvarez, M. E., 137, 138
Ames, B., 88n10
Andrews, W. G., 130, 131
Argentina, 37, 92, 102, 134, 144n4, 152, 154, 159, 164, 166
Armenia, 101–2
Austen-Smith, D., 66
Australia, 163
Austria, 144n4, 154, 163
Austro-Hungarian empire, 150
authoritarian regimes. *See also* regime transition
    civilian leadership of, 163–4
    civilian vs. military, 141
    consolidation rule and, 28–9
    coups in, 149
    decision making in, 161
    effective ruler in, 161–2
    in Latin America, 159
    military: coups in, 149, 154; in democratic breakdown, 144, 154; democratic governments following, 22–3, 156
    military legacy as variable in, 160–4
    military–presidential nexus in: causal explanation for, 145–6; vs. civilian dictatorship nexus, 141; in fragility of presidential democracies, 22–4; as historical coincidence, 147–8, 153–4
    military rulers in, 162
    monarchies as, 161, 162

multipartism as risk factor for, 95
succession in, 162
titles of rulers in, 153

Bangladesh, 162
Banks, J., 66
Belgium, 76, 163
Benin, 102
Bolivia, 35, 36, 154, 159
Bongho-Nouarra, Stéphane Maurice, 41
Botswana, 31
Brazil, 4n3, 43, 53, 74, 75n3, 76, 101n21, 102, 128, 133, 146, 152, 153, 159, 164, 166, 169, 171
budget process
    legislative amendment in, 101–3
    presidential dominance in: default situation, 103–4; power of amendment, 101–3; power of initiation, 101
    reversal point in, 103
Bulgaria, 43, 54n7, 144n4, 154
Burundi, 102

Canada, 163
Cape Verde, 43
Cardoso, Fernando Henrique, 53, 74
Carey, J. M., 5, 34, 100n20, 112, 121, 127, 133
Central African Republic, 41, 43, 147n5, 162
Cheibub, J. A., 30, 95, 122, 137, 138
Chile, 37, 100, 101, 102, 144n4, 159, 164, 171
China, 162
civilian rulers, 163–4. *See also* authoritarian regimes
coalition governments, 17–18, 52
    analysis of, 69–72
    electoral vs. portfolio, 74–5

Index

Index

Other Books in the Series *(continued from page iii)*

Kathleen Thelen, *How Institutions Evolve: The Political Economy of Skills in Germany, Britain, the United States, and Japan*

Charles Tilly, *Trust and Rule*

Joshua Tucker, *Regional Economic Voting: Russia, Poland, Hungary, Slovakia, and the Czech Republic, 1990–1999*

Ashutosh Varshney, *Democracy, Development, and the Countryside*

Stephen I. Wilkinson, *Votes and Violence: Electoral Competition and Ethnic Riots in India*

Jason Wittenberg, *Crucibles of Political Loyalty: Church Institutions and Electoral Continuity in Hungary*

Elisabeth J. Wood, *Forging Democracy from Below: Insurgent Transitions in South Africa and El Salvador*

Elisabeth J. Wood, *Insurgent Collective Action and Civil War in El Salvador*